Contents

Dad and I

Dad rakes
the lawn.

I rake the lawn, too!

Dad pulls the weeds.

I pull the weeds, too.

Dad washes the car.

I wash the car, too.

Dad takes a nap.

I take a nap,
too. Almost!

What Did It Say?

Mark the things that the girl and her dad did in the story.

_____ 1. They baked a cake.

_____ 2. They raked the leaves.

_____ 3. They read a book.

_____ 4. They pulled the weeds.

_____ 5. They washed the dog.

_____ 6. They washed the car.

Draw something the dad did that the little girl did <u>not</u> do.

Before and After

Cut and paste to show how each thing looked before and after.

Before

After

The Lawn

paste

We raked the leaves.

paste

The Weeds

paste

We pulled the weeds.

paste

The Car

paste

We washed the car.

paste

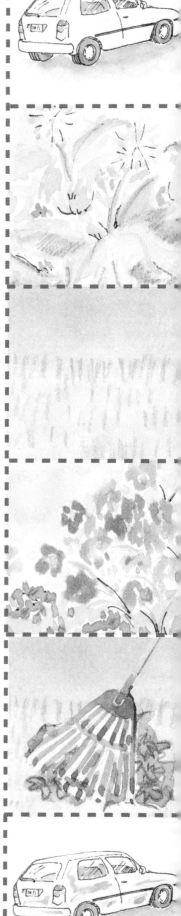

The Sound of p

Color the pictures that start with the sound **p** stands for.

poodle	pear	key
ball	penguin	purse
penny	cupcake	pizza
porcupine	pig	paint

This Is the Way to Wash a Car

Color the pictures. Cut and paste in order the directions for washing a car.

paste

paste

paste

paste

Wash off the dirt.

Dry off the car.

Rinse with clean water.

Get the car wet.

What Do You Hear?

Fill in the circle under the vowel sound you hear.

a   e   i   o   u

Working with Word Families

ap

n + ap = __ __ __   c + ap = __ __ __

m + ap = __ __ __   scr + ap = __ __ __ __ __

tr + ap = __ __ __ __   str + ap = __ __ __ __ __

Finish the pictures. Then color them.

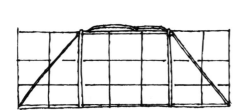

Draw a mouse in the trap.

Draw a strap on the helmet.

Show the baby taking a nap.

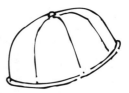

Add a feather and a flower.

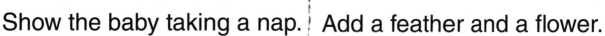

My Cocoon

It's cold out there.

It's warm in here.

It's bright out there.

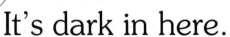

It's dark in here.

It's loud out there.

It's quiet in here.

It's busy out there.

It's still in here.

My sleeping bag is like a cocoon.

What Did It Say?

Circle the words that tell about the cocoon and the sleeping bag.

cold	quiet	warm	bright
loud	busy	still	dark

Fill in the circle in front of the answer.

1.
   ○ It is warm here.
   ○ It is cold here.

2.
   ○ It is dark here.
   ○ It is bright here.

3.
   ○ It is loud here.
   ○ It is quiet here.

Opposites

Words like **loud** and **quiet** are called **opposites**.
Draw a line to connect the opposites.

My hat is on.

up   clean

high   busy

bright   down

still   slow

fast   dark

dirty   low

My hat is off.

Draw pictures to show the **opposites**.

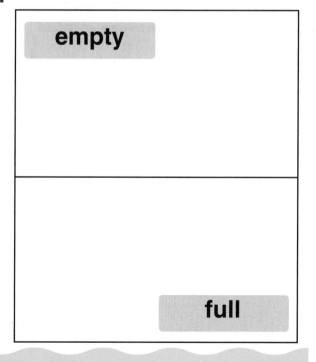

off	empty
on	full

Real or Make-Believe?

Circle **real** or **make-believe**.

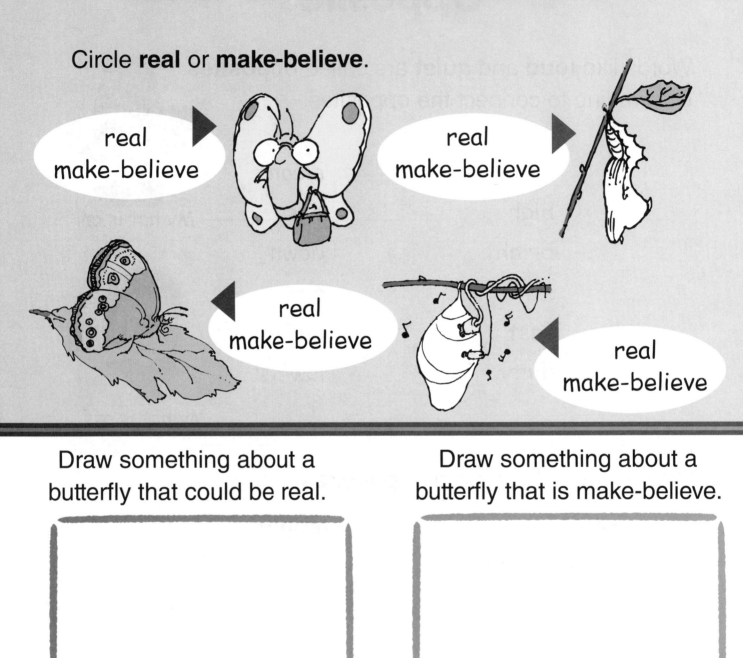

real
make-believe

real
make-believe

real
make-believe

real
make-believe

Draw something about a butterfly that could be real.

Draw something about a butterfly that is make-believe.

Skills: Sequencing Events; Writing a Description

Put It in Order

Color, cut, and paste to put the pictures in order.
Write about each picture.

1. *paste*

____

____

____

____

2. *paste*

____

____

____

____

3. *paste*

____

____

____

____

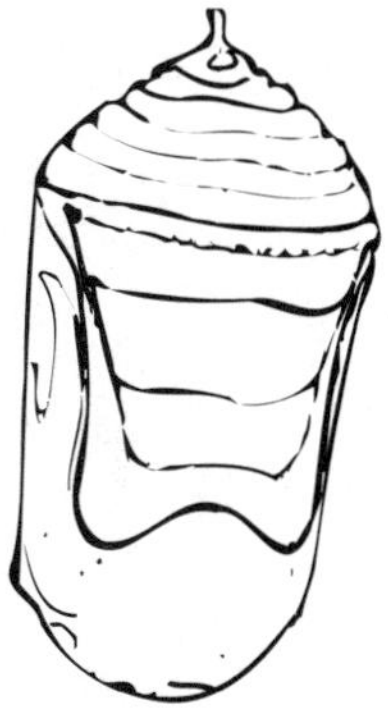

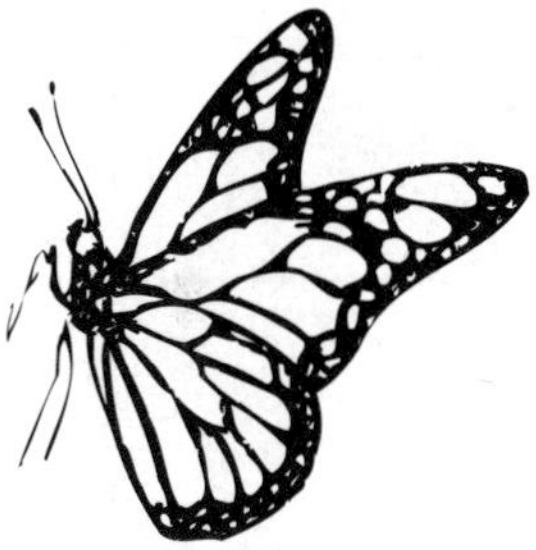

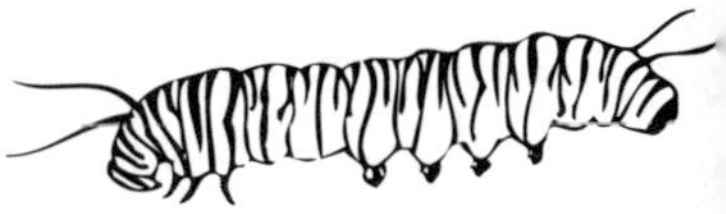

Working with Word Families

ill

h + ill = __ __ __ __

f + ill = __ __ __ __

ch + ill = __ __ __ __ __

dr + ill = __ __ __ __ __

Use the new words to complete these sentences.

1. Please _____ my glass with milk.

2. I need a _____ to fix the door.

3. He lives at the top of the _____.

4. If you go out in the cold you will get

   a _____.

Finish the Picture

Draw the other side of the butterfly. Then color the picture.

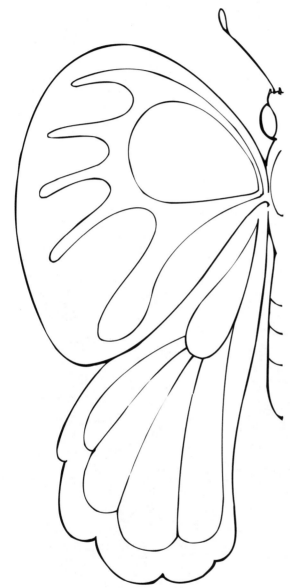

Write about the butterfly.

My butterfly _____

_____

_____ .

Who Can Fix It?

The button came off my pants. Who can fix it?

I know! Sis can sew.

Sharpen Your Skills—Reading • EMC 9719 • © Evan-Moor Corp.

What Did It Say?

Draw a picture of each thing. Then draw lines to tell who fixed it.

button	Mr. Snow

wheel	Sis

knob	Uncle Joe

Which thing could <u>not</u> be fixed quickly?

Words That Rhyme

Write the four words in the story that rhyme with **know**.

_____   _____

_____   _____

The Same Sound

Color the pictures that begin with the same sound as **button**.

Working with Word Families

ar

j + ar = __ __ __   st + ar = __ __ __ __

c + ar = __ __ __   b + ar = __ __ __

sc + ar = __ __ __ __   f + ar = __ __ __

Use the new words to complete these sentences.

I will look at the _____.

I can hang from the high _____.

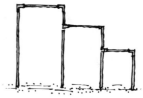

I will put the bug in a _____.

I don't want to have a _____.

Will It Work?

Fill in the circle to answer **yes** or **no**.

1. You can fix the pants with a needle and thread.

   ○ yes   ○ no

2. You can fix the toy car with a rubber band.

   ○ yes   ○ no

3. You can fix the doorknob with tape.

   ○ yes   ○ no

4. You can fix the flower with glue.

   ○ yes   ○ no

What would you use to fix a cut on your hand?

   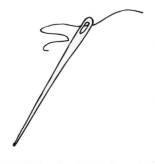

Reading Color Words

Read the words. Color the buttons.

blue

red

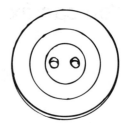

orange

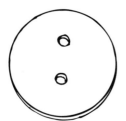

green

purple

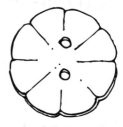

brown

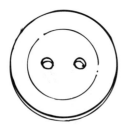

pink

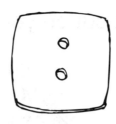

yellow

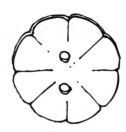

black

What Do You Hear?

Fill in the circle under the vowel sound you hear.

Giant Tortoise

Step by step—see it go.
Step by step—soooo slow.

Heavy shell on its back.
Heavy shell—like a pack.

Plodding on in the sand.
Plodding on over land.

Step by step—see it go.
Step by step—soooo slow.

 After You Read

Practice reading the poem.
Make it sound slow like a tortoise.
Read it to an adult.

What Did It Say?

Fill in the circle for the correct answer.

1. How does the tortoise move?
   - ○ It moves fast.
   - ○ It moves quickly.
   - ○ It moves slowly.

2. What is the tortoise's shell like?
   - ○ It's like a tent.
   - ○ It's like a pack.
   - ○ It's like a suitcase.

3. Where does the tortoise walk?
   - ○ It walks in the woods.
   - ○ It walks in the snow.
   - ○ It walks in the sand.

Draw a picture of a giant tortoise here.

Working with Word Families

ell

b + ell = __ __ __ __   t + ell = __ __ __ __

sh + ell = __ __ __ __ __   w + ell = __ __ __ __

sm + ell = __ __ __ __ __   sp + ell = __ __ __ __ __

Write one of the new words in each sentence. Then draw a picture to show what the sentence says.

The snail has a hard _____.	I can _____ the pretty rose.
The _____ rings when school starts.	I threw a penny in the wishing _____.

Skills: Categorizing; Understanding Opposites (Antonyms)

Heavy or Light?

Color, cut, and paste. Show which things are **heavy** and which things are **light**.

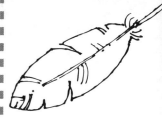

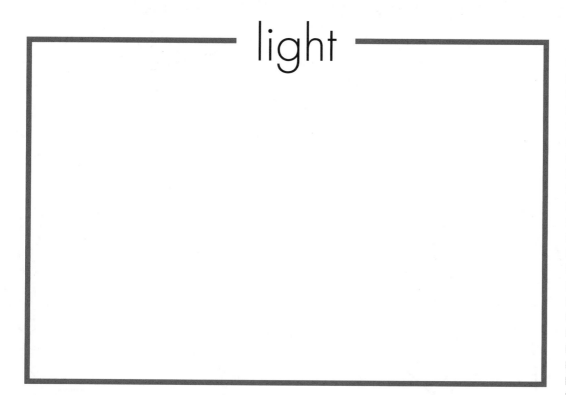

light

heavy

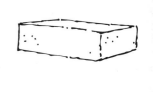

Cool, Man, Cool!

The tortoise wants to look cool. Can you color its shell in a special way? Add shoes and a hat.

Tell what the tortoise looks like.

_____

_____.

In a Shell

Draw another animal that lives in a shell.
Draw the place where it lives, too.

I am a _____.

I live _____

_____

_____.

Put It in the Pack

I'm going on a camping trip.
I will put the things
I need in my pack.

I'll need socks.

I'll need a shirt.

I'll need shorts.

I'll need a sweatshirt.

Put it in the pack.

I'll need a hat.

I'll need food.

I'll need my sleeping bag.

I'll need a flashlight.

I'll need Teddy.

Put me in the pack!

I'll put the pack on my back.
Help! I can't move.

I can't hike to the camp.
I'll take out a few things.

I don't have to have socks.

I don't have to have a shirt.

I don't have to have shorts.

I don't have to have a sweatshirt.

I don't have to have a hat.

I don't have to have food.

I don't have to have a sleeping bag.

I don't have to have a flashlight.

Teddy and I are ready!

Let's go!

After You Read

Practice reading this page.
When you can read it with no
mistakes, read it to an adult.

What Did It Say?

Fill in a circle to answer each question.

1. Where is the little girl going?

○   ○   ○

2. How will the little girl carry her things?

○   ○   ○

3. What is the little girl's problem?

○   ○   ○

4. What does the little girl take out that she will need?

○   ○   ○

Sharpen Your Skills—Reading • EMC 9719 • © Evan-Moor Corp.

Working with Word Families

ack

b + ack = __ __ __ __

p + ack = __ __ __ __

cr + ack = __ __ __ __ __

qu + ack = __ __ __ __ __

sn + ack = __ __ __ __ __

tr + ack = __ __ __ __ __

s + ack = __ __ __ __

r + ack = __ __ __ __

Read the sentence in each box. Draw what it tells you to do.

Draw a dish with a crack.	Draw a snack you like to eat.

What Would You Do?

Fill in the circle for the correct answer.

What would you do if your pack was too heavy?
○ Take something out.   ○ Put something in.

What would you do if it got dark?
○ Turn off the flashlight.   ○ Turn on the flashlight.

What would you do if you got hungry?
○ Eat a snack.   ○ Go to bed.

What would you do to stay dry in the rain?
○ Go outside.   ○ Go in the tent.

What would you cook on the fire?
○ Hot dogs and marshmallows   ○ Jello and ice cream

Take It Camping!

Circle the things you would take camping.
Draw a line under the ones you would need for school.

Connect the Dots

Start with 1. Make something you might see on a camping trip.

Make a list of animals you might see on a camping trip.

_____   _____   _____

_____   _____   _____

An Ant on the Rug

There's an ant on the rug, on the rug.

There's an ant on the rug, on the rug.

What a tiny bug, little ant on the rug.

There's an ant on the rug, on the rug.

There's an ant on my toe, on my toe.

There's an ant on my toe, on my toe.

Where will it go, that ant on my toe?

There's an ant on my toe, on my toe.

Sharpen Your Skills—Reading • EMC 9719 • © Evan-Moor Corp.

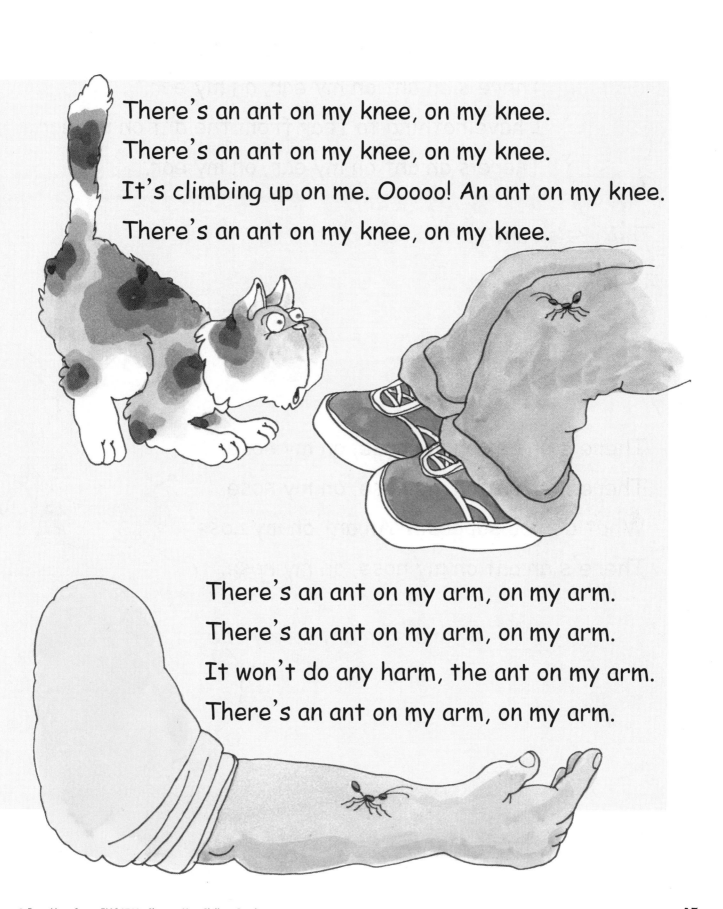

There's an ant on my knee, on my knee.

There's an ant on my knee, on my knee.

It's climbing up on me. Ooooo! An ant on my knee.

There's an ant on my knee, on my knee.

There's an ant on my arm, on my arm.

There's an ant on my arm, on my arm.

It won't do any harm, the ant on my arm.

There's an ant on my arm, on my arm.

There's an ant on my ear, on my ear.

There's an ant on my ear, on my ear.

I have nothing to fear from the ant on my ear.

There's an ant on my ear, on my ear.

There's an ant on my nose, on my nose.

There's an ant on my nose, on my nose.

What do you suppose? An ant on my nose!

There's an ant on my nose, on my nose.

There's an ant in my hair, in my hair.
There's an ant in my hair, in my hair.
I am very aware there's an ant in my hair.
There's an ant in my hair, in my hair.

There's an ant in a jar, in a jar.
There's an ant in a jar, in a jar.
It traveled near and far,
    but now it's in a jar.
There's an ant in a jar, in a jar.

After You Read

Practice your favorite part of the story.
When you can read it quickly, read it
to an adult.

What Did It Say?

Draw a line to show where the ant was.

First

Next

Next

Next

Next

Next

Next

At the end

Do you think the boy was happy to have the ant in the jar?

yes   no

Why do you think the way you do?

_____

_____

Working with Word Families

ug

r + ug = __ __ __   b + ug = __ __ __

d + ug = __ __ __   h + ug = __ __ __

pl + ug = __ __ __ __   sn + ug = __ __ __ __

Use the new words to complete these sentences.

Be careful when you

touch the _____.

Look at the hole

I _____.

Dad gave me

a _____.

He's as _____ as a

_____ in a _____.

Same Sound

Color the pictures that have the same (a) sound as  .

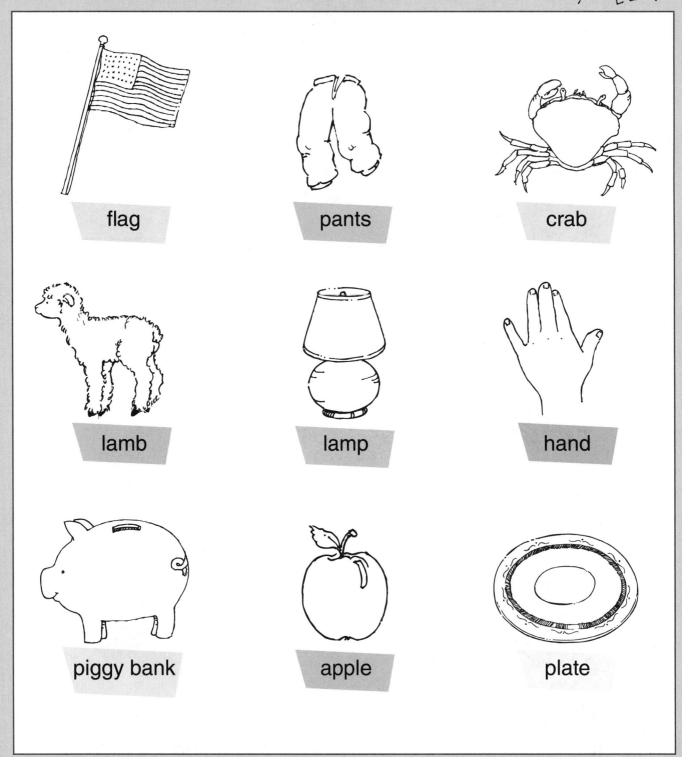

flag

pants

crab

lamb

lamp

hand

piggy bank

apple

plate

Skills: Understanding Word Meaning

What Does It Mean?

Cut and paste to label the picture.

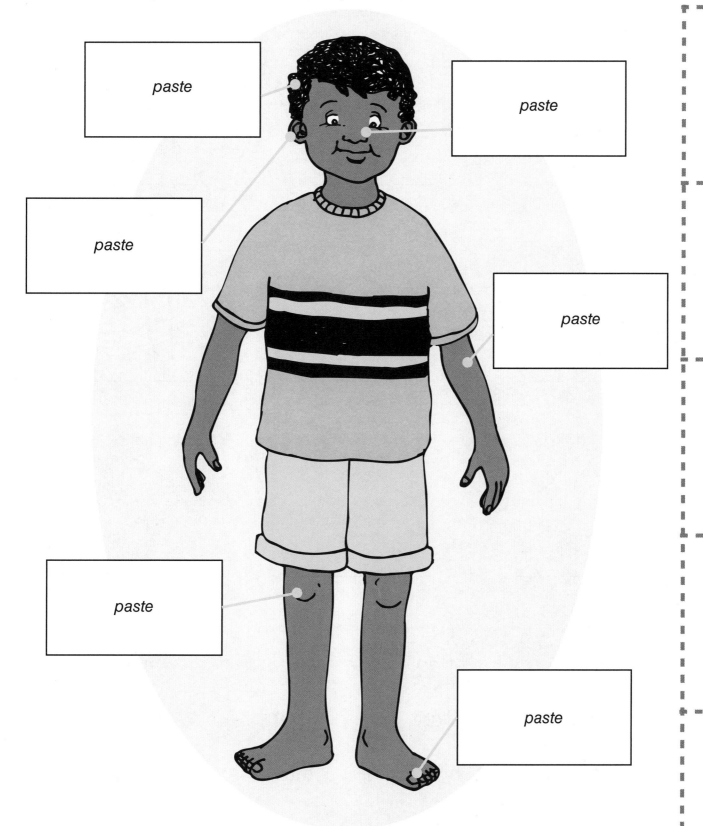

paste

paste

paste

paste

paste

paste

hair

nose

ear

arm

knee

toe

Rhyme Time

Color the pictures in each row that rhyme.
Write the words under the pictures.

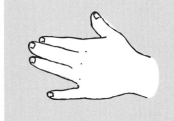

_____   _____   _____

_____   _____   _____

_____   _____   _____

bell	flag	hen	rug
bug	fan	pen	sand
car	hand	plate	skate

Who Lives in the Barn?

Cut out the flaps on the other side of this page.
Paste them on the story pages to make a flap book.

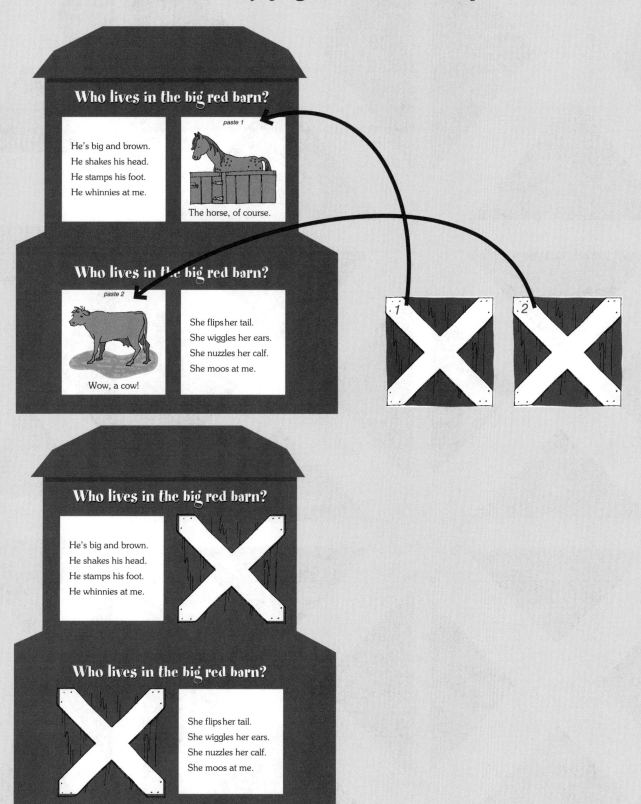

Who lives in the big red barn?

He's big and brown.
He shakes his head.
He stamps his foot.
He whinnies at me.

paste 1

The horse, of course.

Who lives in the big red barn?

paste 2

Wow, a cow!

She flips her tail.
She wiggles her ears.
She nuzzles her calf.
She moos at me.

1

2

Who lives in the big red barn?

He's big and brown.
He shakes his head.
He stamps his foot.
He whinnies at me.

Who lives in the big red barn?

She flips her tail.
She wiggles her ears.
She nuzzles her calf.
She moos at me.

Who lives in the big red barn?

He's big and brown.

He shakes his head.

He stamps his foot.

He whinnies at me.

paste 1

The horse, of course.

Who lives in the big red barn?

paste 2

Wow, a cow!

She flips her tail.

She wiggles her ears.

She nuzzles her calf.

She moos at me.

Who lives in the big red barn?

She wears her winter coat.

She has a little bell.

She wakes her lamb.

She baas at me.

paste 3

My sheep's asleep.

Who lives in the big red barn?

paste 4

*Let's follow
the swallow.*

It flies from the roof.

It builds a small nest.

It sits on its eggs.

It peeps at me.

Who lives in the big red barn?

He stands by the door.

He runs to me.

He licks my hand.

He barks at me.

paste 5

Not a frog! It's my dog.

Who lives in the big red barn?

She laps the milk.

She licks her paws.

She feeds her kittens.

She purrs at me.

paste 6

Mother cat!
Think of that.

Who lives in the big red barn?

It runs so fast.

It hides so well.

It nibbles food.

It squeaks at me.

paste 7

The barn is a house for the mouse.

Who lives in the big red barn?

paste 8

A horse,
A cow,
A sheep,
A swallow,
A dog,
A cat,
And a mouse.
  That's who!

paste 9

What Did It Say?

Fill in the circle under the correct answer.

1. Who builds a small nest?

sheep	swallow	cat	mouse
○	○	○	○

2. Who nibbles food?

sheep	swallow	cat	mouse
○	○	○	○

3. Who has a lamb?

sheep	swallow	cat	mouse
○	○	○	○

4. Who flips her tail?

horse	cow	dog	cat
○	○	○	○

5. Who licks a paw?

horse	cow	dog	cat
○	○	○	○

6. Who barks?

horse	cow	dog	cat
○	○	○	○

7. Who stamps a foot?

horse	cow	dog	cat
○	○	○	○

Working with Word Families

ake

c + ake = __ __ __ __

sn + ake = __ __ __ __ __

r + ake = __ __ __ __

sh + ake = __ __ __ __ __

fl + ake = __ __ __ __ __

br + ake = __ __ __ __ __

Write the correct **-ake** word to finish each sentence.
Draw a picture to show what the sentence says.

I _____ up the leaves.

A _____ of snow is
on my nose.

Which Came First?

Cut and paste to put the animals in order.
Use the rhyme to help.

Who lives in the barn?

The [*paste*] , of course.

Wow, a [*paste*] !

My [*paste*] is asleep.

Let's follow the [*paste*] .

Not a frog! It's my [*paste*] .

Think of that, Mother [*paste*] !

The barn is a house for the [*paste*] .

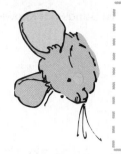

mouse

sheep

dog

swallow

cat

cow

horse

What Does It Say?

Match the noise word to the animal that makes that noise.

baa

whinny

purr

squeak

chirp

moo

woof

Draw another animal here.
What noise does it make?
It says

_____.

Think About It

Which animals live mainly on a farm?
Which animals live mainly in the jungle?
Write the names of the animals in the correct list.

goat   lion   elephant   chicken

horse   zebra   cow   monkey

On a farm   In the jungle

_____   _____

_____   _____

_____   _____

_____   _____

The Big Red Barn

Read the color words. Then color the picture.

The Fix-It Man

Hello, Mr. Fix-It.
Could you come to my house?

The fix-it man came to my house.
He fixed the stove.

Hello, Mr. Fix-It.
We need you to come.

The fix-it man came to my house.
He fixed the sink.

Hello, Mr. Fix-It. The door is stuck.

The fix-it man came to my house.
He fixed the door.

Hello, Mr. Fix-It. My window broke.

The fix-it man came to my house. He fixed the window.

Hello, Mr. Fix-It. Please come fast.

The fix-it man came to my house.
We had cookies and milk.

What Did It Say?

Fill in the circle by the correct answer.

1. Who did the boy call for help?
   ○ Mother   ○ a friend   ○ Mr. Fix-It

2. What was wrong with the window?
   ○ It was stuck.   ○ It broke.   ○ It needed washing.

3. Was Mr. Fix-It a good fixer?
   ○ No, he had to keep coming back.
   ○ Yes, he won a prize.
   ○ Yes, he fixed everything.

4. Why do you think the boy called Mr. Fix-It the last time?
   ○ There were too many cookies in the jar.
   ○ The milk was going to spoil.
   ○ Mr. Fix-It should have a treat.

Write an answer.
Who fixes things at your house?

_____

_____

_____

Put It in Order

Mr. Fix-It will fix the wagon. Color the pictures.
Cut and paste to put them in the correct order.

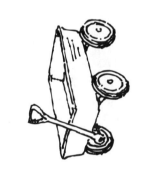

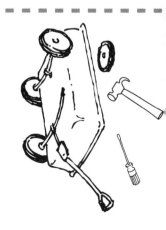

1

paste

2

paste

3

paste

4

paste

Can It Be Fixed?

Some things cannot be put back together.
Write It can be fixed or It can't by each
of the pictures below. Use your best
handwriting.

It can't

Working with Word Families

ink

p + ink = __ __ __ __   s + ink = __ __ __ __

bl + ink = __ __ __ __ __   dr + ink = __ __ __ __ __

shr + ink = __ __ __ __ __ __   th + ink = __ __ __ __ __

Draw a toy boat in a sink.	Draw a muddy pig that's pink.

More Than One

Add **s** to each word to mean more than one.
Then draw what the words say.

one door

two _____

one house

three _____

one bird

four _____

one flower

five _____

Rhyme Time

Color the pictures. Circle the words that rhyme.

house   mouse   cat

window   sink   ink

door   bear   chair

dish   milk   fish

cake   snake   hat

What a

Monday
I have muffins.
Munch! Munch!

Tuesday
I have tuna.
Tasty!

Wednesday
I have waffles.
Wow!

Thursday
I have Thanksgiving turkey.
Thanks!

M
T
W
Th

Sharpen Your Skills—Reading • EMC 9719 • © Evan-Moor Corp.

Week!

Friday
I have fries.
Free fries!

F

Saturday
I have sodas.
Sip it!

S

Sunday
I have soup.
See it simmer.

S

Ummmm—What can I eat next week?

What Did I Have?

Fill in the circle under the correct answer.

1. What did I have on Tuesday?

turkey   tuna   soup
○   ○   ○

2. What did I have on Friday?

waffles   muffins   fries
○   ○   ○

3. What did I have on Sunday?

soup   soda   turkey
○   ○   ○

4. What did I have on Monday?

waffles   fries   muffins
○   ○   ○

5. What did I have on Saturday?

soup   soda   tuna
○   ○   ○

My Favorite Foods

Rewrite the story. Draw or write what you would like to eat each day. Then read the story using your foods.

Monday

I have

Tuesday

I have

Wednesday

I have

Thursday

I have

Friday

I have

Saturday

I have

Sunday

I have

Working with Word Families

unch

l + unch = __ __ __ __ __   m + unch = __ __ __ __ __ __

b + unch = __ __ __ __ __   p + unch = __ __ __ __ __

cr + unch = __ __ __ __ __ __ __

Circle each word from the **-unch** family in the story below.
Draw pictures to show the animals eating.

See the goats?
They like to eat.
Munch, munch,
Hay for lunch.

See the squirrels?
They like to eat.
Munch, munch,
Hear the crunch.

See the monkeys?
They like to eat.
Munch, munch,
What a bunch!

Noisy Foods

Some foods are noisy. Color the things that make crunchy noises when you eat them. Write **munch** under the ones you like to eat.

_____   _____   _____

_____   _____   _____

_____   _____   _____

_____   _____   _____

How Does It Taste?

Write one letter of the food name in each box. When all the boxes have been filled in, read the secret message in the pink boxes.

Foods

milk	apple	custard
fruit	cookie	bread
eggs	chocolate	pudding

Write the secret message here: _____

Food Word Search

See how many of the foods in the Word Box you can find.

Word Box		
☐ apple	☐ banana	☐ spaghetti
☐ cookie	☐ pizza	☐ cheese
☐ grapes	☐ pancake	☑ hamburger
☐ orange	☐ carrot	☐ tuna
☐ potatoes	☐ eggs	☐ corn

```
h  a  m  b  u  r  g  e  r  t  w
a  p  p  l  e  c  a  r  p  u  p
n  c  g  r  a  p  e  s  i  n  o
c  a  t  r  u  c  k  s  z  a  t
o  r  c  h  e  e  s  e  z  x  a
o  r  j  c  o  r  n  z  a  m  t
k  o  p  a  n  c  a  k  e  y  o
i  t  r  a  b  b  i  t  u  p  e
e  r  b  a  n  a  n  a  x  t  s
p  s  p  a  g  h  e  t  t  i  z
o  r  a  n  g  e  w  e  g  g  s
```

Molly and Max

This is Molly.

This is Max.

They played together all week.

Monday they played hide and seek.

Molly hid under the blanket.

Max hid behind the plant.

Tuesday they dug holes in the yard.

Molly buried a bone.

Max picked some flowers.

Wednesday they went for a walk.

Molly walked and sniffed.

Max walked round and round.

Thursday they learned to open doors.

Molly went in and out.

Max found the trash.

Friday they practiced jumping.

Molly jumped high.

Max jumped too high.

Saturday they chased balls.

Molly brought the balls back.

Max found a bigger ball.

Sunday is a day for rest.

Molly will rest.

Will Max rest, too?

What Did It Say?

Fill in the circles to answer the questions.

1. Which dog hid under the blanket? ○ Max ○ Molly

2. Which dog found the trash? ○ Max ○ Molly

3. Which dog brought the balls back? ○ Max ○ Molly

4. Which dog buried a bone? ○ Max ○ Molly

5. Which dog popped a balloon? ○ Max ○ Molly

6. Which dog picked some flowers? ○ Max ○ Molly

7. Which dog do you think will try
   to open the gifts? ○ Max ○ Molly

8. Which dog is easier to care for? ○ Max ○ Molly

Max Learns the Hard Way

Color, cut, and paste. Put the pictures in order to tell Max's story.

1

paste

2

paste

3

paste

4

paste

Trouble!

It's easy for Max to get in trouble. Put a check by the things that would mean trouble.

☐ Max chewed the shoe.

☐ Max drank his water.

☐ Max jumped over the gate.

☐ Max chewed on the bone.

☐ Max knocked over the lamp.

☐ Max picked some flowers.

☐ Max took a nap.

☐ Max opened the gifts.

Think about what Max might do next.
Write it here.

_____

Will it mean trouble for Max?   yes   no

Working with Word Families

one

b + one = __ __ __ __   c + one = __ __ __ __

ph + one = __ __ __ __ __   st + one = __ __ __ __ __

thr + one = __ __ __ __ __ __ z + one = __ __ __ __

Write the words to label the pictures.

__ __ __ __ __   __ __ __ __

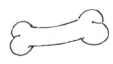

__ __ __ __ __ __   end __ __ __ __

What's at the End?

Write the letter that stands for the sound you hear at the end of each word.

do___   doo___

ba___   boo___

cu___   ja___

tu___   ma___

ca___   bo___

Draw a Pup

Follow the steps to draw a puppy.

How is the pup like Max?

_____

How is the pup different from Max?

_____

New Friends

Cookie lived with Amy. She had a dish for water. She had a dish for food. She had a purple mouse with a long tail. She had all that she needed. Cookie loved her home.

One day Amy came home. She had a surprise for Cookie. It was not a new mouse. It was not a new dish. It was a new friend. It was a little gray kitten.

Cookie didn't need a new friend. Cookie ran from Amy. She hid behind the chair.

Sharpen Your Skills—Reading • EMC 9719 • © Evan-Moor Corp.

The new kitten sniffed Cookie's dish. Cookie hissed at the kitten.

The new kitten tasted Cookie's water. Cookie swatted at the kitten.

The new kitten batted Cookie's mouse. Cookie chased the kitten away.

The new kitten cried. It was afraid. Cookie looked at the kitten. It was shaking.

Cookie touched the kitten with her paw. The kitten was soft. Cookie licked the kitten's ear. She licked the kitten's face. The little kitten began to purr.

Cookie didn't need a friend. But the new kitten did. Maybe Cookie could be the new kitten's friend.

Cookie sat on Amy's lap. The little kitten sat next to Cookie. Cookie purred. The little kitten purred.

Cookie played with her mouse. The little kitten played, too.

Cookie curled up for a nap. The little kitten slept. The little kitten had a new friend. Cookie had a new friend, too.

 Sharpen Your Skills—Reading • EMC 9719 • © Evan-Moor Corp.

What Did It Say?

Answer each question.

Fill in the circle to mark yes or no.

1. In the beginning Cookie had:

    a dish for water .... ○ yes   ○ no

    a purple bed .... ○ yes   ○ no

    a dish for food .... ○ yes   ○ no

    a yellow mouse .... ○ yes   ○ no

2. Was Cookie happy to see

    Amy's surprise? .... ○ yes   ○ no

3. Cookie

    hissed at the new kitten .... ○ yes   ○ no

    scratched the new kitten .... ○ yes   ○ no

    swatted at the new kitten .... ○ yes   ○ no

    chased the new kitten................... ○ yes   ○ no

4. The new kitten was afraid. .... ○ yes   ○ no

5. Cookie decided to be the new

    kitten's friend. .... ○ yes   ○ no

What Does It Mean?

Look at the pictures. Write the best word in each sentence.

sniffed	tasted	cried
licked	chased	swatted
purred	played	hissed

The kitten _____ the flower.

Cookie _____ at the kitten.

Cookie _____ the kitten.

The little kitten _____ .

The kitten _____ with the yarn.

Cookie _____ the kitten's ear.

Animal Babies

Cut and paste to match the babies with the parents.
Write the names under the pictures.

dog   _____

horse   _____

hen   _____

cow   _____

cat   _____

pig   _____

Word Box

chick   calf   piglet   pup   foal   kitten

The Sound of k

Say the picture name. Write the letter **k** where you hear its sound.

__itten   __ook   __ey

__angaroo   __oala   __oorknob

__aw   __ite   __ing

Working with Word Families

ace

f + ace = _ _ _ _

l + ace = _ _ _ _

r + ace = _ _ _ _

pl + ace = _ _ _ _ _

sp + ace = _ _ _ _ _

tr + ace = _ _ _ _ _

Finish each picture. The words tell you what to do.

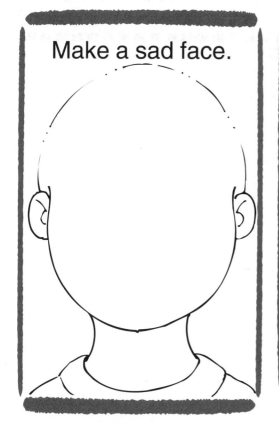

Make a sad face.

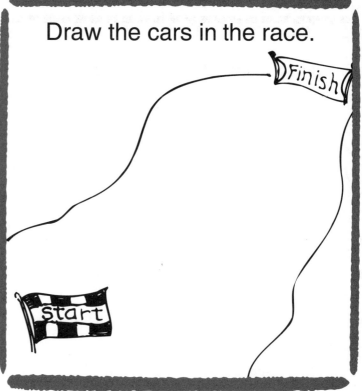

Draw the cars in the race.

What Do You Think?

Fill in the circle in front of yes or no.

Can two cats be friends?	○ yes	○ no
Can two cats drive to the mall?	○ yes	○ no
Can two cats like the same toy?	○ yes	○ no
Can two cats chase one another?	○ yes	○ no
Can two cats lap the milk?	○ yes	○ no
Can two cats write a letter?	○ yes	○ no

Draw something two cats could really do.

The Missing Mitten

One day Tommy got ready to go outside. It was a cold, snowy day. Tommy put on his snow pants. He put on his jacket. He put on his long green stocking hat. His mother gave him a scarf to keep his neck warm. Next he pulled on his shiny yellow snow boots. They were new. Tommy couldn't wait to try them out. He was almost ready. All that he needed were his mittens.

Tommy reached into his jacket pocket. He pulled out one fuzzy blue mitten. One mitten? Where was the other mitten? Tommy looked all over. He looked like a marshmallow man stumbling around his room. Where was the missing mitten?

Tommy yelled to his mom, "Hey, Mom! I can only find one blue mitten. Will you help me find the other one?"

Sharpen Your Skills—Reading • EMC 9719 • © Evan-Moor Corp.

Tommy's mom came into his room. She took one look at Tommy and started to laugh.

Tommy frowned. "What are you laughing at?" he asked.

Tommy's mom pulled Tommy in front of the mirror. She pointed to his long stocking hat. Peeking out from under the hat was a blue thumb. A hat with a blue thumb?

Tommy reached up and pulled off the hat. There was the missing mitten!

What Did It Say?

Fill in the circle or write words to answer the questions.

1. What was missing?
   ○ hat   ○ scarf   ○ mittens

2. Who did the missing thing belong to?
   ○ Mom   ○ Tommy   ○ Dad

3. Where was the missing thing found?

   _____

Draw something that belongs to you that was missing.

Put It in Order

Color, cut, and paste. Show the order that Tommy put on his things before he went outside.

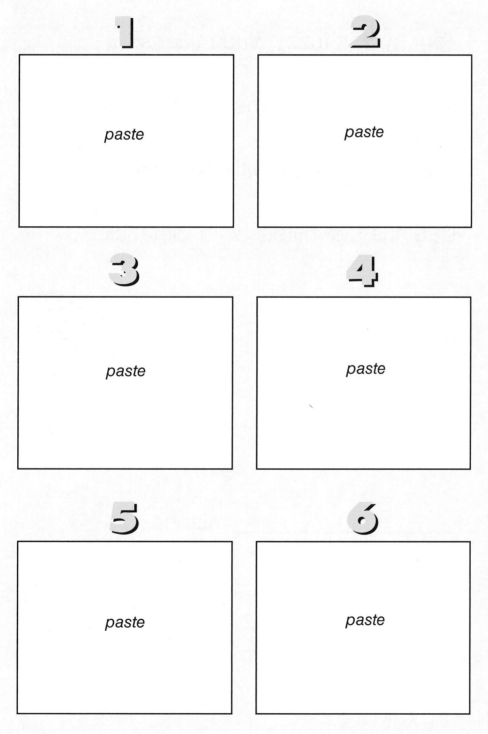

1

paste

2

paste

3

paste

4

paste

5

paste

6

paste

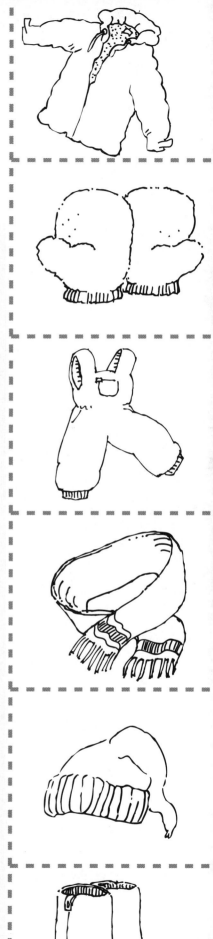

Whose Mittens?

Read the sentences. Then label the mittens.
Use **'s** after the name of the owner.

Tommy has fuzzy blue mittens.

Molly has red mittens with blue stripes.

Baby has mittens with dog ears on them.

Dad has big mittens with metal clips.

____Molly's_____ mittens

_____ mittens

_____ mittens

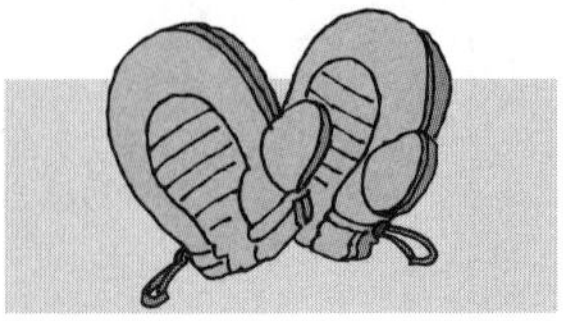

_____ mittens

Working with Word Families

itten

Write the letters to make new words.

m + itten = __ __ __ __ __ __

k + itten = __ __ __ __ __ __

b + itten = __ __ __ __ __ __

wr + itten = __ __ __ __ __ __ __

Use the new words to complete these sentences.

1. The dog was _____ by a flea.

2. My name is _____ in this book.

3. The _____ has soft fur and a nice meow.

4. The _____ keeps my hand warm when it's cold.

Make Them the Same

Color the second mitten to match the first.
List three words that tell about the mittens.

1. _____

2. _____

3. _____

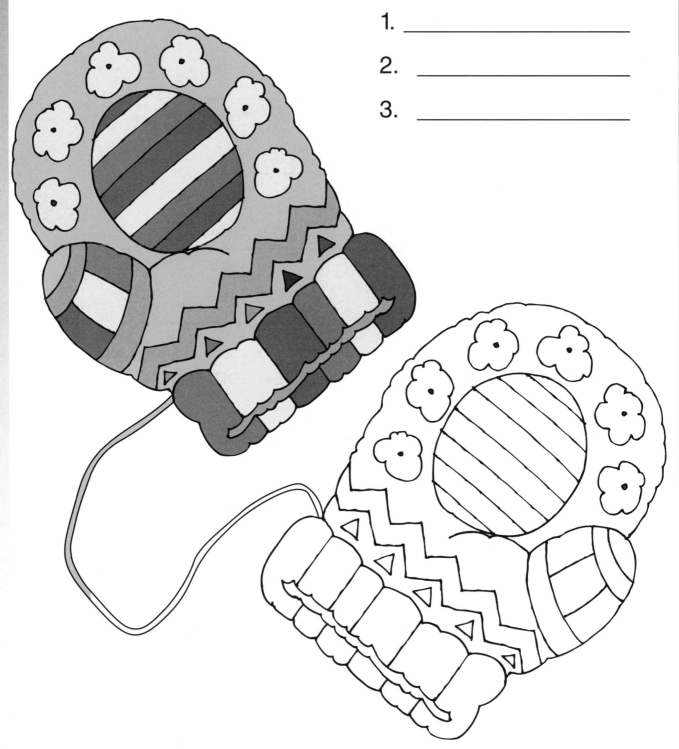

Color Crossword

Use color words to fill in the blanks of this crossword.

Across

3. What color is grape juice and an eggplant?
5. What color is the sky on a sunny day?
7. What color is soot from a fire?
8. What color are ripe tomatoes?
9. What color is the snow?
10. What color is hot chocolate?

Down

1. What color is a ripe pumpkin?
2. What color is a lemon?
3. What color is a cat's tongue?
4. What color is made from black and white?
6. What color is spinach?

black
blue
brown
gray
green
orange
pink
purple
red
white
yellow

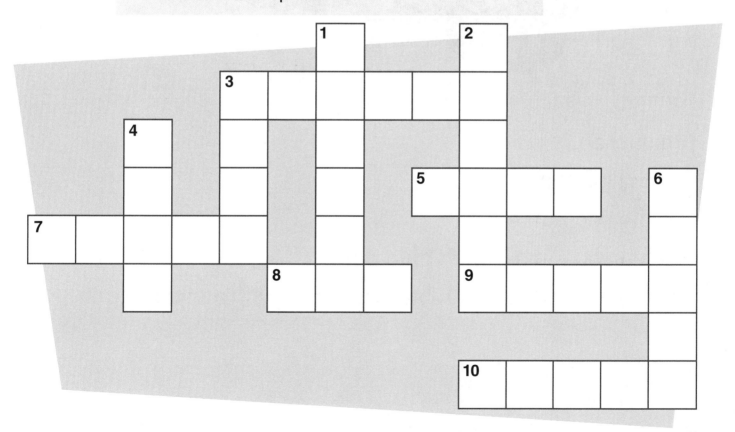

A Mitten

Practice this page until you can read it with no mistakes.
Read it to an adult.

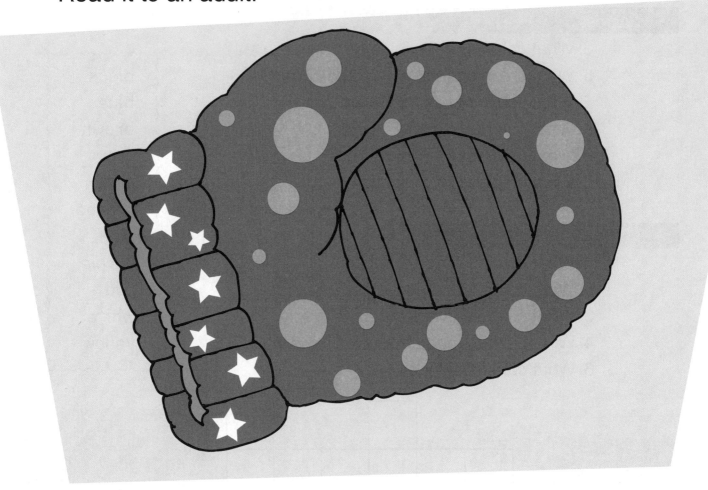

a mitten

a big mitten

a big red mitten

a big red mitten with blue dots

a big red mitten with blue dots and white stars

A New Neighbor

Peter looked down from his window. There was a big moving van next door. He watched as the man unloaded the van.

Peter wanted a new friend—a new friend who could play ball, ride bikes, and build things. Peter watched. The man unloaded a bike, a wagon, and a big bear.

Peter smiled. The new family must have a boy.

Just then a car pulled in behind the moving van. It was the new family. Peter watched. The family got out of the car. There was a boy! He had on a blue ball cap. Peter cheered. He watched the new family go inside their house.

Peter ran downstairs. He grabbed his ball and mitt. He ran next door. He knocked on the door. A man opened the door. Peter said, "Hi, I'm Peter. I live next door. Can your kid come out and play ball?"

The man smiled and said, "I'm glad to meet you, Peter. Sam was hoping to meet a new ball-playing friend. Sam loves to play ball. Sam can catch any ball you throw."

Peter smiled. He couldn't wait to meet Sam. It would be fun to have a pal next door.

The man called, "Sam, come meet our new neighbor. This is Peter. Peter, this is Samantha. We call her Sam."

Peter gulped. Samantha? That was a girl's name. His new neighbor was a girl! The kid with the blue ball cap was a girl? Peter didn't know what to do. He wanted a new friend. He wanted a pal who could play ball. He had thought that pal would be a boy.

Sam smiled at Peter. "Hi, Peter, want to play some catch?"

Peter nodded. He wondered if Sam could really catch. Her dad said she could catch anything.

Later Peter and Sam drank milk and ate cookies. Peter shook his head and smiled. "Sam, your dad was right. You can catch anything I throw. And you throw a mean fast ball, too. I'm glad that you moved next door to me."

After You Read

Practice pages 116 and 117. Use a different voice for each person that is talking. Read the pages to an adult.

What Did It Say?

Fill in the circle to show the answer.

1. How did Peter feel when he met Sam?
   ○ surprised   ○ happy   ○ mad

2. How did Peter feel after he played ball with Sam?
   ○ sad   ○ glad   ○ upset

3. Why did Peter think a new boy had moved in next door?
   ○ The mailman brought a letter.
   ○ His mother told him.
   ○ The moving man unloaded a bike and a wagon.

4. Why did Peter think that the new "boy" liked to play ball?
   ○ The new kid was holding a suitcase.
   ○ The moving man unloaded some bats.
   ○ The new kid was wearing a blue ball cap.

5. What did the new kid's dad boast?
   ○ He said that Sam was a good hitter.
   ○ He said that Sam was a good pitcher.
   ○ He said that Sam could catch any ball Peter threw.

Baseball Words

Use the words below to label the drawing.

baseball	mitt	ball cap	cleats
home plate	bat	backstop	batting glove

The Sound of gr

Color the pictures whose names begin with the sound that gr stands for.

 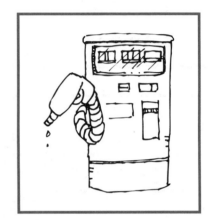

 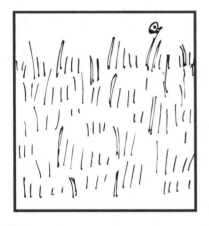 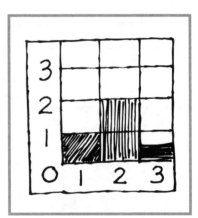

What grade are you in? _____

Is the grass green? _____

Are you ever grumpy? _____

Draw a Story

Cut and paste the sentences in order. Then draw the story.

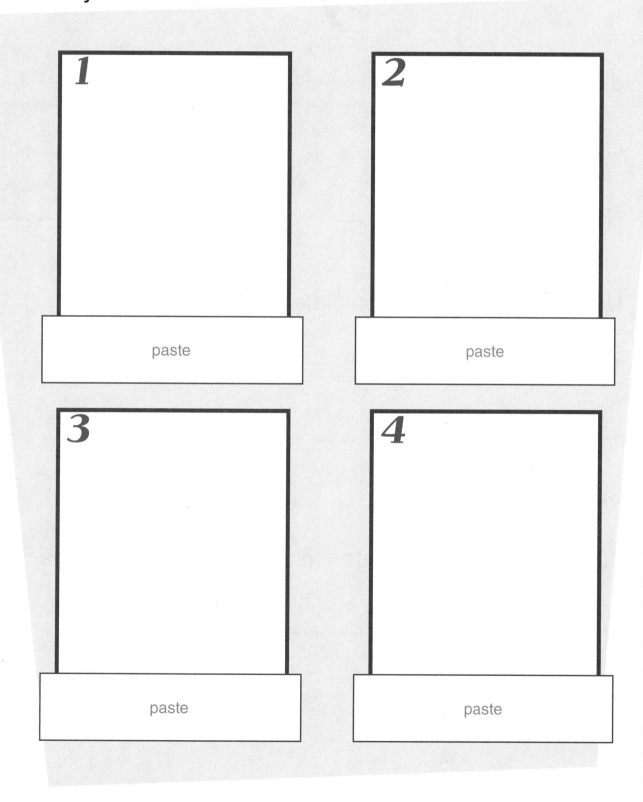

| 1 | 2 |
| paste | paste |

| 3 | 4 |
| paste | paste |

The ball was thrown.

Billy hit the ball hard.

Billy came to the plate.

It was a home run.

Working with Word Families

ay

d + ay = __ __ __   h + ay = __ __ __

cl + ay = __ __ __ __   pl + ay = __ __ __ __

spr + ay = __ __ __ __ __   str + ay = __ __ __ __ __

Use the new words to complete these sentences.

1. The frog is made of _____.

2. The cow sleeps on the _____.

3. I want to go out and _____.

4. _____ the water on the flowers.

5. It's a bright sunny _____.

6. That pup looks like a _____.

George Washington's Barn

George Washington was an important man. Most people know him because he was the first president. Others, because he was a brave soldier.

But George Washington was an important farmer, too. He had a big farm in Virginia. He studied farming. He learned the best way to plant crops. He also learned the best way to harvest crops.

One of the crops that Mr. Washington planted was wheat. Kernels of wheat grow on stalks. When the wheat is ripe, the stalks are cut. The kernels are taken off the stalk. That's a hard job. The stalks are used as straw. The kernels are ground for making bread.

Mr. Washington had a plan. He wanted to make getting the wheat kernels easier. He built a special barn. The barn had 16 sides. It had a ramp up to the door. It was built on a hill so that it had a basement.

Workers cut the wheat. Then they spread it on the floor of the barn. Two mules walked up the ramp into the barn. They walked around and around on the wheat. The kernels of wheat came off the stalks. The kernels fell through holes in the floor to the basement. In the basement, workers swept up the wheat.

George Washington's plan worked. The mules did a good, fast job. The workers were happy. Mr. Washington's wheat was ready for grinding. They could all have bread for dinner!

 Sharpen Your Skills—Reading • EMC 9719 • © Evan-Moor Corp.

What Did It Say?

Think about what you read. Choose the best answer for each question. Look at the story again if you need to.

1. Why do most people know George Washington?
   - ○ He was a brave soldier.
   - ○ He was the first U.S. president.
   - ○ He was a good farmer.

2. Where was George Washington's farm?
   - ○ Washington, D.C.
   - ○ New York
   - ○ Virginia

3. How do you know farming was important to Mr. Washington?
   - ○ He liked to eat bread.
   - ○ He wanted to learn the best way to farm.
   - ○ He fought in a war.

4. Why did Mr. Washington's barn make harvesting wheat easier?
   - ○ It had a ramp so the workers didn't have to go up steps.
   - ○ The mules did most of the work.
   - ○ The workers didn't have to worry about rain.

What Does It Mean?

Read the information below. Use what you learn to fill in the blanks.

George Washington used five different kinds of fences on his farms.

- The **split rail fence** was a moveable fence. It could be laid in a zigzag pattern around trees.
- The **post and rail fence** was a permanent fence. It was used to make boundary lines.
- The **hurdle fence** was a small moveable fence. It was used to keep animals in an area for grazing.
- The **waddle fence** was a tightly woven split rail fence. It was used to pen birds and small animals.
- The **living hedge** was made of bushes. It was used between fields and pastures.

A split rail fence

Write the name of the fence that would be best.

1. A fence between your property and your neighbor's property _____

2. A fence around the chicken yard _____

3. A fence along a border with rocks and trees _____

4. A fence to keep the sheep in one area of the pasture _____

Reading a Map

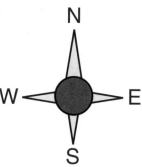

George Washington's big farm was called a plantation. This is a map of his plantation.

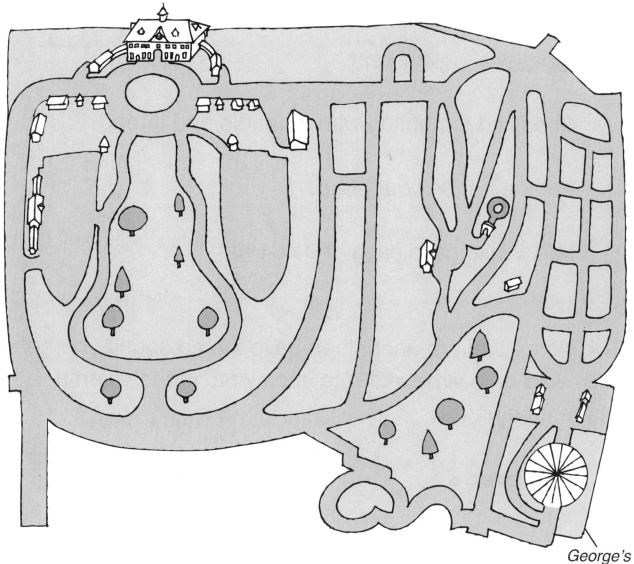

George's barn

Draw a line that shows how George might walk on pathways from his house to his barn.

In which directions would he have to go? _____

The Sounds of ea

The letters **ea** can stand for different sounds. Read the words and listen for two different **ea** sounds.

I am <u>ready</u> to plant the seeds.

<u>Please</u> take your <u>seat</u>.

She fixed the button with a needle and <u>thread</u>.

Put the hat on your <u>head</u>.

Mrs. White gave <u>each</u> of us a <u>treat</u>.

The words that are underlined have the **ea** sound you hear in **bread** or in **wheat**. Write each word in the column where it belongs.

bread

wheat

_____

_____

_____

_____

_____

_____

_____

_____

Put the Steps in Order

Cut and paste.

paste

paste

paste

paste

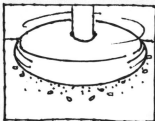

paste

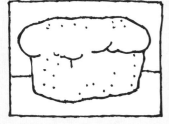

paste

Make some bread.

Plant the wheat seeds.

Take the kernels off the stalk.

Water the seeds.

Cut the wheat stalks.

Grind the kernels into flour.

Working with Word Families

alk

w + alk = __ __ __ __   st + alk = __ __ __ __ __

t + alk = __ __ __ __   ch + alk = __ __ __ __ __

Draw something you would see on a **walk** by a lake.

Draw a place where you cannot **talk**.

Puzzle Page

Cut out the puzzle pieces. Put them together.

What do you have? _____

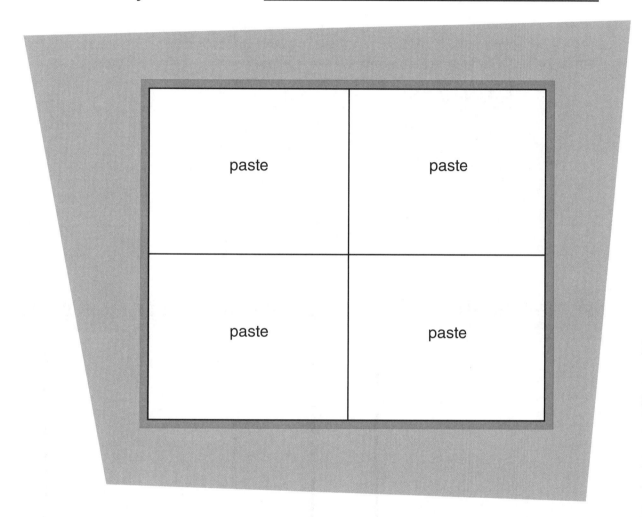

Match the Opposites

Draw a line to match each pair of opposites.

plant	down
hard	slow
fast	harvest
up	less
more	easy

Draw something that is fast.

Draw something that is slow.

Tracking Form

Topic	Color in each page you complete.					
Dad and I	6	7	8	9	10	11
My Cocoon	14	15	16	17	18	19
Who Can Fix It?	24	25	26	27	28	29
Giant Tortoise	31	32	33	34	35	
Put It in the Pack	40	41	42	43		
An Ant on the Rug	48	49	50	51	52	
Who Lives in the Barn?	59	60	61	62	63	64
The Fix-It Man	70	71	72	73	74	75
What a Week!	78	79	80	81	82	83
Molly and Max	88	89	90	91	92	93
New Friends	97	98	99	100	101	102
The Missing Mitten	106	107	108	109	110	111
	112					
A New Neighbor	118	119	120	121	122	
George Washington's Barn	125	126	127	128	129	130
	131	132				

Answer Key

Checking your child's work is an important part of learning. It allows you to see what your child knows well and what areas need more practice. It also provides an opportunity for you to help your child understand that making mistakes is a part of learning.

When an error is discovered, ask your child to look carefully at the question or problem. Errors often occur through misreading. Your child can quickly correct these errors. Help your child with items she or he finds difficult.

The answer key pages can be used in several ways:

- Remove the answer pages and give the book to your child. Go over the answers as each story and the accompanying activity pages are completed.
- Leave the answer pages in the book and give the practice pages to your child one story unit at a time.

Page 6

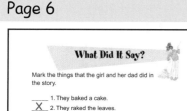

Page 7

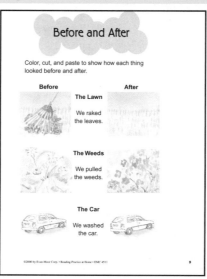

Page 8

Page 9

Page 10

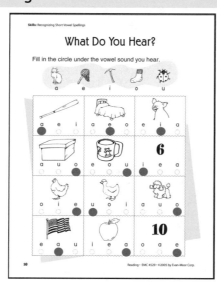

Page 11

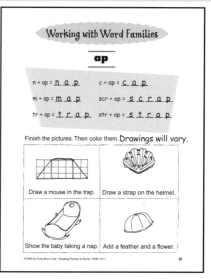

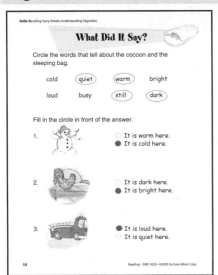

Skills: Recalling Story Details; Understanding Opposites

What Did It Say?

Circle the words that tell about the cocoon and the sleeping bag.

cold (quiet) (warm) bright

loud busy (still) (dark)

Fill in the circle in front of the answer.

1. ○ It is warm here.
   ● It is cold here.

2. ○ It is dark here.
   ● It is bright here.

3. ● It is loud here.
   ○ It is quiet here.

14   Reading • EMC 4529 • ©2005 by Evan-Moor Corp.

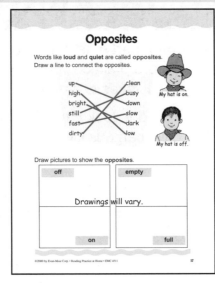

Opposites

Words like **loud** and **quiet** are called **opposites**. Draw a line to connect the opposites.

up — low
high — slow
bright — down
still — busy
fast — dark
dirty — clean

My hat is on.
My hat is off.

Draw pictures to show the **opposites**.

off	empty
Drawings will vary.	
on	full

©2000 by Evan-Moor Corp. • Reading Practice at Home • EMC 4511   17

Real or Make-Believe?

Circle **real** or **make-believe**.

real / make-believe
real / make-believe
real / make-believe
real / make-believe
real / make-believe

Draw something about a butterfly that could be real.

Draw something about a butterfly that is make-believe.

Drawings will vary.

18   ©2000 by Evan-Moor Corp. • Reading Practice at Home • EMC 4511

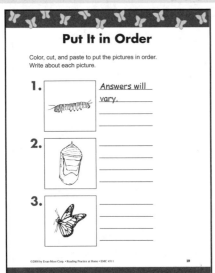

Put It in Order

Color, cut, and paste to put the pictures in order. Write about each picture.

1. Answers will vary.

2.

3.

©2000 by Evan-Moor Corp. • Reading Practice at Home • EMC 4511   19

Working with Word Families

ill

h + ill = h i l l
f + ill = f i l l
ch + ill = c h i l l
dr + ill = d r i l l

Use the new words to complete these sentences.

1. Please ___fill___ my glass with milk.

2. I need a ___drill___ to fix the door.

3. He lives at the top of the ___hill___.

4. If you go out in the cold you will get a ___chill___.

20   ©2000 by Evan-Moor Corp. • Reading Practice at Home • EMC 4511

Skills: Seeing the Whole; Writing a Description

Finish the Picture

Draw the other side of the butterfly. Then color the picture.

Write about the butterfly.

My butterfly ___Responses will vary.___

©2005 by Evan-Moor Corp. • EMC 4529 • Reading   19

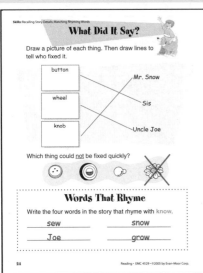

Skills: Recalling Story Details; Matching Rhyming Words

What Did It Say?

Draw a picture of each thing. Then draw lines to tell who fixed it.

button — Mr. Snow
wheel — Sis
knob — Uncle Joe

Which thing could **not** be fixed quickly?

Words That Rhyme

Write the four words in the story that rhyme with know.

sew   snow
Joe   grow

24   Reading • EMC 4529 • ©2005 by Evan-Moor Corp.

The Same Sound

Color the pictures that begin with the same sound as button.

©2000 by Evan-Moor Corp. • Reading Practice at Home • EMC 4511   27

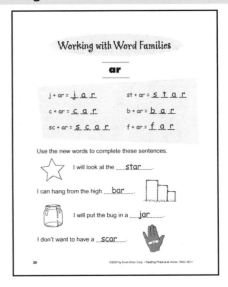

Working with Word Families

ar

j + ar = j a r   st + ar = s t a r
c + ar = c a r   b + ar = b a r
sc + ar = s c a r   f + ar = f a r

Use the new words to complete these sentences.

I will look at the ___star___.

I can hang from the high ___bar___.

I will put the bug in a ___jar___.

I don't want to have a ___scar___.

28   ©2000 by Evan-Moor Corp. • Reading Practice at Home • EMC 4511

Page 27

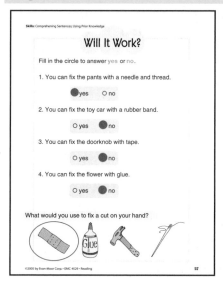

Skills: Comprehending Sentences; Using Prior Knowledge

Will It Work?

Fill in the circle to answer yes or no.

1. You can fix the pants with a needle and thread.
   ● yes   ○ no

2. You can fix the toy car with a rubber band.
   ○ yes   ● no

3. You can fix the doorknob with tape.
   ○ yes   ● no

4. You can fix the flower with glue.
   ○ yes   ● no

What would you use to fix a cut on your hand?

©2005 by Evan-Moor Corp. • EMC 4529 • Reading

Page 28

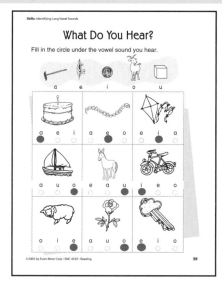

Reading Color Words

Read the words. Color the buttons.

blue   red   orange

Buttons should be correctly colored.

green   purple   brown

pink   yellow   black

©2000 by Evan-Moor Corp. • Reading Practice at Home • EMC 4511

Page 29

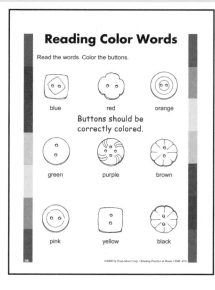

Skills: Identifying Long Vowel Sounds

What Do You Hear?

Fill in the circle under the vowel sound you hear.

a   e   i   o   u

©2005 by Evan-Moor Corp. • EMC 4529 • Reading

Page 31

What Did It Say?

1. How does the tortoise move?
   ○ It moves fast.
   ○ It moves quickly.
   ● It moves slowly.

2. What is the tortoise's shell like?
   ○ It's like a tent.
   ● It's like a pack.
   ○ It's like a suitcase.

3. Where does the tortoise walk?
   ○ It walks in the woods.
   ○ It walks in the snow.
   ● It walks in the sand.

Draw a picture of a giant tortoise here.

Drawings will vary.

©2000 by Evan-Moor Corp. • Reading Practice at Home • EMC 4511

Page 32

Working with Word Families

ell

b + ell = **b e l l**   t + ell = **t e l l**

sh + ell = **s h e l l**   w + ell = **w e l l**

sm + ell = **s m e l l**   sp + ell = **s p e l l**

Write one of the new words in each sentence. Then draw a picture to show what the sentence says.

The snail has a hard **shell**

I can **smell** the pretty rose.

Drawings will vary.

The **bell** rings when school starts.

I threw a penny in the wishing **well**

©2000 by Evan-Moor Corp. • Reading Practice at Home • EMC 4511

Page 33

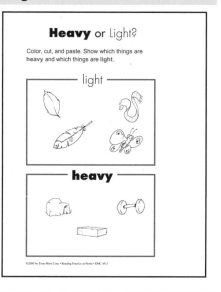

Heavy or Light?

Color, cut, and paste. Show which things are heavy and which things are light.

light

heavy

©2000 by Evan-Moor Corp. • Reading Practice at Home • EMC 4511

Page 34

Skills: Following Directions; Writing a Description

Cool, Man, Cool!

The tortoise wants to look cool. Can you color its shell in a special way? Add shoes and a hat.

Tell what the tortoise looks like.

Responses will vary.

Reading • EMC 4529 • ©2005 by Evan-Moor Corp.

Page 35

Skills: Using Prior Knowledge; Completing Sentences

In a Shell

Draw another animal that lives in a shell. Draw the place where it lives, too.

Drawings will vary.

I am a **Responses will vary.**

I live _____

©2005 by Evan-Moor Corp. • EMC 4529 • Reading

Page 40

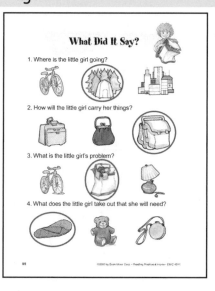

What Did It Say?

1. Where is the little girl going?

2. How will the little girl carry her things?

3. What is the little girl's problem?

4. What does the little girl take out that she will need?

©2000 by Evan-Moor Corp. • Reading Practice at Home • EMC 4511

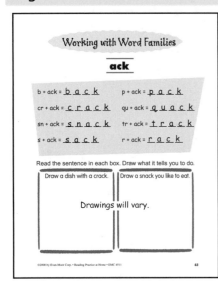

Working with Word Families

ack

b + ack = b a c k   p + ack = p a c k

cr + ack = c r a c k   qu + ack = q u a c k

sn + ack = s n a c k   tr + ack = t r a c k

s + ack = s a c k   r + ack = r a c k

Read the sentence in each box. Draw what it tells you to do.

Draw a dish with a crack.	Draw a snack you like to eat.
Drawings will vary.	

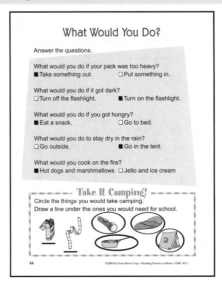

What Would You Do?

Answer the questions.

What would you do if your pack was too heavy?
■ Take something out.   □ Put something in.

What would you do if it got dark?
□ Turn off the flashlight.   ■ Turn on the flashlight.

What would you do if you got hungry?
■ Eat a snack.   □ Go to bed.

What would you do to stay dry in the rain?
□ Go outside.   ■ Go in the tent.

What would you cook on the fire?
■ Hot dogs and marshmallows   □ Jello and ice cream

Take It Camping!
Circle the things you would take camping.
Draw a line under the ones you would need for school.

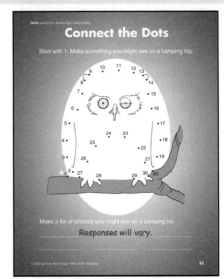

Connect the Dots

Start with 1. Make something you might see on a camping trip.

Make a list of animals you might see on a camping trip.

Responses will vary.

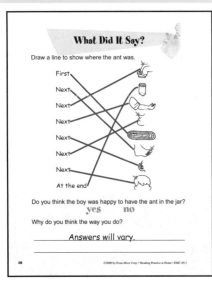

What Did It Say?

Draw a line to show where the ant was.

First
Next
Next
Next
Next
Next
Next
At the end

Do you think the boy was happy to have the ant in the jar?
yes   **no**

Why do you think the way you do?

Answers will vary.

Working with Word Families

ug

r + ug = r u g   b + ug = b u g

d + ug = d u g   h + ug = h u g

pl + ug = p l u g   sn + ug = s n u g

Use the new words to complete these sentences.

Be careful when you touch the plug

Look at the hole I dug

Dad gave me a hug

He's as snug as a bug in a rug

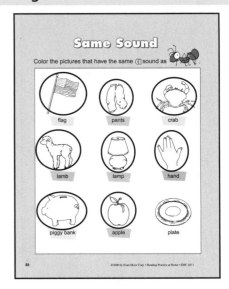

Same Sound

Color the pictures that have the same ă sound as

flag   pants   crab

lamb   lamp   hand

piggy bank   apple   plate

What Does It Mean?

Cut and paste to label the picture.

hair   nose

ear

arm

knee

toe

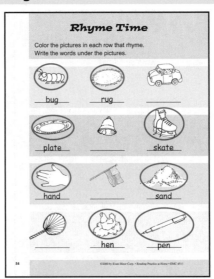

Rhyme Time

Color the pictures in each row that rhyme.
Write the words under the pictures.

bug   rug

plate   skate

hand   sand

hen   pen

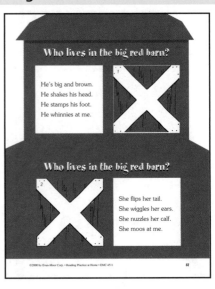

Who lives in the big red barn?

He's big and brown.
He shakes his head.
He stamps his foot.
He whinnies at me.

Who lives in the big red barn?

She flips her tail.
She wiggles her ears.
She nuzzles her calf.
She moos at me.

Page 56

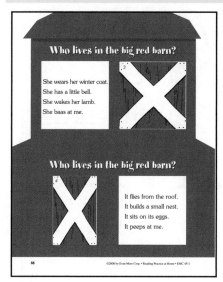

Who lives in the big red barn?

She wears her winter coat.
She has a little bell.
She wakes her lamb.
She baas at me.

Who lives in the big red barn?

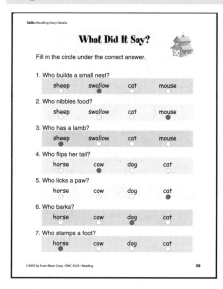

It flies from the roof.
It builds a small nest.
It sits on its eggs.
It peeps at me.

Page 57

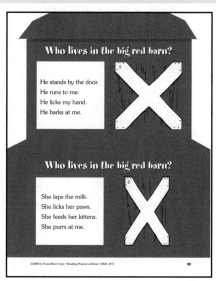

Who lives in the big red barn?

He stands by the door.
He runs to me.
He licks my hand.
He barks at me.

Who lives in the big red barn?

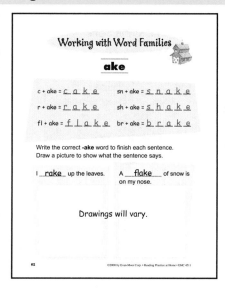

She laps the milk.
She licks her paws.
She feeds her kittens.
She purrs at me.

Page 58

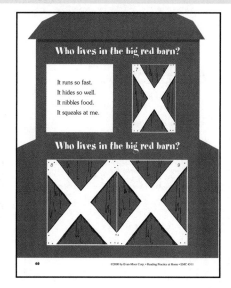

Who lives in the big red barn?

It runs so fast.
It hides so well.
It nibbles food.
It squeaks at me.

Who lives in the big red barn?

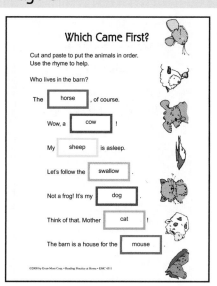

Page 59

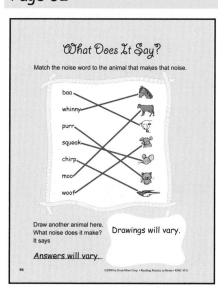

Skills: Recalling Story Details

What Did It Say?

Fill in the circle under the correct answer.

1. Who builds a small nest?
   sheep   **swallow**   cat   mouse

2. Who nibbles food?
   sheep   swallow   cat   **mouse**

3. Who has a lamb?
   sheep   swallow   cat   mouse

4. Who flips her tail?
   horse   **cow**   dog   cat

5. Who licks a paw?
   horse   cow   dog   **cat**

6. Who barks?
   horse   cow   **dog**   cat

7. Who stamps a foot?
   horse   cow   dog   cat

©2005 by Evan-Moor Corp. • EMC 4529 • Reading

Page 60

Working with Word Families

ake

c + ake = c a k e   sn + ake = s n a k e
r + ake = r a k e   sh + ake = s h a k e
fl + ake = f l a k e   br + ake = b r a k e

Write the correct **-ake** word to finish each sentence.
Draw a picture to show what the sentence says.

I __rake__ up the leaves.   A __flake__ of snow is on my nose.

Drawings will vary.

Page 61

Which Came First?

Cut and paste to put the animals in order.
Use the rhyme to help.

Who lives in the barn?

The [horse], of course.

Wow, a [cow] !

My [sheep] is asleep.

Let's follow the [swallow]

Not a frog! It's my [dog]

Think of that. Mother [cat] !

The barn is a house for the [mouse]

Page 62

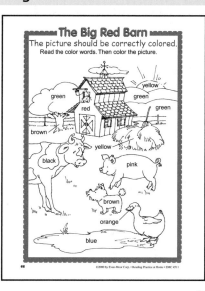

What Does It Say?

Match the noise word to the animal that makes that noise.

baa
whinny
purr
squeak
chirp
moo
woof

Draw another animal here.
What noise does it make?
It says

__Answers will vary__

Page 63

Think About It

Which animals live mainly on a farm?
Which animals live mainly in the jungle?
Write the names of the animals in the correct list.

goat   lion   elephant   chicken
horse   zebra   cow   monkey

On a farm	In the jungle
goat	lion
chicken	elephant
horse	zebra
cow	monkey

Page 64

The Big Red Barn

The picture should be correctly colored.
Read the color words. Then color the picture.

yellow   green   green   red   yellow   green   brown   black   yellow   pink   brown   orange   blue

What Did It Say?

Fill in the circle by the correct answer.

1. Who did the boy call for help?
   ○ Mother   ○ a friend   ● Mr. Fix-It

2. What was wrong with the window?
   ○ It was stuck.   ● It broke.   ○ It needed washing.

3. Was Mr. Fix-It a good fixer?
   ○ No, he had to keep coming back.
   ○ Yes, he won a prize.
   ● Yes, he fixed everything.

4. Why do you think the boy called Mr. Fix-It the last time?
   ○ There were too many cookies in the jar.
   ○ The milk was going to spoil.
   ● Mr. Fix-It should have a treat.

Write an answer.
Who fixes things at your house?

Answers will vary.

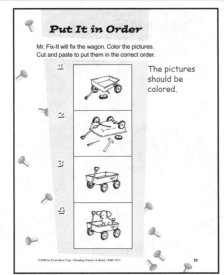

Put It in Order

Mr. Fix-It will fix the wagon. Color the pictures.
Cut and paste to put them in the correct order.

The pictures should be colored.

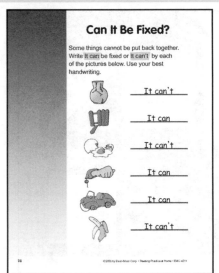

Can It Be Fixed?

Some things cannot be put back together.
Write It can be fixed or It can't by each of the pictures below. Use your best handwriting.

It can't

It can

It can't

It can

It can

It can't

Working with Word Families

ink

p + ink = p i n k   s + ink = s i n k

bl + ink = b l i n k   dr + ink = d r i n k

shr + ink = s h r i n k   th + ink = t h i n k

Draw a toy boat in a sink.	Draw a muddy pig that's pink.
Drawings will vary.	

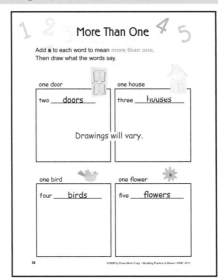

More Than One

Add **s** to each word to mean more than one.
Then draw what the words say.

one door   one house
two doors   three houses

Drawings will vary.

one bird   one flower
four birds   five flowers

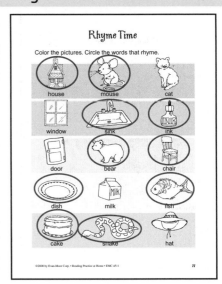

Rhyme Time

Color the pictures. Circle the words that rhyme.

house	mouse	cat
window	sink	ink
door	bear	chair
dish	milk	fish
cake	snake	hat

Skills: Recalling Story Details

What Did I Have?

Fill in the circle under of the correct answer.

1. What did I have on Tuesday?
   turkey   tuna   soup

2. What did I have on Friday?
   waffles   muffins   fries

3. What did I have on Sunday?
   soup   soda   turkey

4. What did I have on Monday?
   waffles   fries   muffins

5. What did I have on Saturday?
   soup   soda   tuna

My Favorite Foods

Rewrite the story. Draw or write what you would like to eat each day beside the name of the day. Then read the story using your foods.

Monday I have	Answers will vary.
Tuesday I have	
Wednesday I have	
Thursday I have	
Friday I have	
Saturday I have	
Sunday I have	

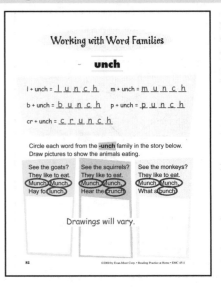

Working with Word Families

- unch

l + unch = l u n c h   m + unch = m u n c h

b + unch = b u n c h   p + unch = p u n c h

cr + unch = c r u n c h

Circle each word from the **-unch** family in the story below.
Draw pictures to show the animals eating.

See the goats? They like to eat. Munch, Munch. Hay for lunch.	See the squirrels? They like to eat. Munch, Munch. Hear the crunch.	See the monkeys? They like to eat. Munch, Munch. What a bunch.

Drawings will vary.

Page 81

Noisy Foods

Some foods are noisy. Color the things that make crunchy noises when you eat them. Write **munch** under the ones you like to eat.

Answers will vary.

©2000 by Evan-Moor Corp. • Reading Practice at Home • EMC 4511   83

Page 82

How Does It Taste?

Write one letter of the food name in each box. When all the boxes have been filled in, read the secret message in the pink boxes.

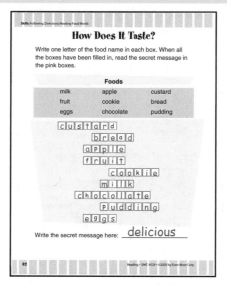

Foods		
milk	apple	custard
fruit	cookie	bread
eggs	chocolate	pudding

c u s t a r d
b r e a d
a p p l e
f r u i t
c o o k i e
m i l k
c h o c o l a t e
P u d d i n g
e g g s

Write the secret message here: __delicious__

82   Reading • EMC 4529 • ©2005 by Evan-Moor Corp.

Page 83

Food Word Search

See how many of the foods in the Word Box you can find.

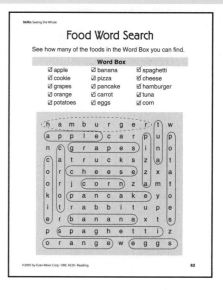

Word Box		
☑ apple	☑ banana	☑ spaghetti
☑ cookie	☑ pizza	☑ cheese
☑ grapes	☑ pancake	☑ hamburger
☑ orange	☑ carrot	☑ tuna
☑ potatoes	☑ eggs	☑ corn

h a m b u r g e r t w
a p p l e c a r t u n
n c g r a p e s i n o
c a t r u c k s z n a
o r c h e e s e z x m
o r j c o r n z a m
k i t p a n c a k e
i e r a b b i t u p e
e r b a n a n a x t
p s p a g h e t t i z
o r a n g e w e g g s

©2005 by Evan-Moor Corp. • EMC 4529 • Reading   83

Page 88

What Did It Say?

Fill in the circles to answer the questions.

1. Which dog hid under the blanket? ○ Max ● Molly
2. Which dog found the trash? ● Max ○ Molly
3. Which dog brought the balls back? ○ Max ● Molly
4. Which dog buried a bone? ○ Max ● Molly
5. Which dog popped a balloon? ● Max ○ Molly
6. Which dog picked some flowers? ● Max ○ Molly
7. Which dog do you think will try to open the gifts? ● Max ○ Molly
8. Which dog is easier to care for? ○ Max ● Molly

88   Reading • EMC 4529 • ©2005 by Evan-Moor Corp.

Page 89

Max Learns the Hard Way

Color, cut, and paste. Put the pictures in order to tell Max's story.

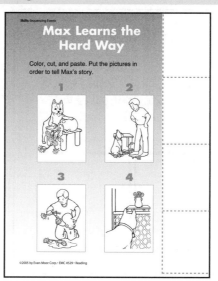

1   2
3   4

©2005 by Evan-Moor Corp. • EMC 4529 • Reading

Page 90

Trouble!

It's easy for Max to get in trouble. Put a check by the things that would mean *trouble*.

☑ Max chewed the shoe.
☐ Max drank his water.
☑ Max jumped over the gate.
☐ Max chewed on the bone.
☑ Max knocked over the lamp.
☑ Max picked some flowers.
☐ Max took a nap.
☑ Max opened the gifts.

Think about what Max might do next. Write it here.

____Answers will vary.____

Will it mean trouble for Max?   yes   no

90   ©2000 by Evan-Moor Corp. • Reading Practice at Home • EMC 4511

Page 91

Working with Word Families

one

b + one = b o n e   c + one = c o n e
ph + one = p h o n e   st + one = s t o n e
thr + one = t h r o n e   z + one = z o n e

Write the words to label the pictures.

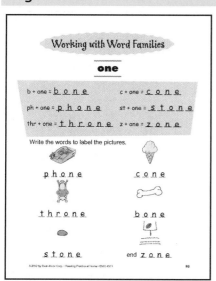

p h o n e   c o n e

t h r o n e   b o n e

s t o n e   end z o n e

©2002 by Evan-Moor Corp. • Reading Practice at Home • EMC 4511   83

Page 92

What's at the End?

Write the letter that stands for the sound you hear at the end of each word.

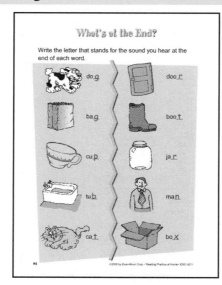

do_g   doo_r
ba_g   boo_t
cu_p   ja_r
tu_b   ma_n
              bo_x

94   ©2000 by Evan-Moor Corp. • Reading Practice at Home • EMC 4511

Page 93

Draw a Pup

Follow the steps to draw a puppy.

Responses will vary.

How is the pup like Max?
____Responses will vary.____

How is the pup different from Max?

©2005 by Evan-Moor Corp. • EMC 4529 • Reading   93

© Evan-Moor Corp. • EMC 9719 • Sharpen Your Skills—Reading

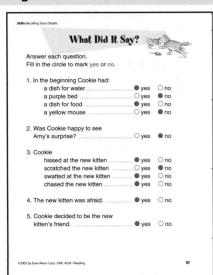

Skills: Recalling Story Details

What Did It Say?

Answer each question.
Fill in the circle to mark yes or no.

1. In the beginning Cookie had:
   a dish for water .... ● yes ○ no
   a purple bed .... ○ yes ● no
   a dish for food .... ● yes ○ no
   a yellow mouse .... ○ yes ● no

2. Was Cookie happy to see
   Amy's surprise? .... ○ yes ● no

3. Cookie
   hissed at the new kitten .... ● yes ○ no
   scratched the new kitten .... ○ yes ● no
   swatted at the new kitten .... ● yes ○ no
   chased the new kitten .... ● yes ○ no

4. The new kitten was afraid. .... ● yes ○ no

5. Cookie decided to be the new
   kitten's friend. .... ● yes ○ no

©2005 by Evan-Moor Corp. • EMC 4529 • Reading   97

What Does It Mean?

Look at the pictures. Write the best word in each sentence.

sniffed	tasted	cried
licked	chased	swatted
purred	played	hissed

The kitten __sniffed__ the flower.

Cookie __hissed__ at the kitten.

Cookie __chased__ the kitten.

The little kitten __cried__ .

The kitten __played__ with the yarn.

Cookie __licked__ the kitten's ear.

100   ©2000 by Evan-Moor Corp. • Reading Practice at Home • EMC 4511

Animal Babies

Cut and paste to match the babies with the parents.
Write the names under the pictures.

dog	__pup__	horse	__foal__
hen	__chick__	cow	__calf__
cat	__kitten__	pig	__piglet__

Word Box
chick   calf   piglet   pup   foal   kitten

©2000 by Evan-Moor Corp. • Reading Practice at Home • EMC 4511   101

Skills: Listening for the /k/ Sound; Adding the Letter k to Complete Words

The Sound of k

Say the picture name. Write the letter k where you hear
its sound.

__K__itten   ____ook   __k__ey

__k__angaroo   __k__oala   ____oorknob

____aw   __k__ite   __k__ing

100   Reading • EMC 4529 • ©2005 by Evan-Moor Corp.

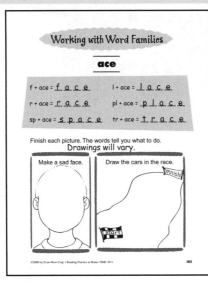

Working with Word Families

ace

f + ace = __f a c e__   l + ace = __l a c e__

r + ace = __r a c e__   pl + ace = __p l a c e__

sp + ace = __s p a c e__   tr + ace = __t r a c e__

Finish each picture. The words tell you what to do.
Drawings will vary.

Make a sad face.   Draw the cars in the race.

©2000 by Evan-Moor Corp. • Reading Practice at Home • EMC 4511   103

Skills: Using Prior Knowledge; Using Real-Life Experiences

What Do You Think?

Fill in the circle in front of yes or no.

Can two cats be friends?   ● yes ○ no
Can two cats drive to the mall?   ○ yes ● no
Can two cats like the same toy?   ● yes ○ no
Can two cats chase one another?   ● yes ○ no
Can two cats lap the milk?   ● yes ○ no
Can two cats write a letter?   ○ yes ● no

Draw something two cats could really do.

Drawings will vary.

102   Reading • EMC 4529 • ©2005 by Evan-Moor Corp.

Skills: Recalling Story Details

What Did It Say?

Fill in the circle or write words to answer the questions.

1. What was missing?
   ○ hat   ○ scarf   ● mittens

2. Who did the missing thing belong to?
   ○ Mom   ● Tommy   ○ Dad

3. Where was the missing thing found?
   _____in Tommy's hat_____

Draw something that belongs to you that was missing.

106   Reading • EMC 4529 • ©2005 by Evan-Moor Corp.

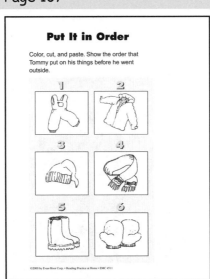

Put It in Order

Color, cut, and paste. Show the order that
Tommy put on his things before he went
outside.

1   2

3   4

5   6

©2000 by Evan-Moor Corp. • Reading Practice at Home • EMC 4511

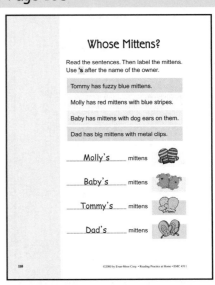

Whose Mittens?

Read the sentences. Then label the mittens.
Use **'s** after the name of the owner.

Tommy has fuzzy blue mittens.

Molly has red mittens with blue stripes.

Baby has mittens with dog ears on them.

Dad has big mittens with metal clips.

__Molly's__ mittens

__Baby's__ mittens

__Tommy's__ mittens

__Dad's__ mittens

110   ©2000 by Evan-Moor Corp. • Reading Practice at Home • EMC 4511

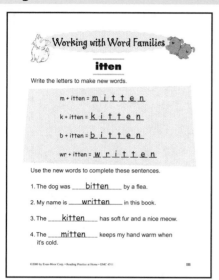

Working with Word Families
itten

Write the letters to make new words.

m + itten = m i t t e n

k + itten = k i t t e n

b + itten = b i t t e n

wr + itten = w r i t t e n

Use the new words to complete these sentences.

1. The dog was __bitten__ by a flea.

2. My name is __written__ in this book.

3. The __kitten__ has soft fur and a nice meow.

4. The __mitten__ keeps my hand warm when it's cold.

©2000 by Evan-Moor Corp. • Reading Practice at Home • EMC 4511   111

Skills: Writing Descriptive Words

Make Them the Same

Color the second mitten to match the first.
List three words that tell about the mittens.

1. __Responses will vary.__

2. _____

3. _____

110   Reading • EMC 4529 • ©2005 by Evan-Moor Corp.

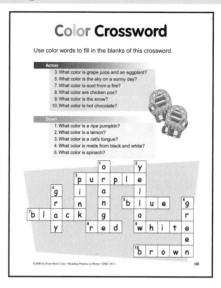

Color Crossword

Use color words to fill in the blanks of this crossword.

Across

3. What color is grape juice and an eggplant?
5. What color is the sky on a sunny day?
7. What color is soot from a fire?
8. What color are chicken pox?
9. What color is the snow?
10. What color is hot chocolate?

Down

1. What color is a ripe pumpkin?
2. What color is a lemon?
3. What color is a cat's tongue?
4. What color is made from black and white?
6. What color is spinach?

©2000 by Evan-Moor Corp. • Reading Practice at Home • EMC 4511   112

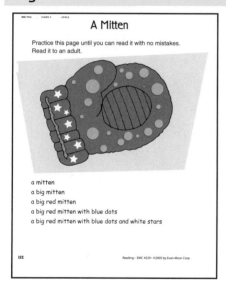

A Mitten

Practice this page until you can read it with no mistakes.
Read it to an adult.

a mitten

a big mitten

a big red mitten

a big red mitten with blue dots

a big red mitten with blue dots and white stars

112   Reading • EMC 4529 • ©2005 by Evan-Moor Corp.

What Did It Say?

1. How did Peter feel when he met Sam?
■ surprised ☐ happy ☐ mad

2. How did Peter feel after he played ball with Sam?
☐ sad ■ glad ☐ upset

3. Why did Peter think a new boy had moved in next door?
☐ The mailman brought a letter.
☐ His mother told him.
■ The moving man unloaded a bike and a wagon.

4. Why did Peter think that the new "boy" liked to play ball?
☐ The new kid was holding a suitcase.
☐ The moving man unloaded some bats.
■ The new kid was wearing a blue ball cap.

5. What did the new kid's dad boast?
☐ He said that Sam was a good hitter.
☐ He said that Sam was a good pitcher.
■ He said that Sam could catch any ball Peter threw.

120   ©2000 by Evan-Moor Corp. • Reading Practice at Home • EMC 4511

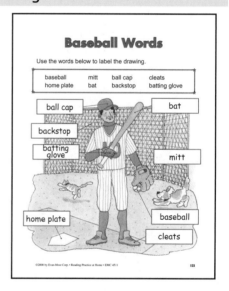

Baseball Words

Use the words below to label the drawing.

| baseball | mitt | ball cap | cleats |
| home plate | bat | backstop | batting glove |

ball cap

bat

backstop

batting glove

mitt

home plate

baseball

cleats

©2000 by Evan-Moor Corp. • Reading Practice at Home • EMC 4511   121

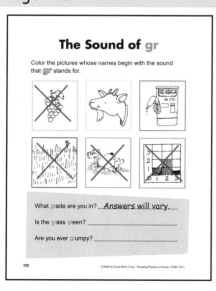

The Sound of gr

Color the pictures whose names begin with the sound that gr stands for.

What grade are you in? __Answers will vary.__

Is the grass green? _____

Are you ever grumpy? _____

122   ©2000 by Evan-Moor Corp. • Reading Practice at Home • EMC 4511

Draw a Story

Cut and paste the sentences in order. Then draw the story.

Drawings will vary.

1 | Billy came to the plate.

2 | The ball was thrown.

3 | Billy hit the ball hard.

4 | It was a home run.

©2000 by Evan-Moor Corp. • Reading Practice at Home • EMC 4511

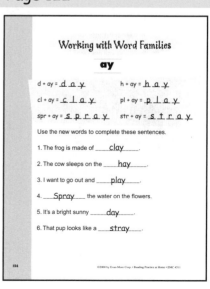

Working with Word Families
ay

d + ay = d a y

h + ay = h a y

cl + ay = c l a y

pl + ay = p l a y

spr + ay = s p r a y

str + ay = s t r a y

Use the new words to complete these sentences.

1. The frog is made of __clay__

2. The cow sleeps on the __hay__

3. I want to go out and __play__.

4. __Spray__ the water on the flowers.

5. It's a bright sunny __day__.

6. That pup looks like a __stray__

124   ©2000 by Evan-Moor Corp. • Reading Practice at Home • EMC 4511

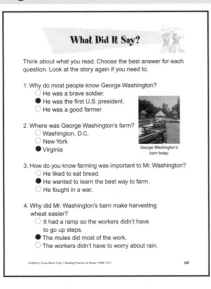

What Did It Say?

Think about what you read. Choose the best answer for each question. Look at the story again if you need to.

1. Why do most people know George Washington?
   ○ He was a brave soldier.
   ● He was the first U.S. president.
   ○ He was a good farmer.

2. Where was George Washington's farm?
   ○ Washington, D.C.
   ○ New York
   ● Virginia

George Washington's barn today

3. How do you know farming was important to Mr. Washington?
   ○ He liked to eat bread.
   ● He wanted to learn the best way to farm.
   ○ He fought in a war.

4. Why did Mr. Washington's barn make harvesting wheat easier?
   ○ It had a ramp so the workers didn't have to go up steps.
   ● The mules did most of the work.
   ○ The workers didn't have to worry about rain.

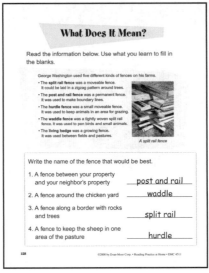

What Does It Mean?

Read the information below. Use what you learn to fill in the blanks.

George Washington used five different kinds of fences on his farms.
- The **split rail fence** was a moveable fence. It could be laid in a zigzag pattern around trees.
- The **post and rail fence** was a permanent fence. It was used to make boundary lines.
- The **hurdle fence** was a small moveable fence. It was used to keep animals in an area for grazing.
- The **waddle fence** was a tightly woven split rail fence. It was used to pen birds and small animals.
- The **living hedge** was a growing fence. It was used between fields and pastures.

A split rail fence

Write the name of the fence that would be best.

1. A fence between your property and your neighbor's property — **post and rail**

2. A fence around the chicken yard — **waddle**

3. A fence along a border with rocks and trees — **split rail**

4. A fence to keep the sheep in one area of the pasture — **hurdle**

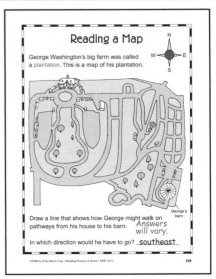

Reading a Map

George Washington's big farm was called a plantation. This is a map of his plantation.

George's barn

Draw a line that shows how George might walk on pathways from his house to his barn. **Answers will vary.**

In which direction would he have to go? **southeast**

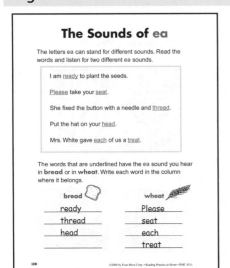

The Sounds of ea

The letters ea can stand for different sounds. Read the words and listen for two different ea sounds.

I am <u>ready</u> to plant the seeds.

<u>Please</u> take your <u>seat</u>.

She fixed the button with a needle and <u>thread</u>.

Put the hat on your <u>head</u>.

Mrs. White gave <u>each</u> of us a <u>treat</u>.

The words that are underlined have the ea sound you hear in **bread** or in **wheat**. Write each word in the column where it belongs.

bread	wheat
ready	Please
thread	seat
head	each
	treat

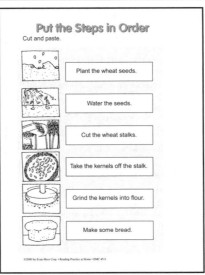

Put the Steps in Order
Cut and paste.

- Plant the wheat seeds.
- Water the seeds.
- Cut the wheat stalks.
- Take the kernels off the stalk.
- Grind the kernels into flour.
- Make some bread.

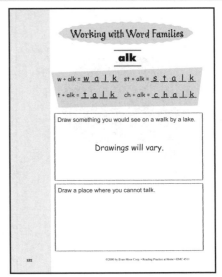

Working with Word Families

alk

w + alk = **w a l k**   st + alk = **s t a l k**

t + alk = **t a l k**   ch + alk = **c h a l k**

Draw something you would see on a walk by a lake.

Drawings will vary.

Draw a place where you cannot talk.

Puzzle Page

Cut out the puzzle pieces. Put them together.

What do you have? **George Washington's Barn**

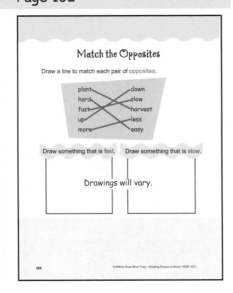

Match the Opposites

Draw a line to match each pair of opposites.

plant — harvest
hard — easy
fast — slow
up — down
more — less

Draw something that is fast.   Draw something that is slow.

Drawings will vary.

Contents

Skills:

Writing &
Counting 0–2

Trace.

O O O O O O

| | | | | |

2 2 2 2 2 2

Count the dogs. Write the numbers.

Gone to the Dogs

Skills:

Writing & Counting 3–5

Gone to the Dogs

Trace.

3   3   3   3   3   3

4   4   4   4   4   4

5   5   5   5   5   5

Count the dogs. Match the dogs to their doghouses.

Skills:
Writing & Counting 6–8

Trace.

6   6   6   6   6   6

7   7   7   7   7   7

8   8   8   8   8   8

Draw the bones.

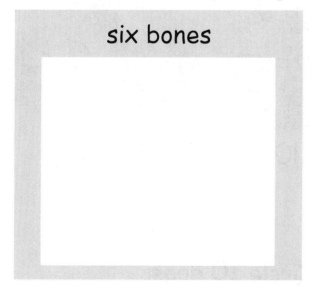

six bones	eight bones

Circle the larger number on each bone.

Gone to the Dogs

Numbers 9 and 10

Gone to the Dogs

Trace.

q q q q q q

10 10 10 10 10 10

How many dogs?

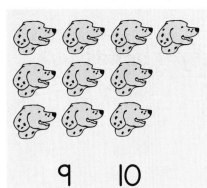

9   10

9   10

9   10

Circle **9** dogs.

Circle **10** dogs.

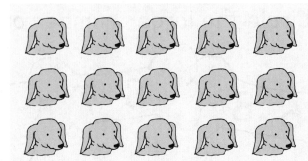

Sharpen Your Skills—Math • EMC 9719 • © Evan-Moor Corp.

Skills:
Counting 0–10

How many puppies?

8 9 10

4 5 6

3 4 5

0 1 2

8 9 10

5 6 7

7 8 9

Gone to the Dogs

Count and Tell

Note: You may need to help your child read the word problems.

Gone to the Dogs

How many legs?

 has _____ legs.

How many ears?

has _____ ears.

How many feet in all?

and have

_____ feet in all.

How many bones?

 has _____ bones.

What is the largest answer? _____

What is the smallest answer? _____

Skills:

One-to-One
Correspondence

Note: You may need to help your child read the word problems.

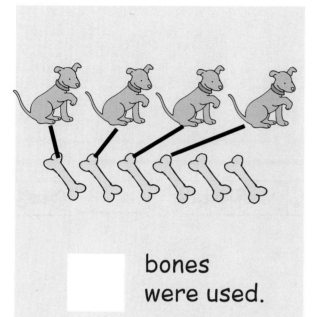

☐ bones
were used.

☐ doghouses
were used.

☐ cans of food
were used.

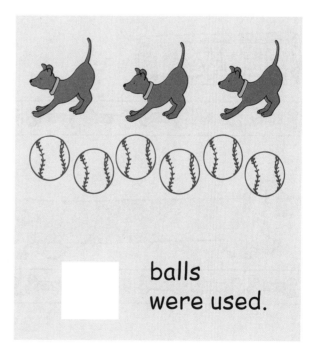

☐ balls
were used.

Gone to the Dogs

What is the largest number of things used? _____

What is the smallest number of things used? _____

Dog Bone Measuring

Skills:

Nonstandard
Measurement

How long is each thing?

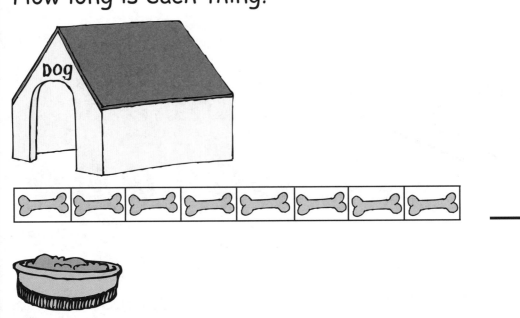

_____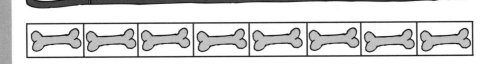

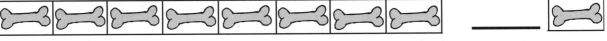

_____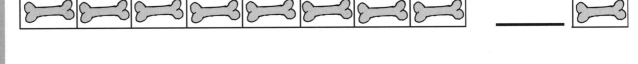

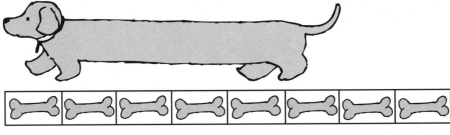

_____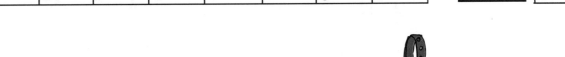

_____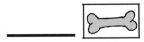

Gone to the Dogs

Sharpen Your Skills—Math • EMC 9719 • © Evan-Moor Corp.

Skills:

Reading
Graphs

Read the graph. Answer the questions.

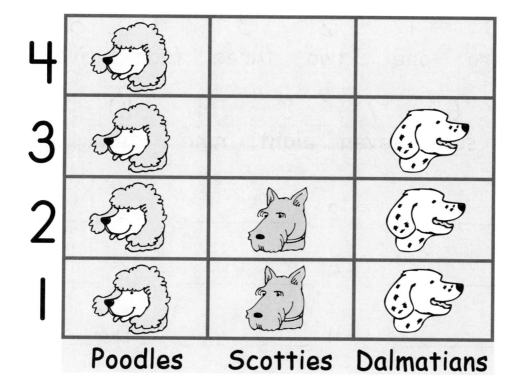

4 3 2 1 — Poodles Scotties Dalmatians

Gone to the Dogs

1. How many dogs are in the store?

 _____   _____    _____

2. How many dogs in all? _____

3. Are there more or ?

4. Which dog is there the most of?

Number Words

Write each number word.

0	1	2	3	4	5
zero	one	two	three	four	five

6	7	8	9	10
six	seven	eight	nine	ten

3 _____   2 _____   1 _____

10 _____   9 _____   6 _____

0 _____   4 _____   5 _____

7 _____   8 _____

Count and match.

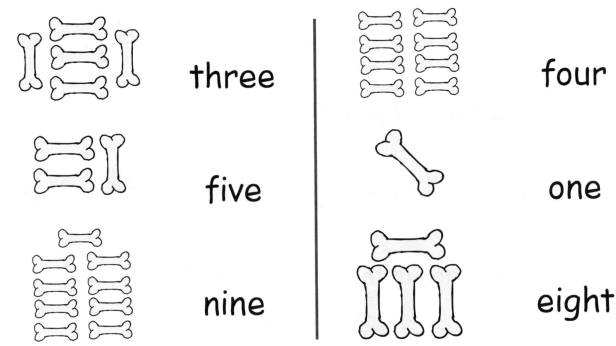

three

five

nine

four

one

eight

Sharpen Your Skills—Math • EMC 9719 • © Evan-Moor Corp.

Gone to the Dogs

Skills:

More, Less
Larger, Smaller

Write the numbers. Circle the set with more.

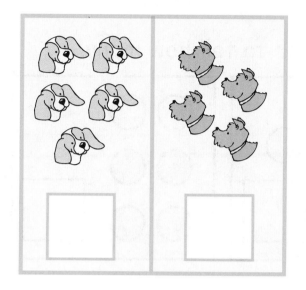

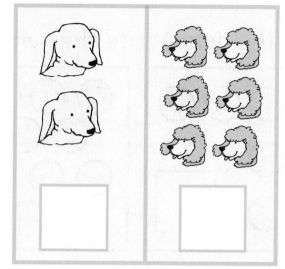

Write the numbers. Circle the set with less.

Which number is larger?

5 or 8   3 or 1

Which number is smaller?

7 or 2   9 or 0

Gone to the Dogs

Count the dots. Write the number to tell how many.

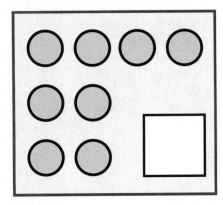
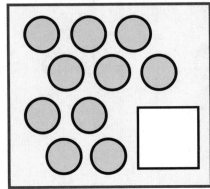
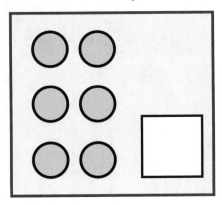

Fill in the circle to show how long it is.

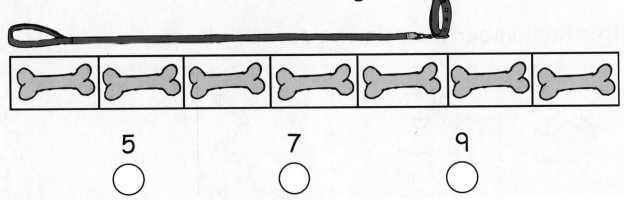

5   7   9
○   ○   ○

Color the shapes.

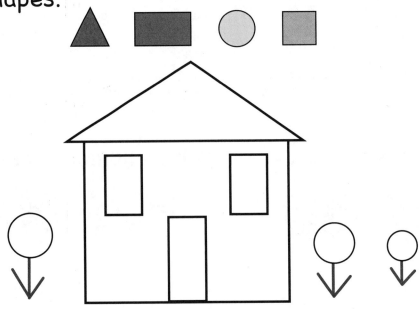

Skills:

Addition to 6

Add.

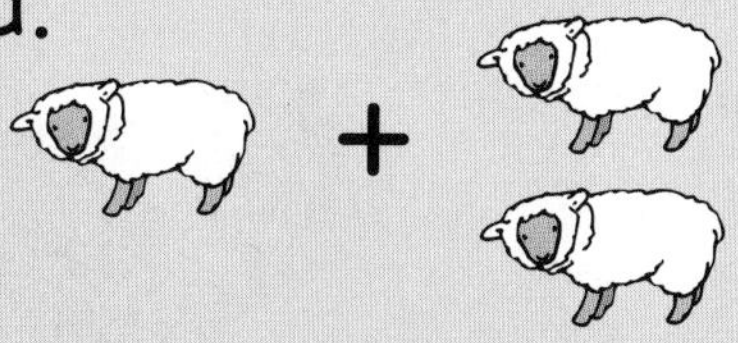

1 + 2 = ____

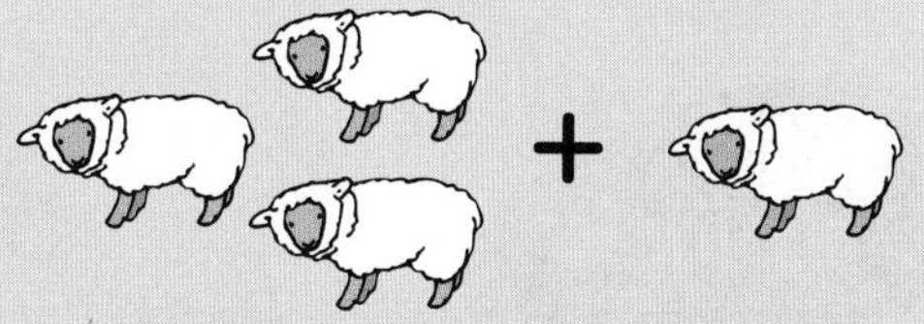

3 + 1 = ____

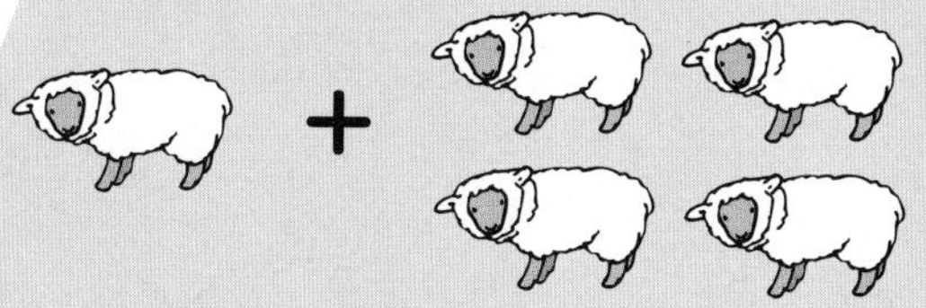

1 + 4 = ____

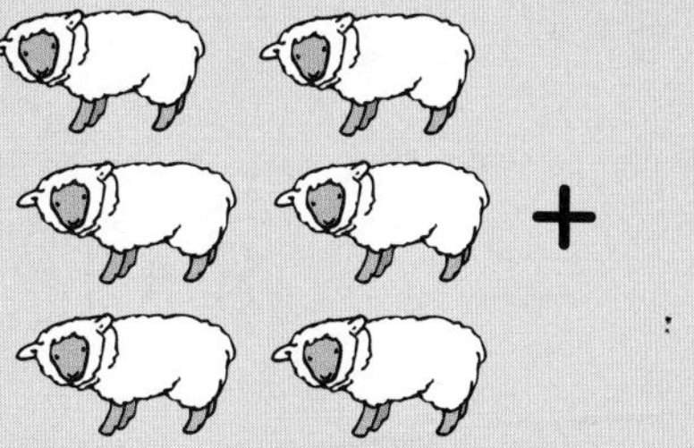

6 + 0 = ____

Write and add.

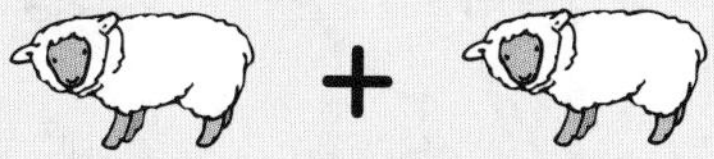

1 + 1 = 2

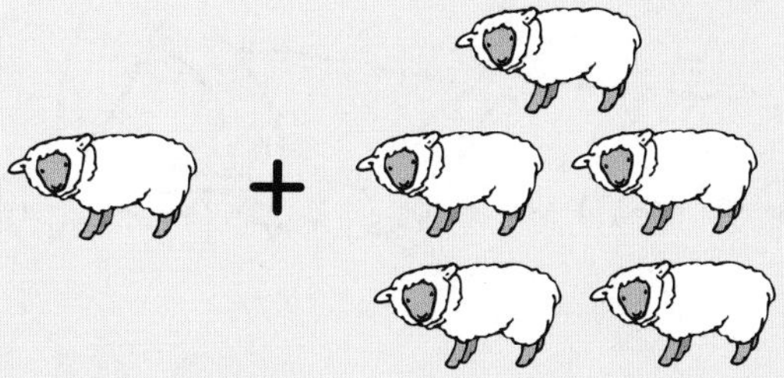

___ + ___ = ___

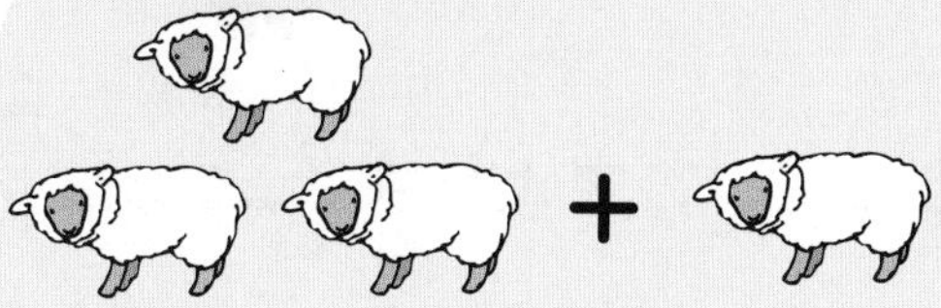

___ + ___ = ___

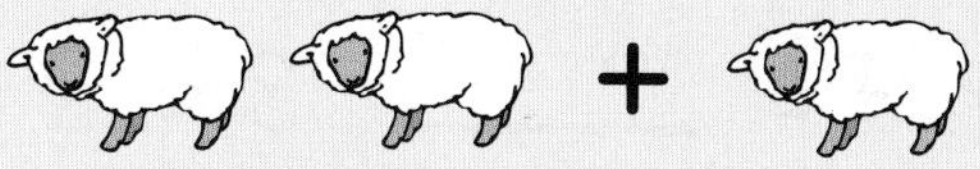

___ + ___ = ___

On the Farm

Skills:
Addition to 6

Add. Color.

1 = black

3 = yellow

5 = brown

2 = pink

4 = green

6 = blue

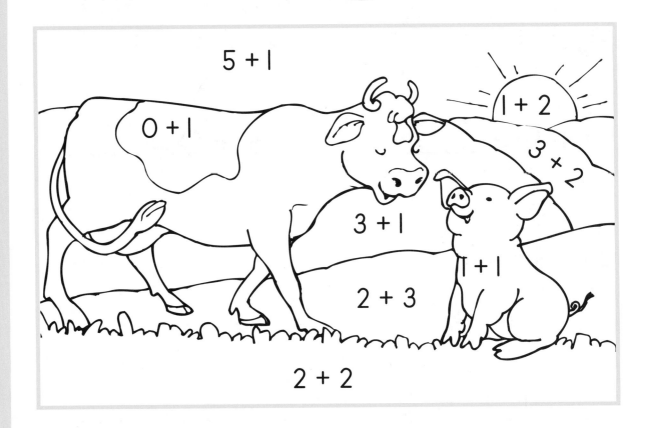

5 + 1

0 + 1

1 + 2

3 + 2

3 + 1

1 + 1

2 + 3

2 + 2

On the Farm

Add.

2 + 4 = _____   3 + 2 = _____   4 + 0 = _____

3 + 3 = _____   1 + 5 = _____   4 + 1 = _____

Skills:

Word Problems:
Addition to 6

Note: You may need to help your child read the word problems.

Add.

2 horses.
2 more horses come.
How many horses?

__2__ + __2__ = __4__

4 horses

---

3 hens.
3 more hens come.
How many hens?

___ + ___ = ___

hens

---

0 pigs in the pen.
5 pigs jump in.
How many pigs?

___ + ___ = ___

pigs

---

2 sheep.
1 more sheep comes.
How many sheep?

___ + ___ = ___

sheep

On the Farm

Add.

$2 + 2 =$ _____ $3 + 2 =$ _____ $4 + 2 =$ _____

$1 + 2 =$ _____ $0 + 2 =$ _____ $1 + 1 =$ _____

$3 + 1 =$ _____ $1 + 0 =$ _____ $0 + 3 =$ _____

$0 + 0 =$ _____ $2 + 3 =$ _____ $3 + 3 =$ _____

3	2	0	3	0
+ 1	+ 3	+ 3	+ 3	+ 0
☐	☐	☐	☐	☐

1	4	4	2	1
+ 0	+ 2	+ 1	+ 2	+ 1
☐	☐	☐	☐	☐

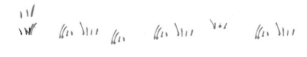

On the Farm

Skills:

Money—Pennies

_____ ¢

_____ ¢

_____ ¢

_____ ¢

_____ ¢

_____ ¢

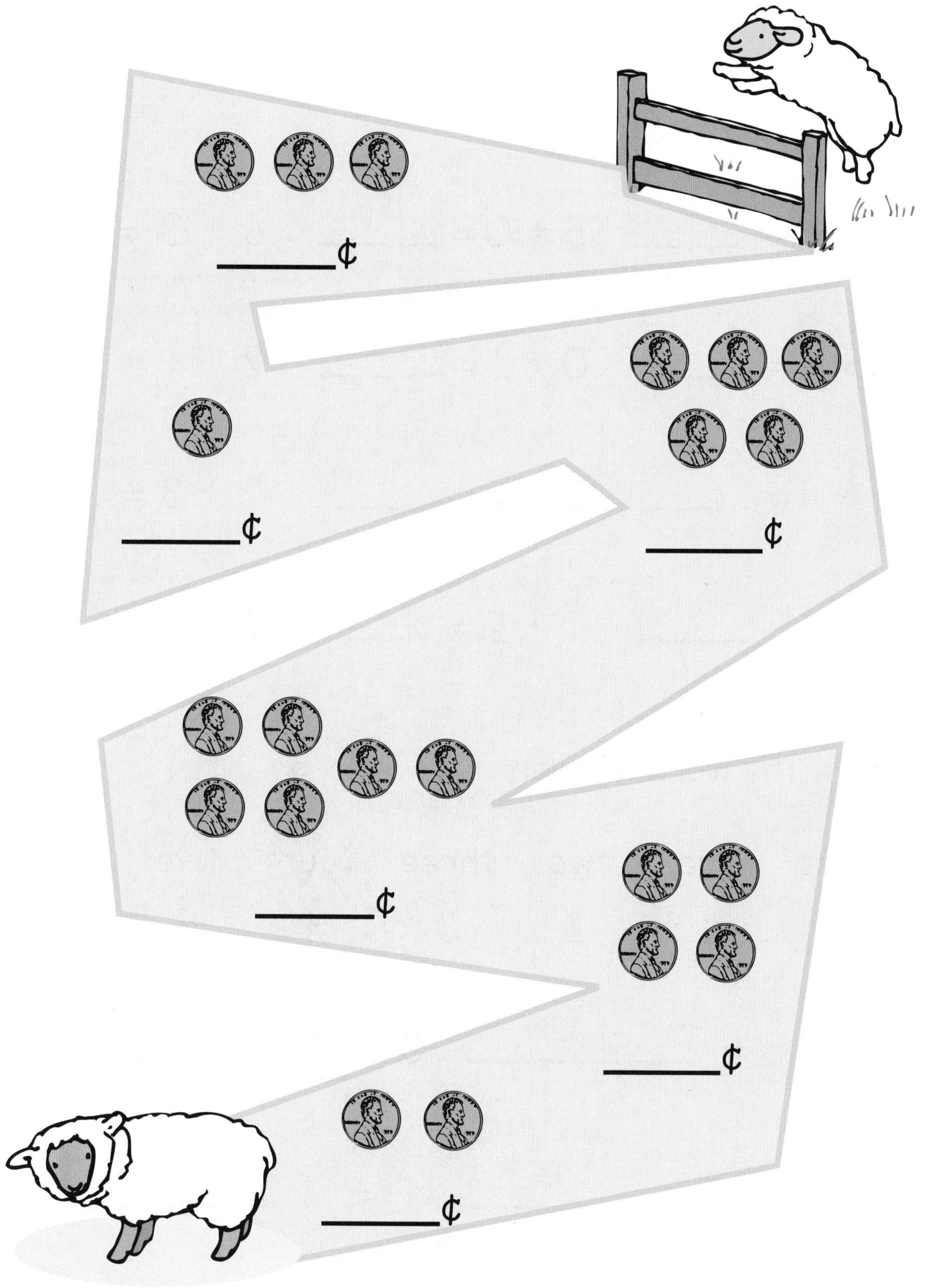

On the Farm

How Many Pigs?

On the Farm

Add.

$5 + 1 =$ _____ $5 + 0 =$ _____ $6 + 0 =$ _____

$3 + 1 =$ _____ $0 + 1 =$ _____ $2 + 1 =$ _____

$0 + 4 =$ _____ $0 + 2 =$ _____ $2 + 3 =$ _____

$0 + 0 =$ _____ $1 + 2 =$ _____ $0 + 6 =$ _____

Write the word answer.

zero	one	two	three	four	five	six
0	1	2	3	4	5	6

$1 + 5 =$ __six__ $3 + 2 =$ _____

$0 + 0 =$ _____ $1 + 1 =$ _____

$1 + 3 =$ _____ $2 + 1 =$ _____

Skills:

Word Problems:
Addition to 6

Note: You may need to help your child read the word problems.

Add.

4 hens.
1 more hen comes.
How many hens?

___ + ___ = ___

☐ hens

---

1 cow.
3 more cows come.
How many cows?

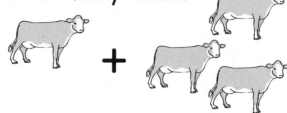

___ + ___ = ___

☐ cows

---

2 chicks.
1 more chick comes.
How many chicks?

___ + ___ = ___

☐ chicks

---

2 donkeys.
3 more donkeys come.
How many donkeys?

___ + ___ = ___

☐ donkeys

On the Farm

On the Farm

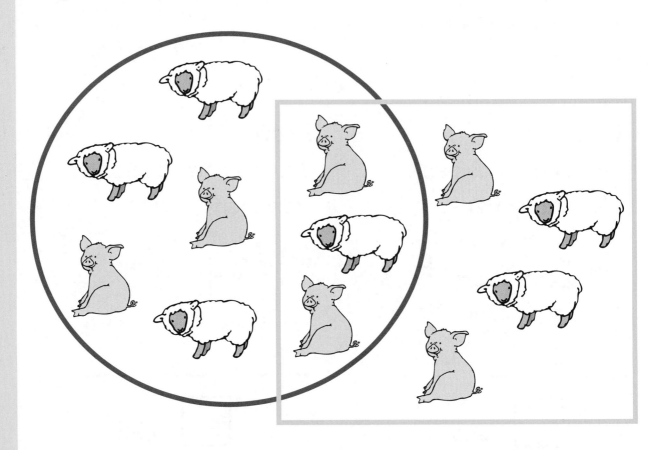

Tell how many.

1. ![sheep] in the ◯ ? _____

2. ![pig] in the ▢ ? _____

3. ![sheep] in **both** the ◯ and the ▢ ? _____

4. ![pig] in **both** the ◯ and the ▢ ? _____

5. ![sheep] in the ▢ but **not** in the ◯ ? _____

Skills:

Ordinal
Numbers

 first
1st

 second
2nd

 third
3rd

 fourth
4th

 fifth
5th

 sixth
6th

1. Which place is the in? _____

2. Which place is the in? _____

3. Which place is the in? _____

4. Which animal is between the 4th and 6th place?

5. Which animal is between the 2nd and 4th place?

6. Mark the 3rd goat.

7. Mark the 5th dog.

On the Farm

The Answer Is the Same

Add.

$3 + 2 = $ _____ $0 + 1 = $ _____ $1 + 2 = $ _____

$2 + 3 = $ _____ $1 + 0 = $ _____ $2 + 1 = $ _____

$0 + 4 = $ _____ $1 + 5 = $ _____ $0 + 6 = $ _____

$4 + 0 = $ _____ $5 + 1 = $ _____ $6 + 0 = $ _____

$3 + 0 = $ _____ $3 + 1 = $ _____ $4 + 2 = $ _____

$0 + 3 = $ _____ $1 + 3 = $ _____ $2 + 4 = $ _____

Make two addition problems.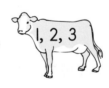

$\underline{1} + \underline{2} = \underline{3}$
$\underline{2} + \underline{1} = \underline{3}$

___ + ___ = ___   ___ + ___ = ___

___ + ___ = ___   ___ + ___ = ___

Skills:

Ordinal
Numbers

4th floor

3rd floor

2nd floor

1st floor

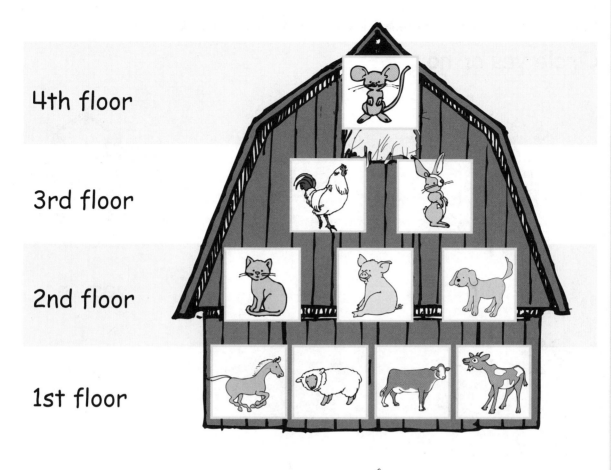

1. On which floor do the  and live? _____

2. Which animal lives on the 4th floor? _____

3. On which floor does the live? _____

4. Which animal lives on the 1st floor? _____

5. Which floor is below the ? _____

6. Which floor is above the ? _____

On the Farm

Skills:

Symmetry

Note: You may need to read the sentence at the bottom of the page to your child.

Circle **yes** or **no**.

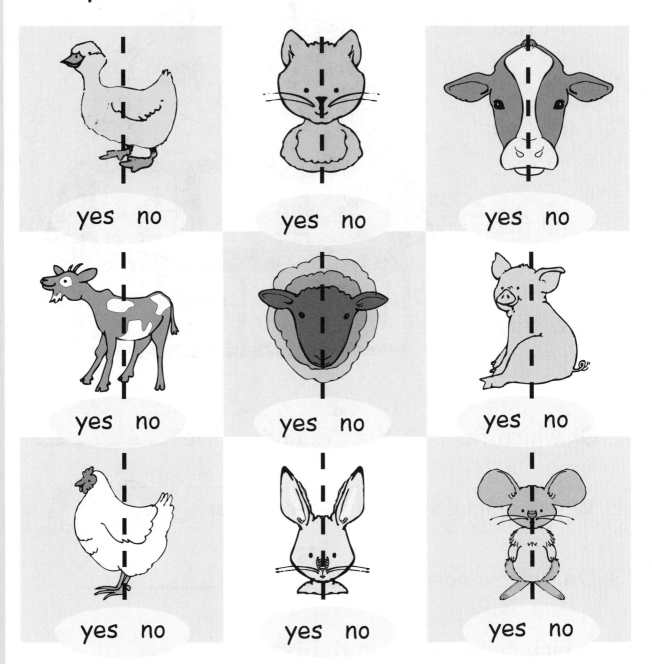

yes   no   yes   no   yes   no

yes   no   yes   no   yes   no

yes   no   yes   no   yes   no

On the Farm

When an object is **symmetrical**, both sides are the same in shape and size.

TEST YOUR SKILLS

Count.

Add.

3 + 3 = _____   4 + 2 = _____   1 + 2 = _____   0 + 0 = _____

1 + 0 = _____   3 + 2 = _____   4 + 1 = _____   1 + 1 = _____

Read the graph. Answer the questions.

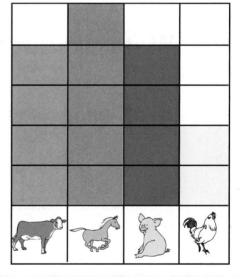

1. How many 🐓 are there? _____

2. How many 🐴 are there? _____

3. Which two have the same number?

Read and answer.

3 🐷 are in the mud. 2 more 🐷 come.

How many 🐷 are in the mud?   _____

How Many Bears?

Subtract.

$$3 - 2 = 1$$

$$5 - 3 = \underline{}$$

$$4 - 0 = \underline{}$$

$$6 - 4 = \underline{}$$

Write and subtract.

$$\underline{5} - \underline{1} = \underline{4}$$

$$\underline{} - \underline{} = \underline{}$$

$$\underline{} - \underline{} = \underline{}$$

$$\underline{} - \underline{} = \underline{}$$

Bears Everywhere

The number of bears is **greater than** the number of fish.

3 > 2

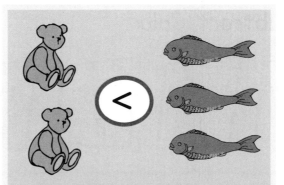

The number of bears is **less than** the number of fish.

2 < 3

Write > or < .

1 ◯ 5   7 ◯ 6

8 ◯ 4   2 ◯ 4

6 ◯ 7   4 ◯ 5

Bears Everywhere

Color the Bear

Skills:

Subtraction to 6

Note: You may need to read the sentence at the bottom of the page to your child.

Subtract. Color.

| orange 0 | brown 1 | blue 2 | red 3 | green 4 | purple 5 | yellow 6 |

Subtract.

6 – 6 = ___   3 – 3 = ___   4 – 4 = ___

1 – 1 = ___   5 – 5 = ___   2 – 2 = ___

When you subtract a number from itself, you get _____.

    Sharpen Your Skills—Math • EMC 9719 • © Evan-Moor Corp.

Bears Everywhere

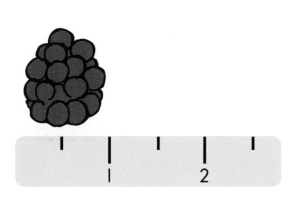

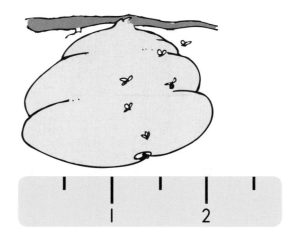

The berry is _____ inch long.

The hive is _____ inches.

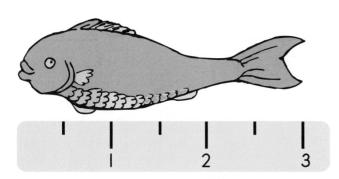

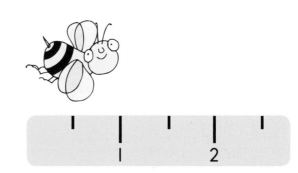

The fish is _____ inches long.

The bee is _____ inch.

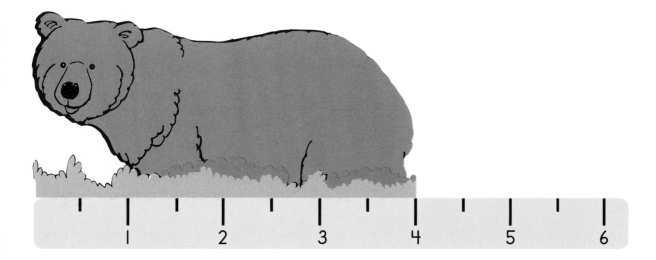

The bear is _____ inches long.

Bears Everywhere

How Many Bears Are Left?

Subtract.

5 − 5 = ____   2 − 1 = ____   6 − 5 = ____

3 − 1 = ____   0 − 0 = ____   4 − 3 = ____

6 − 6 = ____   5 − 2 = ____   3 − 0 = ____

5 − 0 = ____   6 − 2 = ____   1 − 1 = ____

5 − 0	2 − 1	4 − 3	5 − 5	1 − 0
□	□	□	□	□

6 − 3	5 − 2	3 − 0	5 − 4	3 − 1
□	□	□	□	□

Bears Everywhere

The Bear Facts

Note: You may need to help your child read the word problems.

Write the problems. Answer them.

Black Bear had 5 berries. He ate 3 berries.

How many berries were left?

$$\begin{array}{r} 5 \\ -\ 3 \\ \hline 2 \end{array}$$

_2_ berries were left.

Grizzly Bear caught 6 salmon. 1 swam away.

How many salmon were left?

____ salmon were left.

4 baby bears were in the tree. 1 climbed down.

How many baby bears were still in the tree?

____ baby bears were still in the tree.

Sun Bear had 3 honeycombs. Sun Bear ate all 3 of them.

How many honeycombs were left?

____ honeycombs were left.

Skills:

Word Problems: Subtraction to 6

Bears Everywhere

© Evan-Moor Corp. • EMC 9719 • Sharpen Your Skills—Math   UNIT 3   **177**

Hibernating Bears

Subtract.

6 – 0 = _____   4 – 2 = _____   3 – 3 = _____

5 – 1 = _____   6 – 3 = _____   5 – 4 = _____

6 – 1 = _____   4 – 3 = _____   3 – 2 = _____

5 – 3 = _____   4 – 0 = _____   6 – 6 = _____

Write a word answer.

zero	one	two	three	four	five	six
0	1	2	3	4	5	6

5 – 5 = _zero_____   3 – 2 = _____

6 – 0 = _____   6 – 2 = _____

4 – 2 = _____   4 – 1 = _____

Bears Everywhere

Read the graph.

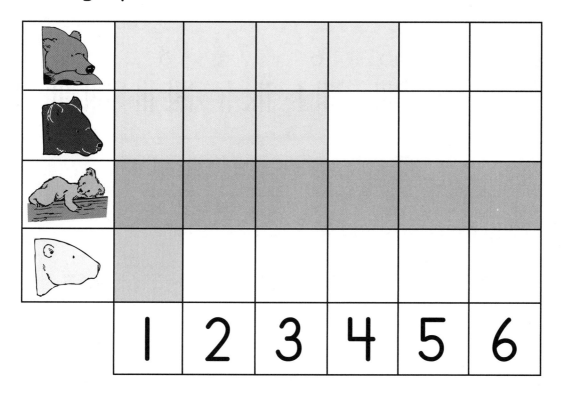

1. How many ?_____

2. How many ? _____

3. How many more than ? _____

4. How many more than ? _____

5. How many more than ? _____

Bears Everywhere

Tally Marks

Tally marks can tell how many.

1	2	3	4	5	6	7	8	9	10
I	II	III	IIII	NI	NI I	NI II	NI III	NI IIII	NI NI

Use tally marks to make each number.

Show 3	Show 10	Show 5
Show 1	Show 7	Show 2
Show 8	Show 4	Show 6

Count. Write the number.

III _____   NI NI _____   I _____

NI _____   NI IIII _____   NI III _____

Sharpen Your Skills—Math • EMC 9719 • © Evan-Moor Corp.

Bears Everywhere

Skills:

Using Tally Marks

Skills:

Subtraction to 6

Subtract.

$6 - 6 =$ ___

$6 - 0 =$ ___

$5 - 4 =$ ___

$5 - 1 =$ ___

$3 - 1 =$ ___

$3 - 2 =$ ___

$2 - 2 =$ ___

$2 - 0 =$ ___

Who is the mystery bear?
Write the letter that goes with each answer.

A
$1 - 1 = \underline{0}$

B
$2 - 1 =$ ___

D
$5 - 3 =$ ___

E
$3 - 0 =$ ___

R
$4 - 0 =$ ___

T
$6 - 1 =$ ___

Y
$6 - 0 =$ ___

___ ___ ___ ___ ___   ___ ___ $\overset{A}{\underline{}}$ ___
5   3   2   2   6   1   3   0   4

Bears Everywhere

Corners and Sides

Count the number of sides and corners.
Write the number.

rectangle

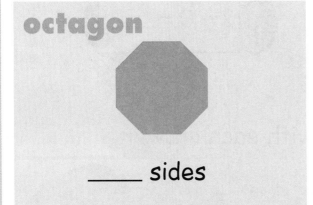

__4__ sides

__4__ corners

hexagon

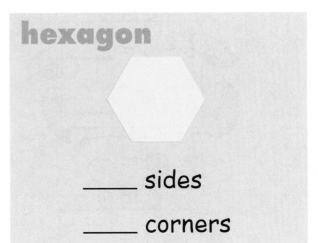

_____ sides

_____ corners

octagon

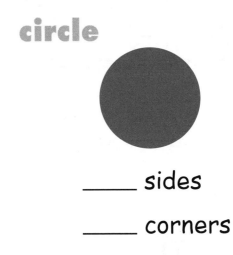

_____ sides

_____ corners

circle

_____ sides

_____ corners

square

_____ sides

_____ corners

triangle

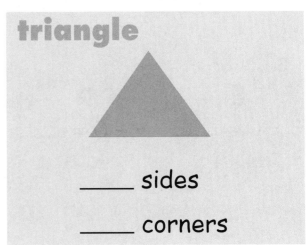

_____ sides

_____ corners

Bears Everywhere

Sharpen Your Skills—Math • EMC 9719 • © Evan-Moor Corp.

TEST YOUR SKILLS

Count. Write the number.

N̶N̶ I   N̶N̶ I I   N̶N̶ N̶N̶

_____   _____   _____

Fill in the circle for the answer.

	0	1	2
$5 - 5 =$	○	○	○
$2 - 0 =$	○	○	○
$4 - 2 =$	○	○	○
$3 - 1 =$	○	○	○

Count the sides and corners.

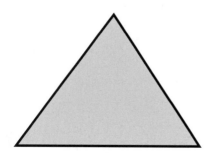

_____ sides

_____ corners

Add.

$$\begin{array}{r} 4 \\ + 3 \\ \hline \end{array}$$

$$\begin{array}{r} 2 \\ + 4 \\ \hline \end{array}$$

$$\begin{array}{r} 8 \\ + 0 \\ \hline \end{array}$$

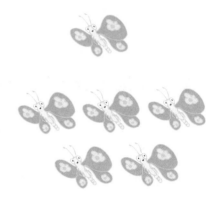

$$\begin{array}{r} 1 \\ + 5 \\ \hline \end{array}$$

Subtract.

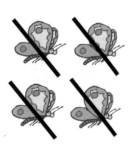

$$\begin{array}{r} 4 \\ - 4 \\ \hline 0 \end{array}$$

$$\begin{array}{r} 6 \\ - 2 \\ \hline \end{array}$$

$$\begin{array}{r} 5 \\ - 3 \\ \hline \end{array}$$

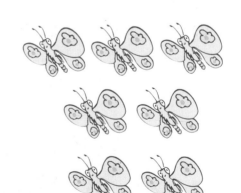

$$\begin{array}{r} 7 \\ - 5 \\ \hline \end{array}$$

creepy Crawlies

Skills:

Patterns

Circle the shape that comes next in each pattern. Label the patterns.

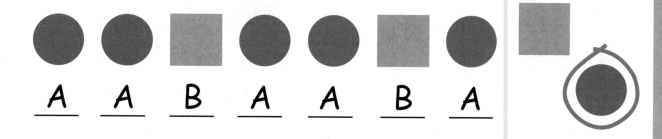

A A B A A B A

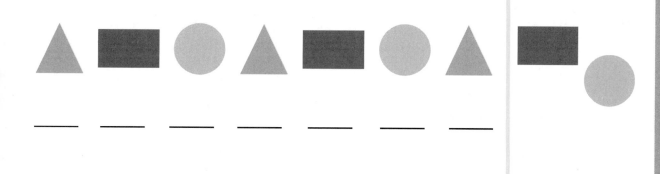

Creepy Crawlies

Skills:

Addition & Subtraction to 8

Note: You may need to help your child read the word problems.

Write the problems. Answer them.

8 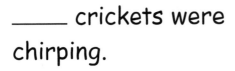 were marching.
3 stopped.

How many ants were still marching?

_____ ants were still marching.

4 were looking for aphids. 3 more ladybugs came.

How many ladybugs in all?

There were _____ ladybugs in all.

6  were chirping.
2 more came.

How many crickets were chirping?

_____ crickets were chirping.

5  were buzzing.
4 stopped.

How many bees were buzzing?

_____ bee was buzzing.

Creepy Crawlies

What's the Time?

Skills:

Telling Time to the Hour

Note: You may need to read the information to your child.

There are 2 hands on a clock.

- The shorter hand is the **hour hand**.
  It points to the hour.

- The longer hand is the **minute hand**.
  It points to 12 when the time is "on the hour."

Write the time.

Creepy Crawlies

The Ant Families

Make 2 addition problems and 2 subtraction problems.

$$\underline{1} + \underline{3} = \underline{4}$$
$$\underline{3} + \underline{1} = \underline{4}$$
$$\underline{4} - \underline{1} = \underline{3}$$
$$\underline{4} - \underline{3} = \underline{1}$$

$$\underline{} + \underline{} = \underline{}$$
$$\underline{} + \underline{} = \underline{}$$
$$\underline{} - \underline{} = \underline{}$$
$$\underline{} - \underline{} = \underline{}$$

$$\underline{} + \underline{} = \underline{}$$
$$\underline{} + \underline{} = \underline{}$$
$$\underline{} - \underline{} = \underline{}$$
$$\underline{} - \underline{} = \underline{}$$

$$\underline{} + \underline{} = \underline{}$$
$$\underline{} + \underline{} = \underline{}$$
$$\underline{} - \underline{} = \underline{}$$
$$\underline{} - \underline{} = \underline{}$$

Circle the one that does **not** belong in this "family."

$$1 + 6 = 7 \qquad 6 + 1 = 7 \qquad 7 - 1 = 6 \qquad 6 - 1 = 5$$

Which 3 numbers are "family members"?

$$\underline{} \quad \underline{} \quad \underline{}$$

Creepy Crawlies

Color the graph to show how many.

🐝							
🦋							
🦟							
🐞							
	1	2	3	4	5	6	7

Creepy Crawlies

1. There were the most

2. There were the least

3. Which 2 bugs had the same number?

Fill in the numbers.

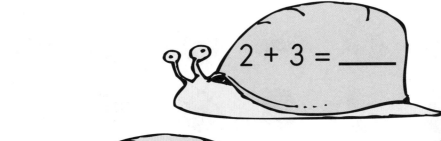

2 + 3 = _____

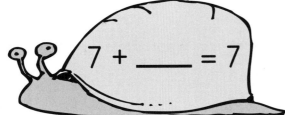

7 + _____ = 7

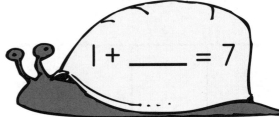

1 + _____ = 7

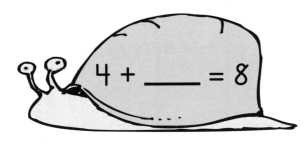

4 + _____ = 8

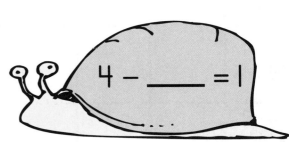

4 − _____ = 1

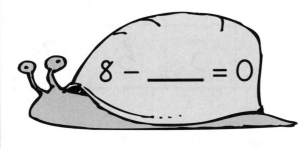

8 − _____ = 0

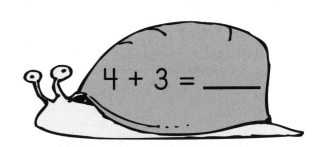

4 + 3 = _____

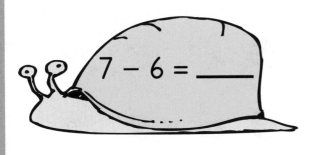

7 − 6 = _____

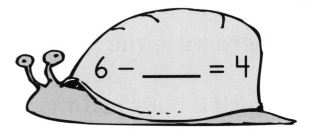

6 − _____ = 4

How many parts?

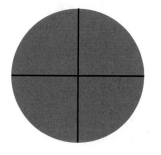 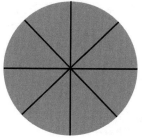  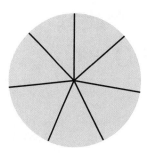

__4__ parts   _____ parts   _____ part   _____ parts

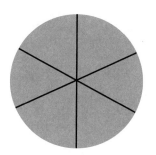 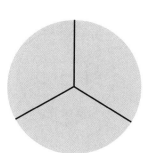  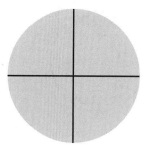

_____ parts   _____ parts   _____ parts   _____ parts

Which ones have **2 equal parts**? Circle them.

Which ones have **3 equal parts**? Circle them.

   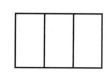

Creepy Crawlies

Skills:

Addition &
Subtraction
to 8

Creepy Crawlies

Add or subtract. Color the ladybugs that = **6**.

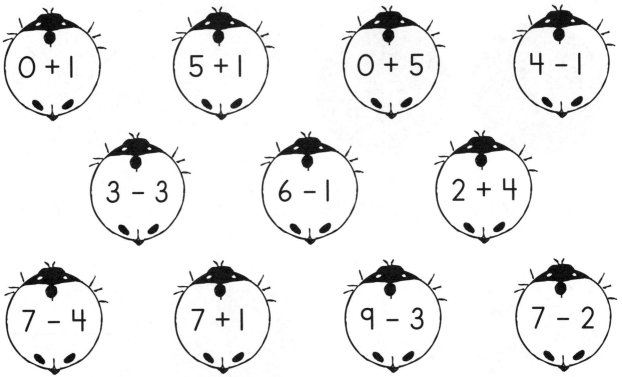

0 + 1   5 + 1   0 + 5   4 – 1

3 – 3   6 – 1   2 + 4

7 – 4   7 + 1   9 – 3   7 – 2

Add or subtract. Color the ladybugs that = **3**.

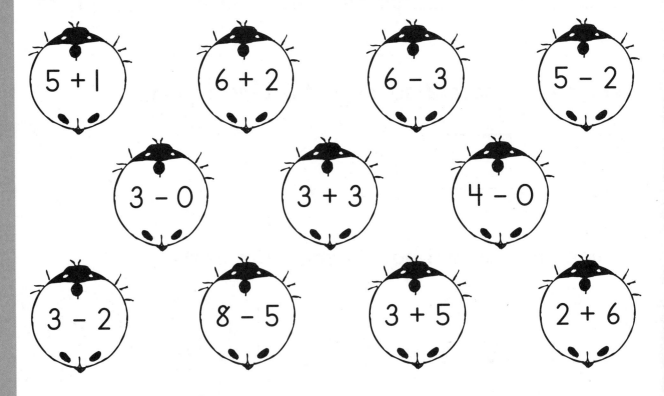

5 + 1   6 + 2   6 – 3   5 – 2

3 – 0   3 + 3   4 – 0

3 – 2   8 – 5   3 + 5   2 + 6

Skills:

Word Problems:
Addition &
Subtraction to 6

Note: You may need to help your child read the word problems.

Write the problems. Answer them.

6 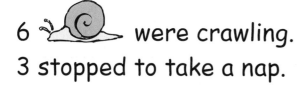 were crawling.
3 stopped to take a nap.

How many
snails were
still crawling?

_____ snails were still
crawling.

1  was flying.
3 more dragonflies
came.

How many
dragonflies
were flying?

_____ dragonflies were
flying.

6  were eating
grass. All 6 hopped away.

How many
grasshoppers
were still
eating grass?

_____ grasshoppers
were still eating grass.

2 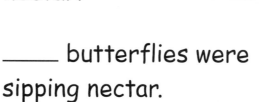 were sipping
nectar. 4 more
butterflies came.

How many
butterflies
were sipping
nectar?

_____ butterflies were
sipping nectar.

Creepy Crawlies

Fraction Fun

Color ½.

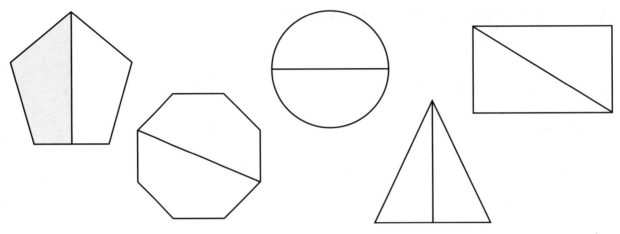

Color ⅓.

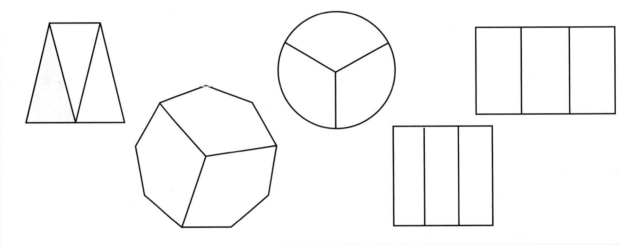

Color ¼.

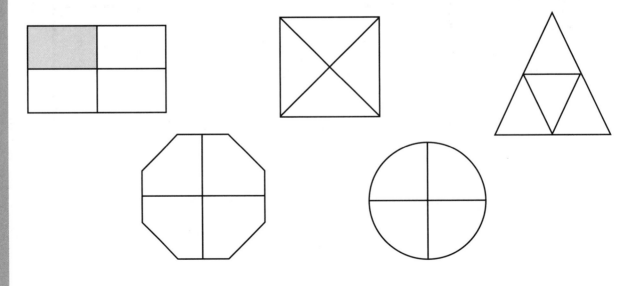

Sharpen Your Skills—Math • EMC 9719 • © Evan-Moor Corp.

Skills:

Addition & Subtraction to 8

Add and subtract.

5 + 2 = _____

5 − 2 = _____

8 + 0 = _____

8 − 0 = _____

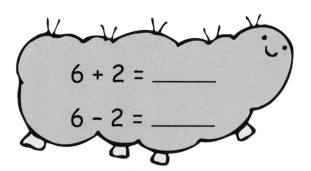

6 + 2 = _____

6 − 2 = _____

4 + 4 = _____

4 − 4 = _____

What Does It Say?

Write the letter that goes with each answer.

B	D	E	G	M	N	O	T	U
7	2	8	3	4	1	4	5	4
− 3	− 2	+ 0	+ 3	+ 3	+ 1	− 3	− 2	+ 1

_____ _____ _____ _____ , _____ B _____ _____ _____ _____

0   1   2   3   4   5   6   7   8

Creepy Crawlies

TEST YOUR SKILLS

Add or subtract.

3 + 5 = _____   6 + 2 = _____   8 − 1 = _____   8 − 5 = _____

8 + 0 = _____   3 + 2 = _____   7 − 4 = _____   7 − 7 = _____

Measure. 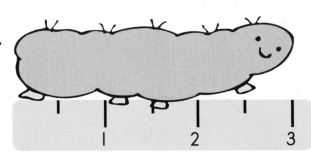   The caterpillar is _____ inches long.

Write the time.

_____ :   _____ :

Symmetrical?

yes   no   yes   no

> or < ?

7 ◯ 4   2 ◯ 8

What is colored?

$\frac{1}{4}$ $\frac{1}{2}$ $\frac{1}{3}$

Finish the pattern. Label it.

____ ____ ____ ____ ____ ____ ____

Skills:

Addition to 10

A number line can help you add.

$$4 + 5 = ?$$

Put a ✏️ on 4.

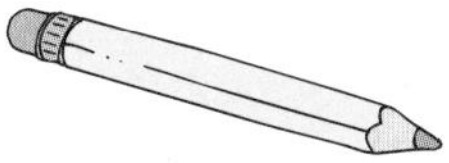

Count forward 5 spaces. The answer is 9.

```
        1    2    3    4    5
 0  1  2  3  4  5  6  7  8  9  10
```

6 + 4 = _____

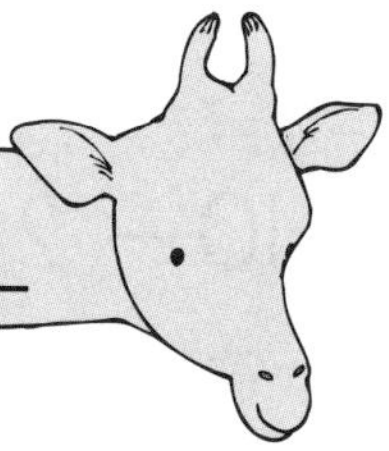

2 + 7 = _____

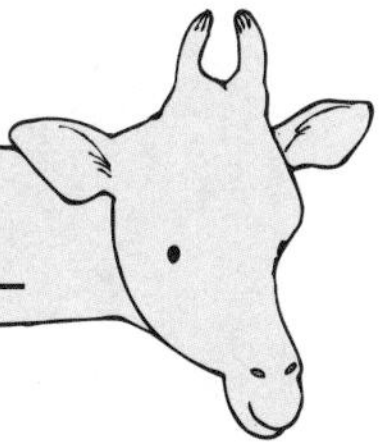

4 + 4 = _____

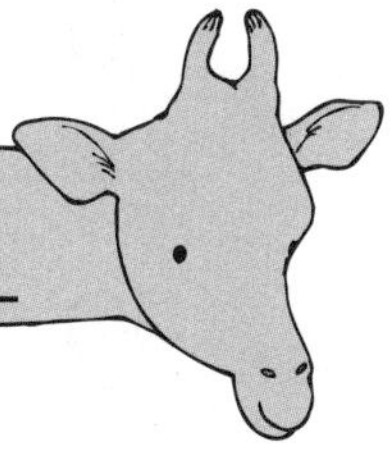

5 + 5 = _____

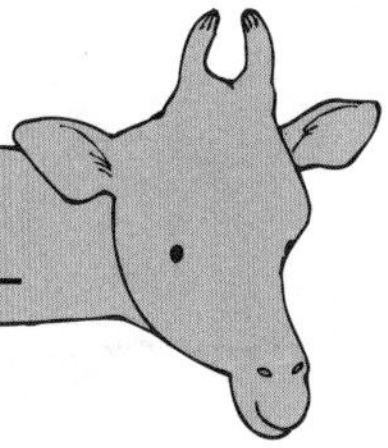

5 + 4 = _____

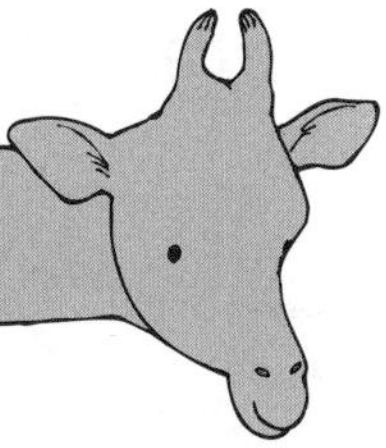

3 + 7 = _____

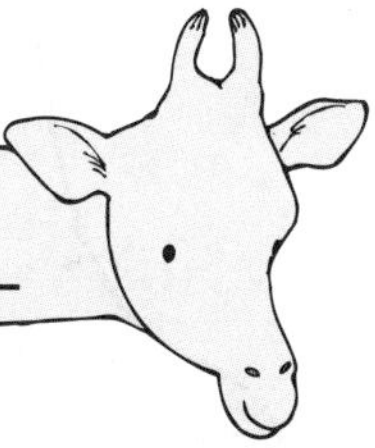

8 + 2 = _____

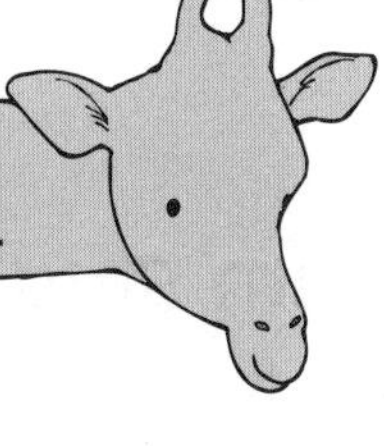

6 + 3 = _____

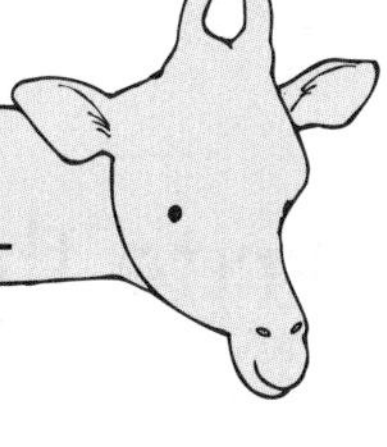

At the Zoo

Skills:

Subtraction
to 10

A number line can help you subtract.

$$9 - 3 = ?$$

Put a 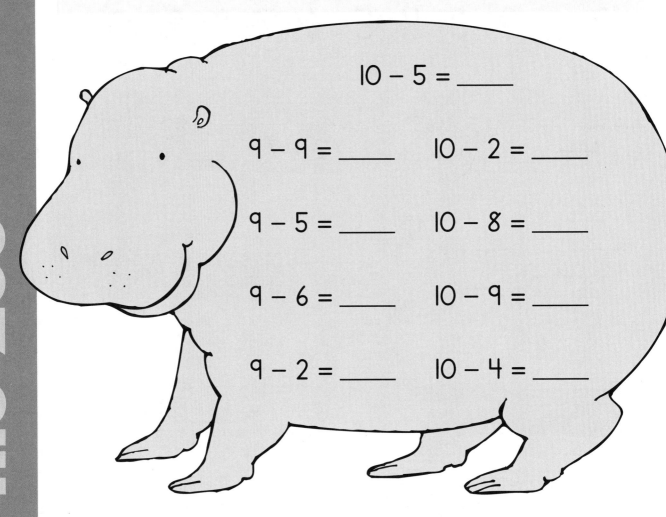 on 9.

Count back 3 spaces. The answer is 6.

3   2   1

0 1 2 3 4 5 6 7 8 9 10

$10 - 5 =$ _____

$9 - 9 =$ _____ $10 - 2 =$ _____

$9 - 5 =$ _____ $10 - 8 =$ _____

$9 - 6 =$ _____ $10 - 9 =$ _____

$9 - 2 =$ _____ $10 - 4 =$ _____

Write the answers in order from smallest to greatest.

_____, _____, _____, _____, _____, _____, _____, _____, _____

At the Zoo

Skills:

Measurement—
Weight

Which animal weighs more?

Which animal weighs less?

At the Zoo

At the Zoo

Note: You may need to help your child read the word problems.

Write the problems. Answer them.

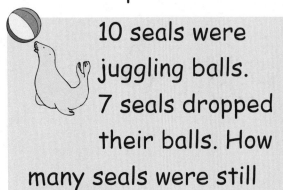

10 seals were juggling balls. 7 seals dropped their balls. How many seals were still juggling?

$$\underline{10} - \underline{7} = \underline{3}$$

| 3 | seals were still juggling. |

9 elephants were eating hay. 8 elephants ran away. How many elephants were left?

$$\underline{} - \underline{} = \underline{}$$

| | elephant was left. |

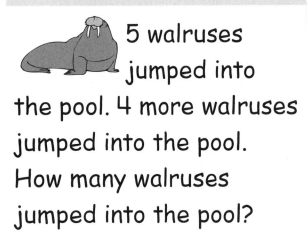

5 walruses jumped into the pool. 4 more walruses jumped into the pool. How many walruses jumped into the pool?

$$\underline{} + \underline{} = \underline{}$$

| | walruses jumped into the pool. |

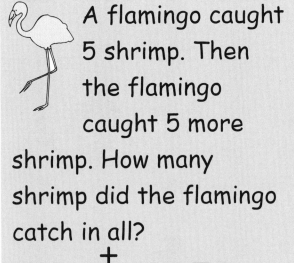

A flamingo caught 5 shrimp. Then the flamingo caught 5 more shrimp. How many shrimp did the flamingo catch in all?

$$\underline{} + \underline{} = \underline{}$$

The flamingo caught | | shrimp in all.

  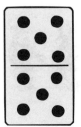 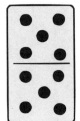 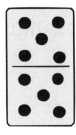

10   20   ___   ___   ___

 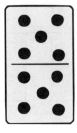   

___   ___   ___   ___   ___

Connect the dots. Start at 10.

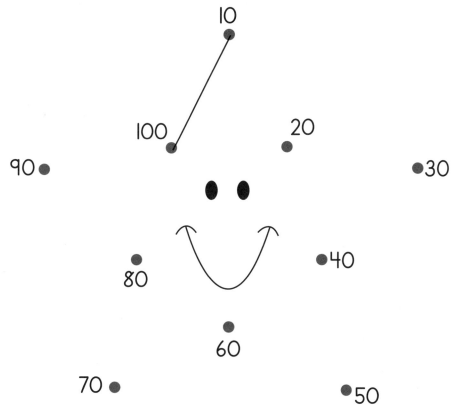

At the Zoo

Add Three Numbers

How many?

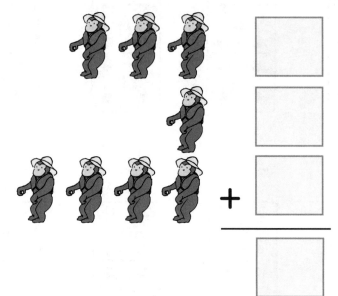

$$\begin{array}{r} 2 \\ 3 \\ + 4 \\ \hline \end{array}$$ $$\begin{array}{r} 3 \\ 5 \\ + 1 \\ \hline \end{array}$$ $$\begin{array}{r} 6 \\ 1 \\ + 2 \\ \hline \end{array}$$ $$\begin{array}{r} 4 \\ 3 \\ + 1 \\ \hline \end{array}$$ $$\begin{array}{r} 8 \\ 0 \\ + 2 \\ \hline \end{array}$$

$$\begin{array}{r} 1 \\ 7 \\ + 1 \\ \hline \end{array}$$ $$\begin{array}{r} 1 \\ 6 \\ + 3 \\ \hline \end{array}$$ $$\begin{array}{r} 2 \\ 5 \\ + 2 \\ \hline \end{array}$$ $$\begin{array}{r} 3 \\ 4 \\ + 3 \\ \hline \end{array}$$ $$\begin{array}{r} 4 \\ 3 \\ + 2 \\ \hline \end{array}$$

$$\begin{array}{r} 5 \\ 2 \\ + 3 \\ \hline \end{array}$$ $$\begin{array}{r} 6 \\ 1 \\ + 2 \\ \hline \end{array}$$ $$\begin{array}{r} 3 \\ 4 \\ + 2 \\ \hline \end{array}$$ $$\begin{array}{r} 5 \\ 2 \\ + 1 \\ \hline \end{array}$$ $$\begin{array}{r} 7 \\ 0 \\ + 2 \\ \hline \end{array}$$

How Many Tens?

Circle groups of 10 animals. How many tens did you make? How many were left?

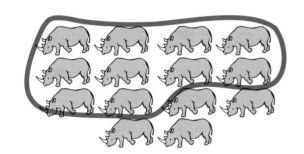

___1___ ten + ___4___ ones = ___14___   ___ ten + ___ ones = ___

___ ten + ___ ones = ___   ___ ten + ___ ones = ___

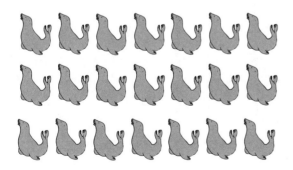

___ tens + ___ ones = ___   ___ ten + ___ ones = ___

At the Zoo

Mystery Boxes

Skills:

Addition to 10

Write the missing numbers.

Make 7

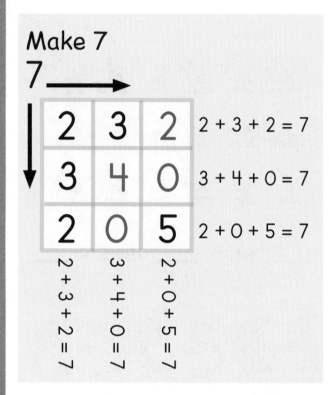

7 →		
2	3	2
3	4	0
2	0	5

2 + 3 + 2 = 7

3 + 4 + 0 = 7

2 + 0 + 5 = 7

2 + 3 + 2 = 7   3 + 4 + 0 = 7   2 + 0 + 5 = 7

Make 8

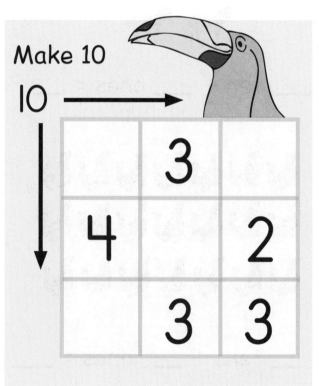

8 →		
	2	3
	5	
3		

Make 9

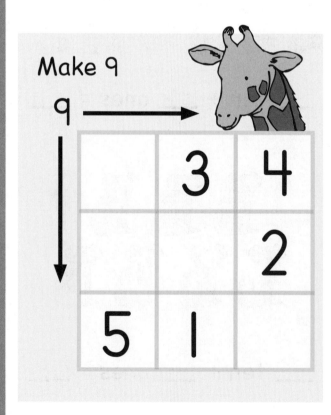

9 →		
	3	4
		2
5	1	

Make 10

10 →		
	3	
4		2
	3	3

Sharpen Your Skills—Math • EMC 9719 • © Evan-Moor Corp.

At the Zoo

Match.

5¢

1¢

nickel

penny

8¢

12¢

10¢

15¢

At the Zoo

Feed the Elephant

Add or subtract.

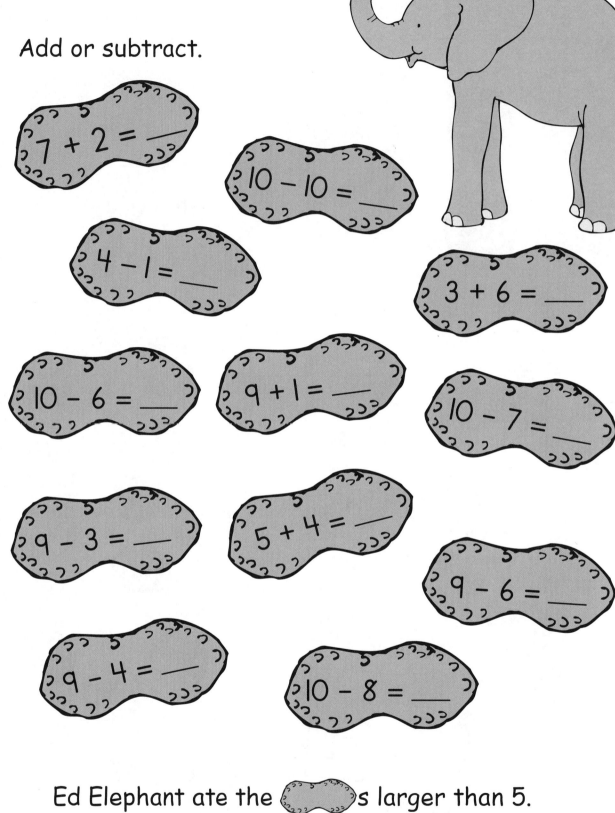

$7 + 2 = \underline{\hspace{1cm}}$

$10 - 10 = \underline{\hspace{1cm}}$

$4 - 1 = \underline{\hspace{1cm}}$

$3 + 6 = \underline{\hspace{1cm}}$

$10 - 6 = \underline{\hspace{1cm}}$

$9 + 1 = \underline{\hspace{1cm}}$

$10 - 7 = \underline{\hspace{1cm}}$

$9 - 3 = \underline{\hspace{1cm}}$

$5 + 4 = \underline{\hspace{1cm}}$

$9 - 6 = \underline{\hspace{1cm}}$

$9 - 4 = \underline{\hspace{1cm}}$

$10 - 8 = \underline{\hspace{1cm}}$

Ed Elephant ate the s larger than 5.

How many s did Ed eat?

At the Zoo

206

Tens and Ones

Each block is one.
Here are **3 ones**.

There are 10 blocks
in this set. This is
1 ten.

How many?

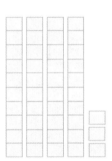

Tens	Ones

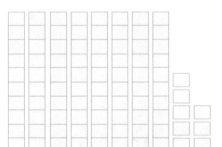

Tens	Ones

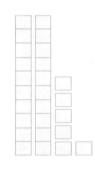

Tens	Ones

Tens	Ones

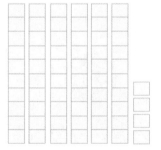

Tens	Ones

Ten	Ones

At the Zoo

How many?

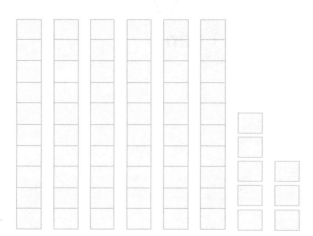

Tens

Ones

Add or subtract.

6 + 4 = _____   10 − 0 = _____

8 + 2 = _____   9 − 4 = _____

Fill in the circle to show how much.

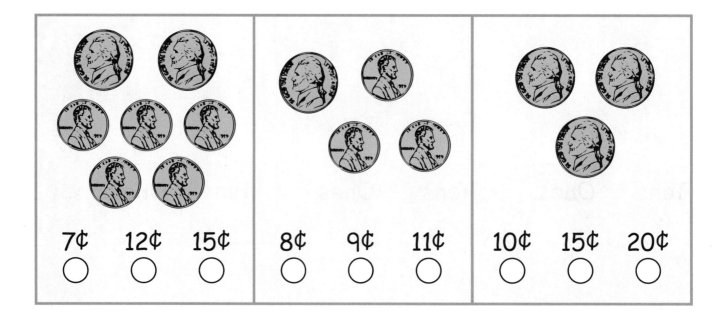

| 7¢ | 12¢ | 15¢ | 8¢ | 9¢ | 11¢ | 10¢ | 15¢ | 20¢ |
| ○ | ○ | ○ | ○ | ○ | ○ | ○ | ○ | ○ |

Skills:

Addition &
Subtraction
to 12

Match each problem to its answer.

6 + 5      10 – 0

9 + 2      12 – 3

9 + 3      12 – 4

4 + 8      11 – 2

8 + 3      12 – 5

7 + 4      11 – 4

Camping

Number families have 2 addition problems and 2 subtraction problems made from 3 numbers.

3 numbers: 7, 5, 12

2 addition problems
7 + 5 = 12
5 + 7 = 12

2 subtraction problems
12 − 7 = 5
12 − 5 = 7

Complete each number family.

8, 3, 11

____ + ____ = ____

____ + ____ = ____

____ − ____ = ____

____ − ____ = ____

9, 2, 11

____ + ____ = ____

____ + ____ = ____

____ − ____ = ____

____ − ____ = ____

8, 4, 12

____ + ____ = ____

____ + ____ = ____

____ − ____ = ____

____ − ____ = ____

9, 3, 12

____ + ____ = ____

____ + ____ = ____

____ − ____ = ____

____ − ____ = ____

Skills:
Addition to 12

How to:

1. Put the larger number in your head.
2. Count on. Write each number on a boot.

$9 + 3 = ?$
Put 9 in your head.
Add the 3 by counting on.

$9 + 3 = \underline{12}$

$8 + 4 = \underline{}$

$7 + 4 = \underline{}$

$7 + 5 = \underline{}$

$6 + 6 = \underline{}$

Camping

Skills:

Subtraction to 12

Use the sleeping bags to help you find the answers.

$$11 - 9 = \underline{} \qquad 11 - 5 = \underline{}$$

$$11 - 7 = \underline{} \qquad 11 - 4 = \underline{}$$

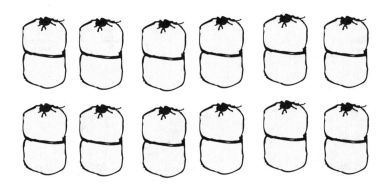

$$12 - 4 = \underline{} \qquad 12 - 6 = \underline{}$$

$$12 - 9 = \underline{} \qquad 12 - 3 = \underline{}$$

Camping

Read the graph. Answer the questions.

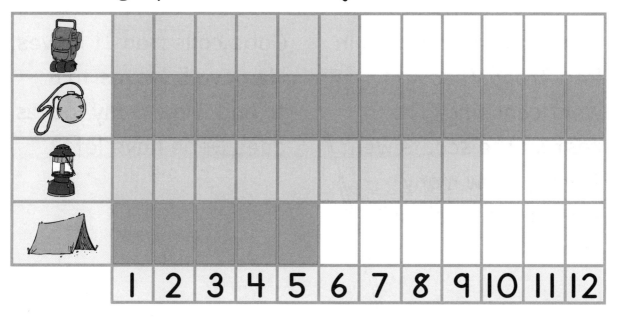

1. How many are there? ☐

2. How many are there? ☐

3. Are there more or more ?

Write the problems. Answer them.

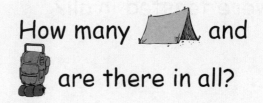

Skills:

Word Problems: Addition & Subtraction to 12

Write the problems. Answer them.

There were 12 scouts in Red Troop. 9 scouts went canoeing. The rest of the scouts went fishing. How many scouts went fishing?

_____ scouts went fishing.

Gabe collected 11 leaves. He gave 5 leaves to a friend. How many leaves does Gabe have left?

Gabe has _____ leaves left.

Katherine toasted 5 marshmallows. Mary toasted 6 marshmallows. How many marshmallows were toasted in all?

_____ marshmallows were toasted in all.

Blue Troop put up 12 tents. The wind blew down 8 tents. How many tents were still standing?

_____ tents were still standing.

Camping

Write the letter that goes with each number.

A
$$12 - 7 = 5$$

F
$$12 - 11$$

K
$$8 + 3$$

M
$$2 + 1$$

N
$$10 - 6$$

O
$$7 - 7$$

R
$$3 + 9$$

S
$$7 + 1$$

T
$$12 - 2$$

U
$$11 - 9$$

W
$$0 + 6$$

Y
$$11 - 4$$

__	__	A	__		__	__	A	__
8	10	5	7		5	6	5	7

__	__	__	__
1	12	0	3

__	__	__	__	__	__ !
8	11	2	4	11	8

Camping

Would you use a **spoon** or a **cup** to fill the containers?

spoon   cup   spoon   cup   spoon   cup

spoon   cup   spoon   cup   spoon   cup

spoon   cup   spoon   cup   spoon   cup

Two-Digit Numbers

Add or subtract the **ones** first.

Then add or subtract the **tens**.

```
tens | ones
  2  |  7     Start on the ones side.
+ 3  |  0
-----------
  5  |  7
```

```
tens | ones
  9  |  8
- 2  |  5
```

```
tens | ones
  1  |  3
+ 3  |  1
```

```
tens | ones
  6  |  4
- 3  |  0
```

```
tens | ones
  6  |  0
+ 2  |  5
```

```
tens | ones
  3  |  7
- 2  |  7
```

```
tens | ones
  8  |  6
- 7  |  5
```

```
tens | ones
  7  |  1
- 5  |  1
```

```
tens | ones
  5  |  1
+ 4  |  4
```

camping

Jobs at Camp

Skills:

Word Problems: Addition & Subtraction to 12

Write the problems. Answer them.

Cassie planted 7 big pine trees and 5 little pine trees. How many pine trees did Cassie plant in all?

Cassie planted _____

Jayme filled 4 canteens with water and 8 canteens with milk. How many canteens did Jayme fill?

Jayme filled _____ canteens.

Green Troop made 6 baskets. Orange Troop made the same number. How many baskets were made by both troops?

_____ baskets were made.

Jake chopped 12 logs. He used 3 of the logs to make a campfire. How many logs were left?

There were _____ logs left.

Camping

This is a long path.
Count by ones.

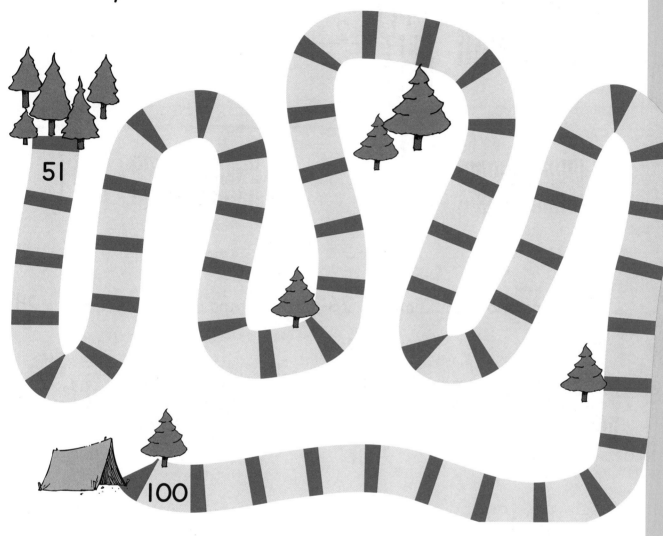

51

100

This is a short path.
Count by tens.

10

Camping

Lots of Sticks

How many tens and ones in these numbers?

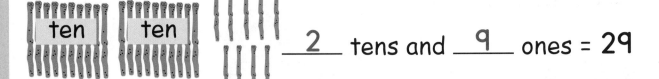

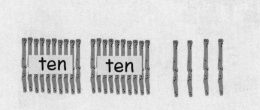

_____2_____ tens and _____9_____ ones = 29

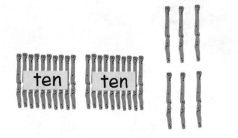

_____ tens and _____ ones = 26

_____ tens and _____ ones = 24

_____ tens and _____ ones = 37

_____ tens and _____ ones = 22

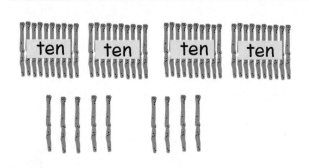

_____ tens and _____ ones = 49

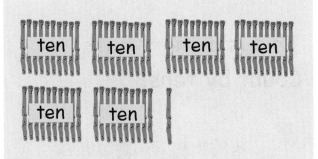

_____ tens and _____ ones = 61

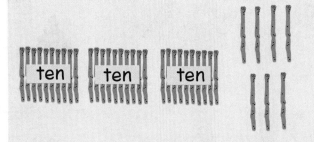

Add or subtract.

12 − 8 = ____   11 − 0 = ____   9 + 3 = ____

7 + 5 = ____   12 − 4 = ____   8 + 4 = ____

Would you use a 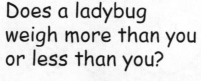 or a to fill the bucket?	Does a ladybug weigh more than you or less than you?	Does a hippo weigh more than you or less than you?

spoon cup	more less	more less

Count by 1s.

<u>75</u> ____ ____

____ ____ ____

____ ____ <u>83</u>

Write the problem and answer it.

Jason had 12 trading cards. He gave 7 to his sister. How many trading cards does Jason have left?

Jason has ____ trading cards left.

Count by 10s to 100.

___, ___, ___, ___, ___, ___, ___, ___, ___, ___

How many tens and ones?

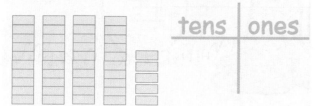

tens	ones

Add or subtract.

```
  22      36      57      61
+ 45    − 14    − 33    + 28
____    ____    ____    ____
```

A Good Crop

Find the answer that is the same as 3 + 3 + 3.
Color that apple red. Color the other apples yellow.

Add Three Numbers

Skills:

Column Addition

Number Words to 14

```
  6        2        5        1        3
  4        8        2        6        8
+ 3      + 1      + 2      + 5      + 2
```

```
  7        4        9        1        3
  0        4        0        5        4
+ 5      + 4      + 4      + 6      + 5
```

Find the Number Words

```
d f o u r t e e n s q f
b s i x e q i i j r u u
n p u x d q k g d w b l
o h z e r o o f i c v d
h e i g h t u x u t p j
w f w f g f i v e o z b
t e n c t w e l v e n l
f o u r c s e v e n g x
n i n e g d d t h r e e
t w o y c b b i x o n e
k l y v t h i r t e e n
e l e v e n n v s k g a
```

1. zero
2. one
3. two
4. three
5. four
6. five
7. six
8. seven
9. eight
10. nine
11. ten
12. eleven
13. twelve
14. thirteen
15. fourteen

Fruity Fun

Skills:

Word Problems: Addition & Subtraction to 14

Read. Find the sentence that isn't needed.
Mark it out. Write the problems. Answer them.

Dana planted 14 watermelon seeds.
9 of the watermelon seeds sprouted.
~~She ate a slice of watermelon.~~
How many watermelon seeds did **not** sprout?

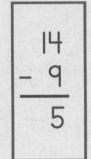

```
  14
-  9
─────
   5
```

___5___ seeds did not sprout.

There were 12 grapes in the bunch.
The grapes were delicious!
Gary ate 6 of the grapes.
How many grapes were left?

_____ grapes were left.

Bobby grew 7 plums and 5 raspberries.
The plums were purple.
How many plums and raspberries did
Bobby grow?

Bobby grew _____ plums and raspberries.

Fruity Fun

Sharpen Your Skills—Math • EMC 9719 • © Evan-Moor Corp.

Skills:

Addition &
Subtraction
to 14

6 + 7 = _____

7 + 6 = _____

13 − 7 = _____

13 − 6 = _____

9 + 4 = _____

4 + 9 = _____

13 − 4 = _____

13 − 9 = _____

8 + 5 = _____

5 + 8 = _____

13 − 8 = _____

13 − 5 = _____

9 + 5 = _____

5 + 9 = _____

14 − 9 = _____

14 − 5 = _____

8 + 4 = _____

4 + 8 = _____

12 − 8 = _____

12 − 4 = _____

8 + 6 = _____

6 + 8 = _____

14 − 6 = _____

14 − 8 = _____

Fruity Fun

Skills:

Reading a Calendar

Look at the calendar. Answer the questions.

JUNE

Sunday	Monday	Tuesday	Wednesday	Thursday	Friday	Saturday
		1	2	3	4	5
6	7	8	9	10	11	
13	14	15	16	17	18	19
20	21	22	23	24	25	26
27	28	29	30			

1. What is the name of this month? _____

2. How many days are in this month? _____

3. Flag Day is on what day? _____

4. There is a birthday on _____ .

5. There is a soccer game on _____ .

6. How many Tuesdays are in this month? _____

7. How many Saturdays are in this month? _____

Fruity Fun

226

What's Missing?

after	before	in between
21 __22__	__46__ 47	29 __30__ 31
39 ___	___ 50	43 ___ 45
45 ___	___ 36	38 ___ 40
50 ___	___ 64	51 ___ 53
64 ___	___ 21	67 ___ 69
77 ___	___ 92	80 ___ 82
99 ___	___ 63	87 ___ 89

Fruity Fun

Skills:
Addition & Subtraction to 14

Barry Banana has a message for you.
Write the letter that goes with each number.

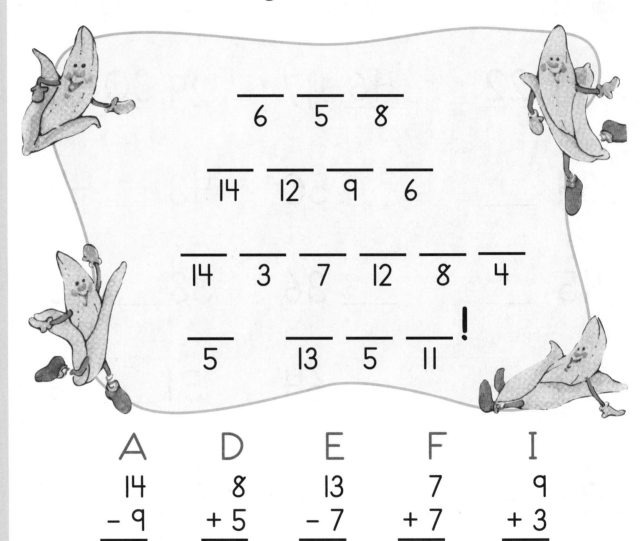

6	5	8

14	12	9	6

14	3	7	12	8	4

				!
5		13	5	11

A
14
− 9

D
8
+ 5

E
13
− 7

F
7
+ 7

I
9
+ 3

R
11
− 8

S
13
− 9

T
13
− 5

U
14
− 7

V
14
− 5

Y
7
+ 4

Fruity Fun

Farmer Fred likes to keep track of the fruit he sells at his stand. Here is what he sold last Saturday.

8 bags of cherries   10 watermelons

7 baskets of berries   5 pears

Color the graph to show what Farmer Fred sold.

	1	2	3	4	5	6	7	8	9	10

1. How many more watermelons sold than pears? _____

2. Which fruit sold the smallest amount? _____

3. How many bags of cherries and baskets of berries? _____

Fruity Fun

TEST YOUR SKILLS

Count by 5s.

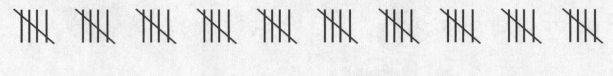

‖‖‖ ‖‖‖ ‖‖‖ ‖‖‖ ‖‖‖ ‖‖‖ ‖‖‖ ‖‖‖ ‖‖‖ ‖‖‖

___ ___ ___ ___ ___ ___ ___ ___ ___ ___

‖‖‖ ‖‖‖ ‖‖‖ ‖‖‖ ‖‖‖ ‖‖‖ ‖‖‖ ‖‖‖ ‖‖‖ ‖‖‖

___ ___ ___ ___ ___ ___ ___ ___ ___ ___

Add.

$$
\begin{array}{r} 6 \\ 4 \\ +3 \\ \hline \end{array}
\qquad
\begin{array}{r} 2 \\ 3 \\ +1 \\ \hline \end{array}
\qquad
\begin{array}{r} 4 \\ 3 \\ +5 \\ \hline \end{array}
\qquad
\begin{array}{r} 9 \\ 0 \\ +4 \\ \hline \end{array}
$$

Read the word. Fill in the circle under the number.

(**zero**)   (**eight**)   (**three**)

7 0 2   9 4 8   10 3 2
○ ○ ○   ○ ○ ○   ○   ○ ○

Answer Key

Page 147

Page 148

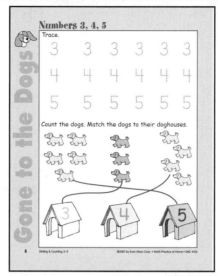

Page 149

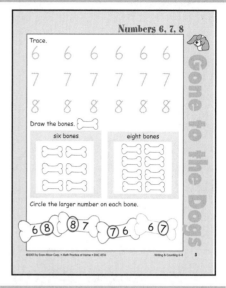

Page 150

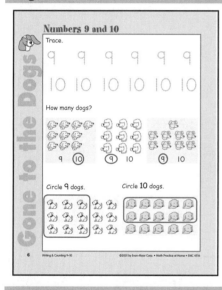

Page 151

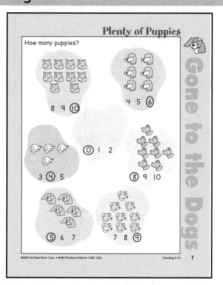

Page 152

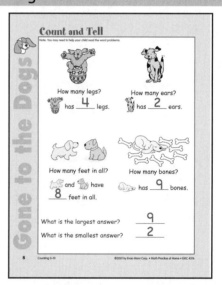

Page 153

Page 154

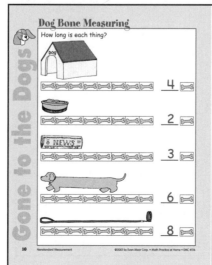

Page 155

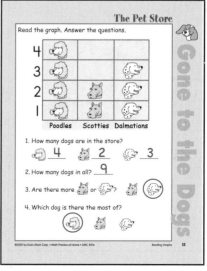

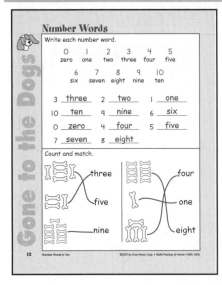

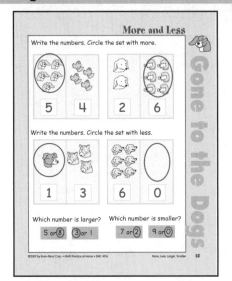

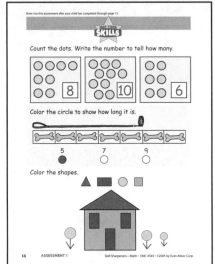

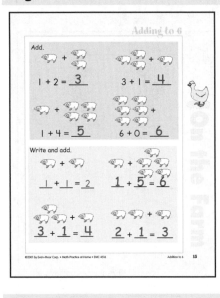

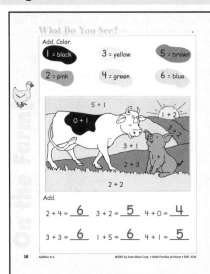

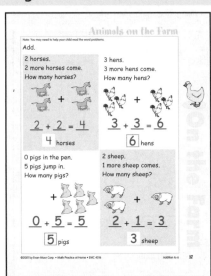

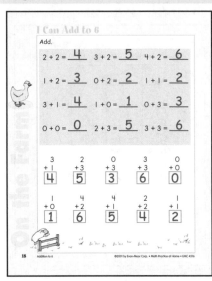

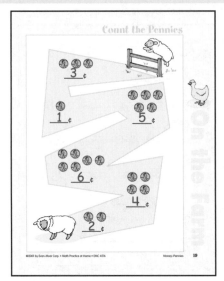

Page 165

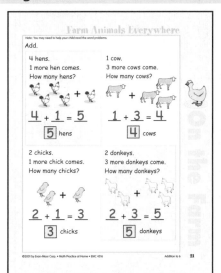

Farm Animals Everywhere

Note: You may need to help your child read the word problems.

Add.

4 hens.
1 more hen comes.
How many hens?

$\underline{4} + \underline{1} = \underline{5}$

$\boxed{5}$ hens

1 cow.
3 more cows come.
How many cows?

$\underline{1} + \underline{3} = \underline{4}$

$\boxed{4}$ cows

2 chicks.
1 more chick comes.
How many chicks?

$\underline{2} + \underline{1} = \underline{3}$

$\boxed{3}$ chicks

2 donkeys.
3 more donkeys come.
How many donkeys?

$\underline{2} + \underline{3} = \underline{5}$

$\boxed{5}$ donkeys

©2001 by Evan-Moor Corp. • Math Practice at Home • EMC 4516 — Addition to 6 — 21

Page 166

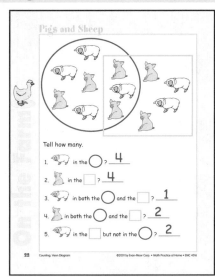

Pigs and Sheep

Tell how many.

1. 🐷 in the ⭕ ? **4**
2. 🐑 in the ⬜ ? **4**
3. 🐷 in both the ⭕ and the ⬜ ? **1**
4. 🐑 in both the ⭕ and the ⬜ ? **2**
5. 🐷 in the ⬜ but not in the ⭕ ? **2**

22 — Counting: Venn Diagram — ©2001 by Evan-Moor Corp. • Math Practice at Home • EMC 4516

Page 167

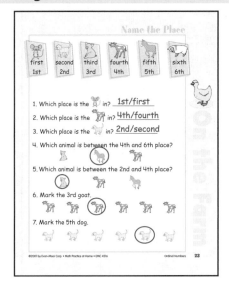

Name the Place

first	second	third	fourth	fifth	sixth
1st	2nd	3rd	4th	5th	6th

1. Which place is the 🐄 in? **1st/first**
2. Which place is the 🐑 in? **4th/fourth**
3. Which place is the 🦙 in? **2nd/second**
4. Which animal is between the 4th and 6th place?
5. Which animal is between the 2nd and 4th place?
6. Mark the 3rd goat.
7. Mark the 5th dog.

©2001 by Evan-Moor Corp. • Math Practice at Home • EMC 4516 — Ordinal Numbers — 23

Page 168

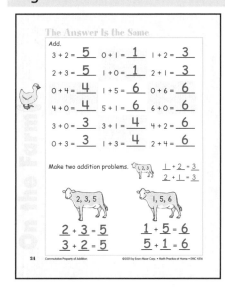

The Answer Is the Same

Add.

$3 + 2 = \underline{5}$ $0 + 1 = \underline{1}$ $1 + 2 = \underline{3}$

$2 + 3 = \underline{5}$ $1 + 0 = \underline{1}$ $2 + 1 = \underline{3}$

$0 + 4 = \underline{4}$ $1 + 5 = \underline{6}$ $0 + 6 = \underline{6}$

$4 + 0 = \underline{4}$ $5 + 1 = \underline{6}$ $6 + 0 = \underline{6}$

$3 + 0 = \underline{3}$ $3 + 1 = \underline{4}$ $4 + 2 = \underline{6}$

$0 + 3 = \underline{3}$ $1 + 3 = \underline{4}$ $2 + 4 = \underline{6}$

Make two addition problems.

1, 2, 3 $\underline{1} + \underline{2} = \underline{3}$
$\underline{2} + \underline{1} = \underline{3}$

2, 3, 5
$\underline{2} + \underline{3} = \underline{5}$
$\underline{3} + \underline{2} = \underline{5}$

1, 5, 6
$\underline{1} + \underline{5} = \underline{6}$
$\underline{5} + \underline{1} = \underline{6}$

24 — Commutative Property of Addition — ©2001 by Evan-Moor Corp. • Math Practice at Home • EMC 4516

Page 169

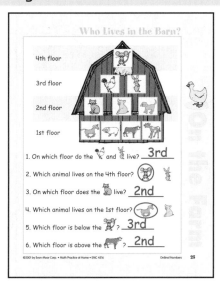

Who Lives in the Barn?

4th floor
3rd floor
2nd floor
1st floor

1. On which floor do the 🐁 and 🐦 live? **3rd**
2. Which animal lives on the 4th floor?
3. On which floor does the 🐱 live? **2nd**
4. Which animal lives on the 1st floor?
5. Which floor is below the 🐭? **3rd**
6. Which floor is above the 🐄? **2nd**

©2001 by Evan-Moor Corp. • Math Practice at Home • EMC 4516 — Ordinal Numbers — 25

Page 170

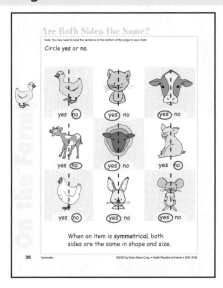

Are Both Sides the Same?

Note: You may need to read the sentence at the bottom of the page to your child.

Circle **yes** or no.

yes **no**   yes no   **yes** no

yes no   **yes** no   yes **no**

yes **no**   **yes** no   **yes** no

When an item is **symmetrical**, both sides are the same in shape and size.

26 — Symmetry — ©2001 by Evan-Moor Corp. • Math Practice at Home • EMC 4516

Page 171

Note: Use this assessment after your child has completed through page 26. Help your child read the directions.

TEST YOUR SKILLS

Count.

$\boxed{6}$ $\boxed{5}$ $\boxed{4}$ $\boxed{7}$

Add.

$3 + 3 = \underline{6}$ $4 + 2 = \underline{6}$ $1 + 2 = \underline{3}$ $0 + 0 = \underline{0}$

$1 + 0 = \underline{1}$ $3 + 2 = \underline{5}$ $4 + 1 = \underline{5}$ $1 + 1 = \underline{2}$

Read the graph. Answer the questions.

1. How many 🐔 are there? **2**
2. How many 🐴 are there? **5**
3. Which two have the same number?

Read and answer.

3 🐷 are in the mud. 2 more come.
How many 🐷 are in the mud? **5**

©2005 by Evan-Moor Corp. • EMC 4545 • Skill Sharpeners—Math — ASSESSMENT 1 — 27

Page 172

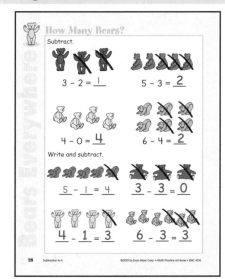

How Many Bears?

Subtract.

$3 - 2 = \underline{1}$ $5 - 3 = \underline{2}$

$4 - 0 = \underline{4}$ $6 - 4 = \underline{2}$

Write and subtract.

$\underline{5} - \underline{1} = 4$ $\underline{3} - \underline{3} = 0$

$\underline{4} - \underline{1} = 3$ $\underline{6} - \underline{3} = 3$

28 — Subtraction to 6 — ©2001 by Evan-Moor Corp. • Math Practice at Home • EMC 4516

Page 173

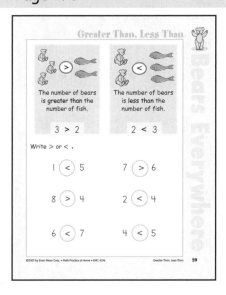

Greater Than, Less Than

🐻 ⭘> 🐟
The number of bears
is greater than the
number of fish.

3 > 2

🐻 ⭘< 🐟 🐟
The number of bears
is less than the
number of fish.

2 < 3

Write > or < .

1 ⭘< 5   7 ⭘> 6

8 ⭘> 4   2 ⭘< 4

6 ⭘< 7   4 ⭘< 5

©2001 by Evan-Moor Corp. • Math Practice at Home • EMC 4516 — Greater Than, Less Than — 29

Page 174

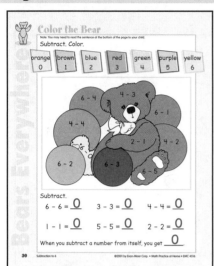

Page 175

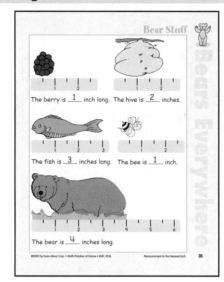

Page 176

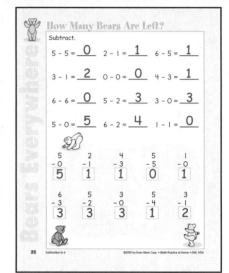

Page 177

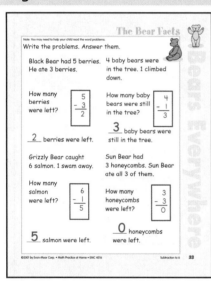

Page 178

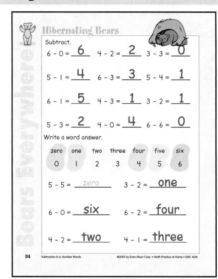

Page 179

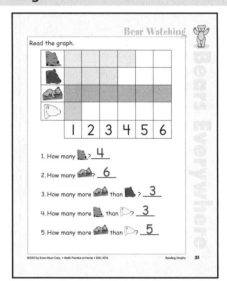

Page 180

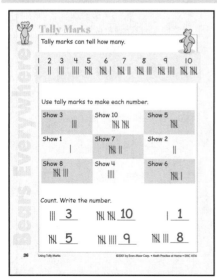

Page 181

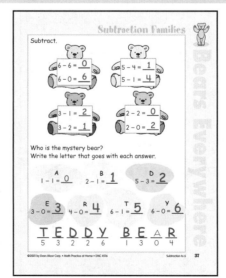

Page 182

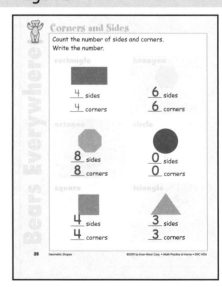

Page 183

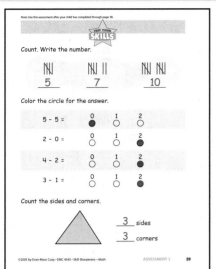

©2005 by Evan-Moor Corp. • EMC 4545 • Skill Sharpeners—Math

ASSESSMENT 3   39

Note: Use this assessment after your child has completed through page 38.

TEST YOUR SKILLS

Count. Write the number.

5   7   10

Color the circle for the answer.

5 - 5 =   ● 0   ○ 1   ○ 2
2 - 0 =   ○ 0   ○ 1   ● 2
4 - 2 =   ○ 0   ○ 1   ● 2
3 - 1 =   ○ 0   ● 1   ○ 2

Count the sides and corners.

3 sides
3 corners

Page 184

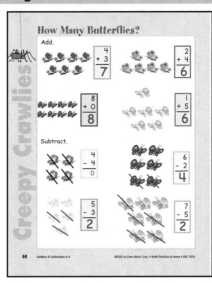

How Many Butterflies?

Add.

4 + 3 = 7
8 + 0 = 8
2 + 4 = 6
1 + 5 = 6

Subtract.

4 - 4 = 0
6 - 2 = 4
5 - 3 = 2
7 - 5 = 2

40   Addition & Subtraction to 8   ©2001 by Evan-Moor Corp. • Math Practice at Home • EMC 4516

Page 185

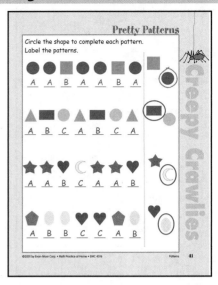

Pretty Patterns

Circle the shape to complete each pattern.
Label the patterns.

A A B A A B A
A B C A B C A
A A B C A A B
A B B C C A B

©2001 by Evan-Moor Corp. • Math Practice at Home • EMC 4516   Patterns   41

Page 186

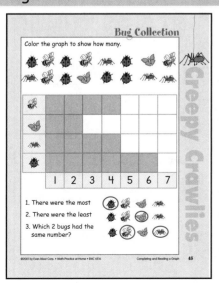

Bug Problems

Note: You may need to help your child read the word problems.

Write the problems. Answer them.

8 were marching. 3 stopped.

How many ants were still marching?   8 - 3 = 5

5 ants were still marching.

4 were looking for aphids. 3 more ladybugs came.

How many ladybugs in all?   4 + 3 = 7

There were **7** ladybugs in all.

6 were chirping. 2 more came.

How many crickets were chirping?   6 + 2 = 8

8 crickets were chirping.

5 were buzzing. 4 stopped.

How many bees were buzzing?   5 - 4 = 1

1 bee was buzzing.

42   Addition & Subtraction to 8   ©2001 by Evan-Moor Corp. • Math Practice at Home • EMC 4516

Page 187

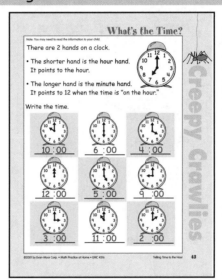

What's the Time?

Note: You may need to read the information to your child.

There are 2 hands on a clock.

• The shorter hand is the **hour hand**. It points to the hour.

• The longer hand is the **minute hand**. It points to 12 when the time is "on the hour."

Write the time.

10:00   6:00   4:00
12:00   5:00   9:00
3:00   11:00   2:00

©2001 by Evan-Moor Corp. • Math Practice at Home • EMC 4516   Telling Time to the Hour   43

Page 188

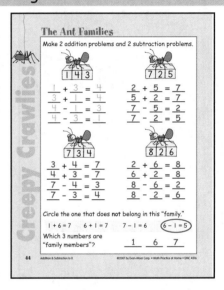

The Ant Families

Make 2 addition problems and 2 subtraction problems.

1 4 3
1 + 3 = 4
3 + 1 = 4
4 - 1 = 3
4 - 3 = 1

7 2 5
2 + 5 = 7
5 + 2 = 7
7 - 5 = 2
7 - 2 = 5

7 3 4
3 + 4 = 7
4 + 3 = 7
7 - 4 = 3
7 - 3 = 4

8 2 6
2 + 6 = 8
6 + 2 = 8
8 - 6 = 2
8 - 2 = 6

Circle the one that does **not** belong in this "family."

1 + 6 = 7   6 + 1 = 7   7 - 1 = 6   (6 - 1 = 5)

Which 3 numbers are "family members"?   1   6   7

44   Addition & Subtraction to 8   ©2001 by Evan-Moor Corp. • Math Practice at Home • EMC 4516

Page 189

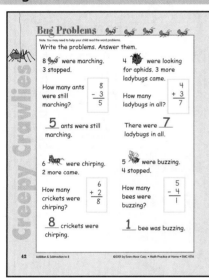

Bug Collection

Color the graph to show how many.

	1	2	3	4	5	6	7

1. There were the most
2. There were the least
3. Which 2 bugs had the same number?

©2001 by Evan-Moor Corp. • Math Practice at Home • EMC 4516   Completing and Reading a Graph   45

Page 190

What's Missing?

Fill in the numbers.

2 + 3 = 5
7 + 0 = 7
1 + 6 = 7
4 + 4 = 8
4 - 3 = 1
8 - 8 = 0
4 + 3 = 7
7 - 6 = 1
6 - 2 = 4

46   Addition & Subtraction to 8   ©2001 by Evan-Moor Corp. • Math Practice at Home • EMC 4516

Page 191

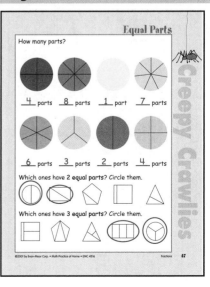

Equal Parts

How many parts?

4 parts   8 parts   1 part   7 parts
6 parts   3 parts   2 parts   4 parts

Which ones have 2 equal parts? Circle them.

Which ones have 3 equal parts? Circle them.

©2001 by Evan-Moor Corp. • Math Practice at Home • EMC 4516   Fractions   47

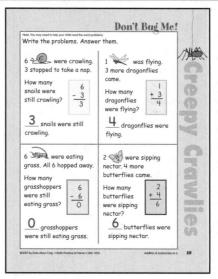

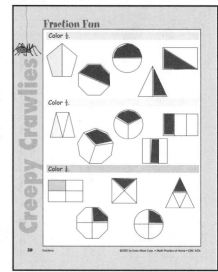

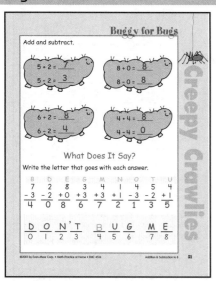

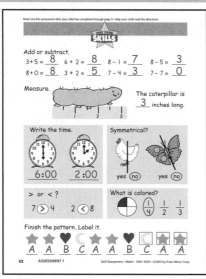

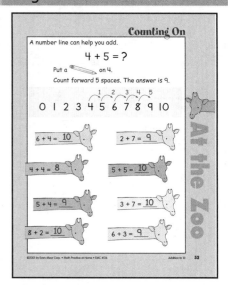

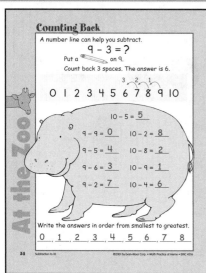

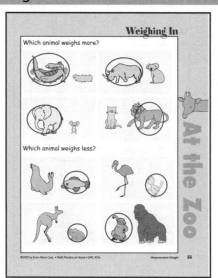

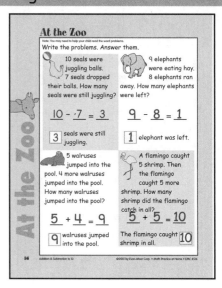

Page 201

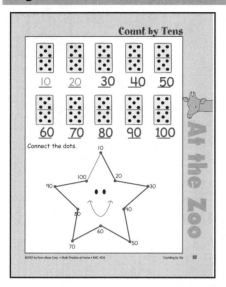

Page 202

Page 203

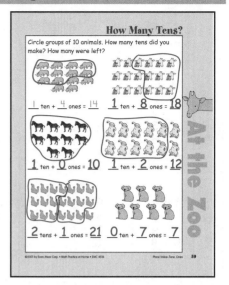

Page 204

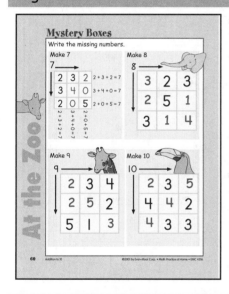

Page 205

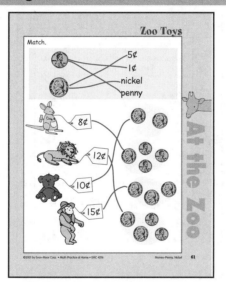

Page 206

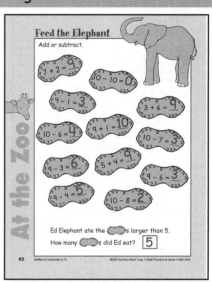

Page 207

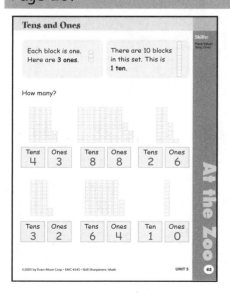

Page 208

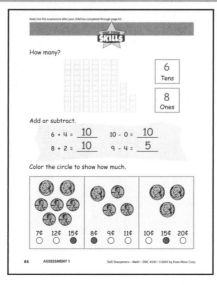

Page 209

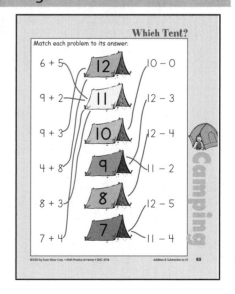

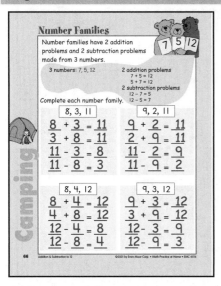

Number Families

Number families have 2 addition problems and 2 subtraction problems made from 3 numbers.

3 numbers: 7, 5, 12

2 addition problems
7 + 5 = 12
5 + 7 = 12

2 subtraction problems
12 − 7 = 5
12 − 5 = 7

Complete each number family.

8, 3, 11
8 + 3 = 11
3 + 8 = 11
11 − 3 = 8
11 − 8 = 3

9, 2, 11
9 + 2 = 11
2 + 9 = 11
11 − 2 = 9
11 − 9 = 2

8, 4, 12
8 + 4 = 12
4 + 8 = 12
12 − 4 = 8
12 − 8 = 4

9, 3, 12
9 + 3 = 12
3 + 9 = 12
12 − 3 = 9
12 − 9 = 3

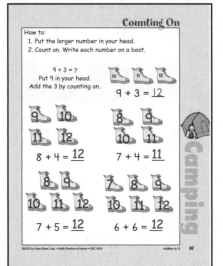

Counting On

How to:
1. Put the larger number in your head.
2. Count on. Write each number on a boot.

9 + 3 = ?
Put 9 in your head.
Add the 3 by counting on.

9 + 3 = 12

8 + 4 = 12

7 + 4 = 11

7 + 5 = 12

6 + 6 = 12

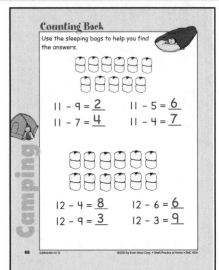

Counting Back

Use the sleeping bags to help you find the answers.

11 − 9 = 2   11 − 5 = 6
11 − 7 = 4   11 − 4 = 7

12 − 4 = 8   12 − 6 = 6
12 − 9 = 3   12 − 3 = 9

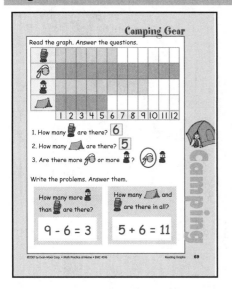

Camping Gear

Read the graph. Answer the questions.

1 2 3 4 5 6 7 8 9 10 11 12

1. How many are there? 6
2. How many are there? 5
3. Are there more or more ?

Write the problems. Answer them.

How many more than are there?
9 − 6 = 3

How many and are there in all?
5 + 6 = 11

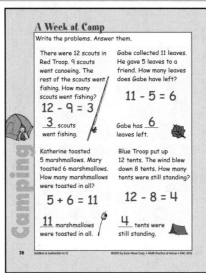

A Week at Camp

Write the problems. Answer them.

There were 12 scouts in Red Troop. 9 scouts went canoeing. The rest of the scouts went fishing. How many scouts went fishing?
12 − 9 = 3
3 scouts went fishing.

Gabe collected 11 leaves. He gave 5 leaves to a friend. How many leaves does Gabe have left?
11 − 5 = 6
Gabe has 6 leaves left.

Katherine toasted 5 marshmallows. Mary toasted 6 marshmallows. How many marshmallows were toasted in all?
5 + 6 = 11
11 marshmallows were toasted in all.

Blue Troop put up 12 tents. The wind blew down 8 tents. How many tents were still standing?
12 − 8 = 4
4 tents were still standing.

Mystery Message

Write the letter that goes with each number.

A
12
− 7
5

F
12
− 11
1

K
8
+ 3
11

M
2
+ 1
3

N
10
− 6
4

O
7
− 7
0

R
3
+ 9
12

S
7
+ 1
8

T
12
− 2
10

U
11
− 9
2

W
0
+ 6
6

Y
11
− 4
7

S T A Y   A W A Y
8 10 5 7   5 6 5 7

F R O M
1 12 0 3

S K U N K S !
8 11 2 4 11 8

Fill Them Up!

Would you use a spoon or a cup to fill the containers?

spoon / cup
spoon / cup
spoon / cup

spoon / cup
spoon / cup
spoon / cup

spoon / cup
spoon / cup
spoon / cup

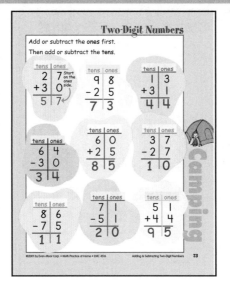

Two-Digit Numbers

Add or subtract the ones first.
Then add or subtract the tens.

tens ones
2 7 Start on the ones side.
+3 0
5 7

tens ones
9 8
−2 5
7 3

tens ones
1 3
+3 1
4 4

tens ones
6 4
−3 0
3 4

tens ones
6 0
+2 5
8 5

tens ones
3 7
−2 7
1 0

tens ones
8 6
−7 5
1 1

tens ones
7 1
−5 1
2 0

tens ones
5 1
+4 4
9 5

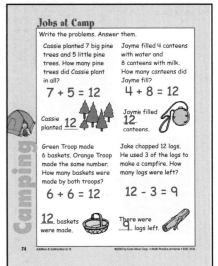

Jobs at Camp

Write the problems. Answer them.

Cassie planted 7 big pine trees and 5 little pine trees. How many pine trees did Cassie plant in all?
7 + 5 = 12
Cassie planted 12

Jayme filled 4 canteens with water and 8 canteens with milk. How many canteens did Jayme fill?
4 + 8 = 12
Jayme filled 12 canteens.

Green Troop made 6 baskets. Orange Troop made the same number. How many baskets were made by both troops?
6 + 6 = 12
12 baskets were made.

Jake chopped 12 logs. He used 3 of the logs to make a campfire. How many logs were left?
12 − 3 = 9
There were 9 logs left.

Page 219

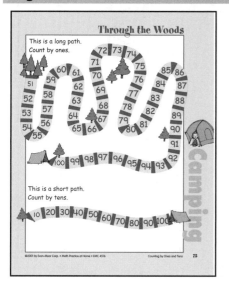

Through the Woods

This is a long path.
Count by ones.

This is a short path.
Count by tens.

10 20 30 40 50 60 70 80 90 100

Page 220

Lots of Sticks

How many tens and ones in these numbers?

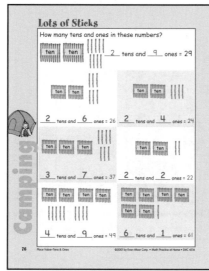

2 tens and 9 ones = 29

2 tens and 6 ones = 26   2 tens and 4 ones = 24

3 tens and 7 ones = 37   2 tens and 2 ones = 22

4 tens and 9 ones = 49   6 tens and 1 ones = 61

Page 221

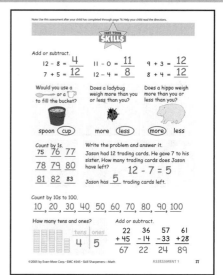

Note: Use this assessment after your child has completed through page 76. Help your child read the directions.

TEST YOUR SKILLS

Add or subtract.

12 - 8 = 4   11 - 0 = 11   9 + 3 = 12

7 + 5 = 12   12 - 4 = 8   8 + 4 = 12

Would you use a ⟶ or a ⟶ to fill the bucket?

spoon (cup)

Does a ladybug weigh more than you or less than you?

more (less)

Does a hippo weigh more than you or less than you?

(more) less

Count by 1s.
75 76 77
78 79 80
81 82 83

Write the problem and answer it.
Jason had 12 trading cards. He gave 7 to his sister. How many trading cards does Jason have left?

12 - 7 = 5

Jason has 5 trading cards left.

Count by 10s to 100.
10, 20, 30, 40, 50, 60, 70, 80, 90, 100

How many tens and ones?

tens	ones
4	5

Add or subtract.

22   36   57   61
+ 45 - 14 - 33 + 28
67   22   24   89

Page 222

A Good Crop

Find the answer that is the same as 3 + 3 + 3.
Color that apple red. Color the other apples yellow.

Page 223

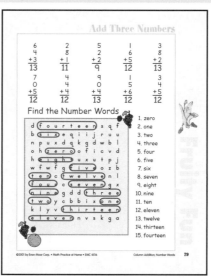

Add Three Numbers

6	2	5	1	3
4	8	2	6	8
+3	+1	+2	+5	+2
13	11	9	12	13

7	4	9	1	3
0	4	0	5	4
+5	+4	+4	+6	+5
12	12	13	12	12

Find the Number Words

d f o u r t e e n s q f
b s i x e q i i j r u u
n p u x d q k g d w b l
o h z e r o o f i c v d
h i g h u x u t p j
w f w f g f i v e o z b
t e n c t w e l v e r
f o u c s e v e n g x
n i n e g d d t h r e e
t w o y c b b i x o n e
k l y v t h i r t e e n
e l e v e n n v s k g a

1. zero
2. one
3. two
4. three
5. four
6. five
7. six
8. seven
9. eight
10. nine
11. ten
12. eleven
13. twelve
14. thirteen
15. fourteen

Page 224

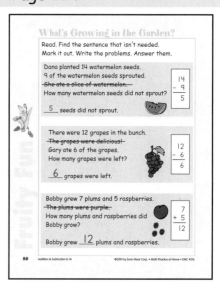

What's Growing in the Garden?

Read. Find the sentence that isn't needed.
Mark it out. Write the problems. Answer them.

Dana planted 14 watermelon seeds.
9 of the watermelon seeds sprouted.
~~She ate a slice of watermelon.~~
How many watermelon seeds did not sprout?

14
- 9
5

5 seeds did not sprout.

There were 12 grapes in the bunch.
~~The grapes were delicious!~~
Gary ate 6 of the grapes.
How many grapes were left?

12
- 6
6

6 grapes were left.

Bobby grew 7 plums and 5 raspberries.
~~The plums were purple.~~
How many plums and raspberries did Bobby grow?

7
+ 5
12

Bobby grew 12 plums and raspberries.

Page 225

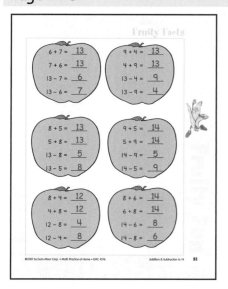

Fruity Facts

6 + 7 = 13	9 + 4 = 13
7 + 6 = 13	4 + 9 = 13
13 - 7 = 6	13 - 4 = 9
13 - 6 = 7	13 - 9 = 4

8 + 5 = 13	9 + 5 = 14
5 + 8 = 13	5 + 9 = 14
13 - 8 = 5	14 - 9 = 5
13 - 5 = 8	14 - 5 = 9

8 + 4 = 12	8 + 6 = 14
4 + 8 = 12	6 + 8 = 14
12 - 8 = 4	14 - 6 = 8
12 - 4 = 8	14 - 8 = 6

Page 226

All About June

Look at the calendar. Answer the questions.

JUNE

Sunday	Monday	Tuesday	Wednesday	Thursday	Friday	Saturday
			1	2	3	4
5	6	7	8	9	10	11
12	13	14	15	16	17	18
19	20	21	22	23	24	25
26	27	28	29	30		

1. What is the name of this month? **June**
2. How many days are in this month? **30**
3. Flag Day is on what day? **14**
4. There is a birthday on **Thursday or June 10**
5. There is a soccer game on **Friday or June 25**
6. How many Tuesdays are in this month? **5**
7. How many Saturdays are in this month? **4**

Page 227

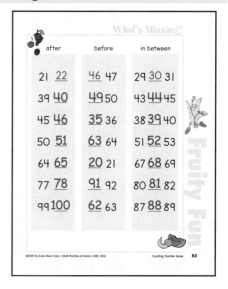

What's Missing?

after	before	in between
21 22	46 47	29 30 31
39 40	49 50	43 44 45
45 46	35 36	38 39 40
50 51	63 64	51 52 53
64 65	20 21	67 68 69
77 78	91 92	80 81 82
99 100	62 63	87 88 89

Page 228

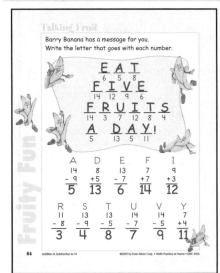

Fruity Fun

Talking Fruit

Barry Banana has a message for you.
Write the letter that goes with each number.

E A T
6 5 8

F I V E
14 12 9 6

F R U I T S
14 3 7 12 8 4

A D A Y !
5 13 5 11

A   D   E   F   I
14   8   13   7   9
- 9   +5   - 7   +7   +3
―――   ――――   ――――   ――――   ――――
5   13   6   14   12

R   S   T   U   V   Y
11   13   13   14   14   7
- 8   - 9   - 5   - 7   - 5   +4
――――   ――――   ――――   ――――   ――――   ――――
3   4   8   7   9   11

84   Addition & Subtraction to 14   ©2005 by Evan-Moor Corp. • Math Practice at Home • EMC 4516

Page 229

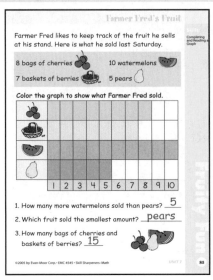

Farmer Fred's Fruit

Farmer Fred likes to keep track of the fruit he sells
at his stand. Here is what he sold last Saturday.

8 bags of cherries   10 watermelons
7 baskets of berries   5 pears

Color the graph to show what Farmer Fred sold.

| | 1 | 2 | 3 | 4 | 5 | 6 | 7 | 8 | 9 | 10 |

1. How many more watermelons sold than pears? __5__
2. Which fruit sold the smallest amount? __pears__
3. How many bags of cherries and
   baskets of berries? __15__

©2005 by Evan-Moor Corp. • EMC 4545 • Skill Sharpeners—Math   UNIT 7   85

Page 230

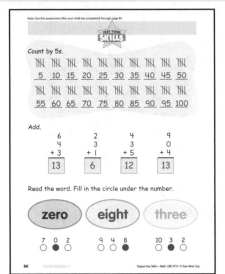

Note: Use this assessment after your child has completed through page 85.

TEST YOUR SKILLS

Count by 5s.

卌 卌 卌 卌 卌 卌 卌 卌 卌 卌
5 10 15 20 25 30 35 40 45 50

卌 卌 卌 卌 卌 卌 卌 卌 卌 卌
55 60 65 70 75 80 85 90 95 100

Add.

```
   6        2        4        9
   4        3        3        0
 + 3      + 1      + 5      + 4
 ────     ────     ────     ────
  13        6       12       13
```

Read the word. Fill in the circle under the number.

(zero)   (eight)   (three)

7 0 2   9 4 8   10 3 2
○ ● ○   ○ ○ ●   ○ ● ○

86   ASSESSMENT 7   Sharpen Your Skills—Math • EMC 9719 • © Evan-Moor Corp.

Contents

At the Circus

May 31, 2005

Dear Grandpa,

    Thank you for taking me to the circus. It was fun. I liked when the man and the big cat sat on a chair. I wish I could ride a horse like the lady in pink. I would stand up and ride.

I like the circus.

Let's go again!

    Love,

    Madison

 **Find It!** Read the spelling words.
Check off the words you can find in the story.

✓ can	✓ pan	✓ man	✓ cat
✓ sat	✓ wish	✓ like	✓ lady

How many spelling words did you find? _____

Skills:

Spelling Words
with **an** and **at**

Spelling
Theme
Vocabulary

Visual Memory

Spelling Practice

Read and Spell	Copy and Spell	Spell It Again!
1. can		
2. pan		
3. man		
4. cat		
5. sat		
6. wish		
7. like		
8. lady		

What's Missing?

Skills:

Spelling Words with **an** and **at**

Spelling Theme Vocabulary

Writing Spelling Words

Using Picture Clues and Sentence Context to Identify Missing Words

Fill in the blanks to write the spelling word that names each picture.

| man | lady | cat | pan | sat | can |

c __ __

__ __ n

__ a __

p __ __

__ __ t

__ __ d __

Finish the spelling word in each sentence.

1. I w_____ I could ride.

2. We l_____ the circus.

Skills:

Spelling Words with **an** and **at**

Spelling Theme Vocabulary

Identifying Rhyming Words

Circus Rhymes

Draw a line to match the words that rhyme.

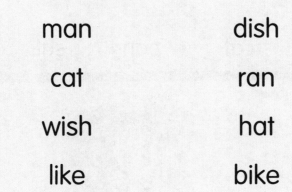

man	dish
cat	ran
wish	hat
like	bike

Write a spelling word to finish each rhyme.

Mrs. Brady
is a _____.

We had Dan
open the _____.

What does Ann
fry in the _____?

That clown _____
on his hat.

can   lady   sat   pan

Sharpen Your Skills—Spell & Write • EMC 9719 • © Evan-Moor Corp.

A Good Start

Skills:

Capitalizing
the First Word
in a Sentence

> **A sentence begins with a capital letter.**
>
> **We went to the circus.**

Circle the sentences that begin with a capital letter.
Fix the letters that should be capitals.

1. Did you like the circus?

2. i wish we could ride the elephant.

3. the clown had a pan on his head.

4. a man rode a bike with one wheel.

5. Can they pack up the big tent?

6. The big cat was in a cage.

7. I saw a lady on a swing.

8. we sat with our friends.

Tell Me Something

A sentence needs ending punctuation.
A sentence that tells something ends with a period. (.)

We see the circus tent.

Unscramble the words to make a sentence.
End each sentence with a period.

1. We circus like the

_____

2. The clown funny is

_____

3. flower He has a

_____

4. It water sprays

_____

5. wet We get

_____

Ask Me Something

▶ **A sentence needs ending punctuation.**
A sentence that asks something ends with
a question mark. (?)

What did you wish for?

Fill in each blank with a word from the box. End each sentence
with a question mark.

| like | chair | cat | circus | ride |

1. What is that big _____

2. Did the big cat sit on a _____

3. How many big cats are in the _____

4. Did you see the lady _____

5. Which circus act do you _____

Skills:

Using a
Question Mark
at the End of a
Question

Using Content
to Complete
Sentences

Fun at the Circus

Ann and Ben went to the circus. Write a sentence telling what each child saw. Use a capital letter and a period.

Ann

_____

_____

_____

Ben

_____

_____

_____

Write a question to ask Ann or Ben about the circus.
Use a capital letter and a question mark.

_____

_____

The Big Show

Skills:

Writing a Creative Story

Using Spelling Words in a Composition

Using Correct Capitalization and Ending Punctuation

Finish the story. Use as many spelling words as you can.

can	pan	man	cat
sat	wish	like	lady

Ann and Ben played circus. They made a tent

in the yard. _____

_____

_____

_____

_____

_____

_____

✔ **Check Your Story**

○ I used a capital letter to begin each sentence.

○ I used a period or question mark at the end of each sentence.

TEST YOUR SKILLS At the Circus

My Spelling Test

Find the correct answer. Fill in the circle.

Ask someone to test you on the spelling words.

1. Which punctuation mark goes at the end of the sentence?

   We like the circus____
   - ○ period (.)
   - ○ question mark (?)

2. Which punctuation mark goes at the end of the sentence?

   Did you see the big cat____
   - ○ period (.)
   - ○ question mark (?)

3. Which sentence has the correct capital letter?
   - ○ here is the circus Tent.
   - ○ Where is your ticket?

1. _____

2. _____

3. _____

4. _____

5. _____

6. _____

7. _____

8. _____

4. Write the sentence correctly.

   did you wich for a kat

   _____

   _____

The Playground

Today is the first day of summer. We are going to the park. Jake's mom will take us. Jake and I are going to have fun. We like to play a ship game. We can get up onto the ship. We can jump off the ship. We can run after another ship. Will we sink it? Yes!

Find It!

Read the spelling words.
Check off the words you can find in the story.

✓ up	✓ us	✓ run	✓ fun
✓ to	✓ ship	✓ jump	✓ game

How many spelling words did you find? _____

Spelling Practice

Read and Spell	Copy and Spell	Spell It Again!
1. up	_____	_____
2. us	_____	_____
3. run	_____	_____
4. fun	_____	_____
5. jump	_____	_____
6. to	_____	_____
7. ship	_____	_____
8. game	_____	_____

Play with Puzzles

Fill in the boxes with the spelling words.

1.

2.

3.

4.

5.

6.

7.

8.

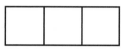

up	us	run	fun
to	ship	jump	game

Circle the spelling word in each bigger word.

funny   running   bus

cup   jumper   onto

Skills:

Spelling Words with Short **u**

Spelling Theme Vocabulary

Spelling Words in Context

Identifying Word Families

Can You Choose?

Choose the correct spelling. Write it on the line.

1. I like to gump/jump. _____

2. How fast can you run/rum? _____

3. We play a ship/shep game. _____

4. We had fen/fun. _____

5. Will you play with uss/us? _____

6. I want to/toe swing. _____

7. Will he play a gam/game? _____

8. She may climb up/op. _____

Make word families. Write the words below in the correct box.

sun	bump	pup
_____	_____	_____
_____	_____	_____

cup
bun
jump
up
run
lump

Find the Sentence

Skills:

Identifying and Writing Complete Sentences

Writing Spelling Words

▶ **A sentence has a whole thought.**

> Sentence: **The three girls jump rope.**
> Not a sentence: **The three girls**

Read the two groups of words. Write the group of words that makes a sentence.

1. Play ball with me   The ball

_____

2. Kim and I   Kim runs to the park

_____

3. Jump rope with us   With me

_____

4. Run fun sun   It is fun to run

_____

Skills:

Capitalizing the First Word in a Sentence

Use a Capital

A sentence begins with a capital letter.

Dogs play in the park.

Does the sentence begin with a capital letter? Circle **yes** or **no**.

1. We run in the park.   yes   no

2. go up the slide.   yes   no

3. we have fun in the jump house.   yes   no

4. Let's play a game.   yes   no

5. I have a ball.   yes   no

Write a sentence that goes with each picture. Use a capital letter to begin each sentence.

_____

_____

_____

_____

Capital I

▶ **The word I is always a capital letter.**

You and I can play a game.

Color the 🙂 if the sentence is correct. Fix the sentences that are <u>not</u> correct.

1. I like the park.

2. Ann and i can swing.

3. I like to go up.

4. Max and I ride bikes.

5. i have a blue bike.

6. May i ride your bike?

7. I can go fast.

8. You and I can race.

What Do You Do?

Write a sentence that begins with capital **I**.

Write a sentence that tells what you like to do at the park.
Use a capital **I**.

_____

Friends Have Fun

Skills:

Writing a
Creative Story

Completing
Sentences

Using Capital I

Finish the story.

My friend's name is _____ .

We like to play _____ .

_____ .

We also like to _____

_____

_____ .

My friend and _____ have fun.

Draw a picture of yourself and your friend playing. Write
a sentence that tells about your picture.

My friend and _____ are _____

_____ .

TEST YOUR SKILLS **The Playground**

My Spelling Test

Find the correct answer. Fill in the circle.

1. Which one is a sentence?
   - ○ A slide
   - ○ A slide is fun

2. Which sentence has the correct capital letter?
   - ○ my bike Is red.
   - ○ Your bike is blue.

3. Which sentence has the correct capital letter?
   - ○ Dad and I like to ride.
   - ○ Dad and i have fun.

Ask someone to test you on the spelling words.

1. _____

2. _____

3. _____

4. _____

5. _____

6. _____

7. _____

8. _____

4. Write the sentence correctly.

    sam and i runn and jum

_____

_____

Note: Help your child read the story.

Fourth of July

Zack and Mia found a note on the door. They read the note. Then they asked Mom for paper. Zack made a red and white hat. Mia made red and blue flowers for her bike. Can you guess why?

Here is what the note said:

Calling All Kids!
Come to Our March!
It is in the Park.
Bring your Bike.
Be there at Noon.
You will get a flag!
You will get drinks
and snacks!

Find It! Read the spelling words.
Check off the words you can find in the story and note.

✓ hat   ✓ hot   ✓ sand   ✓ hand

✓ red   ✓ white   ✓ blue   ✓ flag

How many spelling words did you find? _____

Spelling Practice

Read and Spell	Copy and Spell	Spell It Again!
1. hat	_____	_____
2. hot	_____	_____
3. hand	_____	_____
4. sand	_____	_____
5. red	_____	_____
6. blue	_____	_____
7. white	_____	_____
8. flag	_____	_____

Sharpen Your Skills—Spell & Write • EMC 9719 • © Evan-Moor Corp.

Spell It

Skills:

Spelling Words with Short **a**

Spelling Theme Vocabulary

Visual Discrimination

Writing Spelling Words

Mark an **X** on the misspelled words. Spell them correctly on the lines.

1. What color is the flage?   _____

2. This box is red, whit, and blue. _____

3. The sun is hout.   _____

4. Put on your blue het.   _____

5. Play in the sad with me.   _____

Circle each correct spelling.

1. hamd	hand	hand	hande
2. white	wite	wite	white
3. bue	bloo	blue	blue
4. hawt	haht	hot	howt

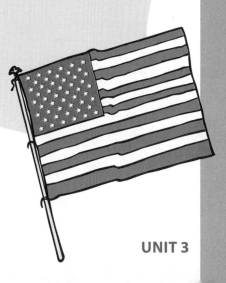

Read and Spell

Skills:

Spelling Words with Short **a**

Spelling Theme Vocabulary

Visual Memory

Using Sentence Context to Identify Missing Words

Write the spelling word that belongs in each sentence.

| hand | sand | hot | flag | white |

It is _____ tonight. We will see colors

in the sky. Put your chair on the _____.

Hold a flag in your _____. Did you hear

a big boom? There is a red and _____ star!

Wave your _____. Happy Fourth of July!

Write the last letter of each spelling word.

re___	whit__	ha___	san___
han___	blu___	ho___	fla___

Is It a Sentence?

▶ **A sentence has a whole thought.**

> Sentence: **Where is my red hat?**
>
> Not a sentence: **My red hat**

If the words make a sentence, color the **YES** star. If the words do <u>not</u> make a sentence, color the **NO** star.

1. Your hat is nice

2. Blue hat

3. The flag is blue and white

4. Dad put the chair on the sand

5. Red, white, and blue

6. The sand is hot

7. Hand sand band land

8. Please hand me a hot dog

Capital Letters

Skills:

Capitalizing
the First Word
of a Sentence

A sentence begins with a capital letter.

We saw the band march.

Circle the sentences that begin with a capital letter.
Fix the letters that should be capitals.

1. do you know what today is?

2. today is a holiday.

3. Our country has a birthday.

4. fly your flag.

5. wear red, white, and blue.

6. wear a hat in the hot sun.

7. We can hear the band play.

8. my brother plays a big drum.

Asking or Telling?

A sentence needs ending punctuation.
A sentence that tells something ends with
a period. (.)

The band plays music.

A sentence that asks something ends with
a question mark. (?)

What songs do they play?

Read each sentence. Draw a line to show if it is an asking
sentence or a telling sentence. The first one has been done
for you.

Do you play in a band?

I like to march.

We all have red hats.

**Asking
Sentence**

Where is your hat?

Can you carry the flag?

**Telling
Sentence**

Here is the flag.

Can you wave your flag?

Fun on the Fourth

Sam and Lisa had fun on the Fourth of July. Write a sentence telling what each child did. Use a capital letter and a period.

Sam

_____

_____

_____

Lisa

_____

_____

_____

Write a question asking each child about his or her day. Use a capital letter and a question mark.

Sam _____

_____

Lisa _____

_____

Holiday Fun

Skills:

Writing a Creative Story

Using Spelling Words in a Composition

Using Correct Capitalization and Ending Punctuation

What do you like to do on the Fourth of July? Write about it. Use as many spelling words as you can.

hat	hot	hand	sand
red	blue	white	flag

_____

_____

_____

_____

_____

_____

_____

_____

✔ Check Your Story

○ I used a capital letter to begin each sentence.

○ I used a period or question mark at the end of each sentence.

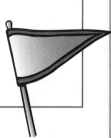

TEST YOUR SKILLS — Fourth of July

My Spelling Test

Find the correct answer. Fill in the circle.

1. Which punctuation mark goes at the end of the sentence?

   Did you march with the band____

   ○ period (.)
   ○ question mark (?)

2. Which one is a sentence?

   ○ The white sand
   ○ The sand is hot

3. Which sentence has the correct capital letter?

   ○ This hat is too big for me.
   ○ my Red hat is just right.

Ask someone to test you on the spelling words.

1. _____

2. _____

3. _____

4. _____

5. _____

6. _____

7. _____

8. _____

4. Write the sentence correctly.

   my flag is rad, white, and blu

   _____

   _____

Note: Help your child read the story.

Story of the Year

The story of the year goes like this:

In the **spring**, baby birds and lambs are born. The days get warmer. Little plants begin to grow.

Summer brings long days of hot sun. The garden is full of flowers and bees. We go to the beach.

In the **fall**, leaves turn yellow, red, and brown. They fall from the trees. We rake them up.

Winter comes and brings the cold. A bear sleeps. The lake has a cover of ice. We have fun in the snow. We make tracks.

Year after year, the story goes on. First spring comes, then summer, fall, and winter.

Find It! Read the spelling words.
Check off the words you can find in the story.

✓ make	✓ shake	✓ lake	✓ rake
✓ sun	✓ snow	✓ grow	✓ after

How many spelling words did you find? _____

Spelling Practice

Read and Spell	Copy and Spell	Spell It Again!
1. make	_____	_____
2. shake	_____	_____
3. lake	_____	_____
4. rake	_____	_____
5. sun	_____	_____
6. snow	_____	_____
7. grow	_____	_____
8. after	_____	_____

Sharpen Your Skills—Spell & Write • EMC 9719 • © Evan-Moor Corp.

Write Your Words

Skills:

Spelling Words with **ake** and **ow**

Spelling Theme Vocabulary

Writing Spelling Words

Visual Memory and Discrimination

Spelling Words in Context

Fill in the boxes with the spelling words.

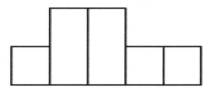

after   sun   snow   grow

1.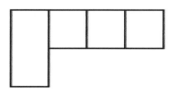

3.

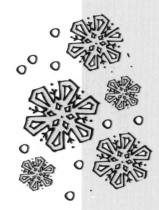

2.

4.

Finish the missing spelling words.

shake   rake   lake   make

1. Please hand me the r_____.

2. Let's m_____ a big pile of leaves.

3. I can sh_____ an apple off the tree.

4. It is too cold to swim in the l_____.

Skills:

Spelling Words with **ake** and **ow**

Spelling Theme Vocabulary

Spelling Words in Context

Identifying Word Families

Choose One

Choose the correct spelling. Write it on the line.

1. The sum/sun is hot. _____

2. Dad will take us to the lake/lak. _____

3. We can mack/make a sand pile. _____

4. See it groo/grow. _____

5. I will sake/shake off the sand. _____

6. Alan has a pail and a rake/roke. _____

7. The sand is as white as snow/snoe. _____

8. Let's play aftr/after we swim. _____

Make word families. Write the words below in the correct box.

| sun | grow | shake | snow | lake | run |

low	fun	make
_____	_____	_____
_____	_____	_____

Nouns Name Things

▶ **Some words name things. These words are called** nouns.

The lady **has a blue** hat.

Color each apple that names something.

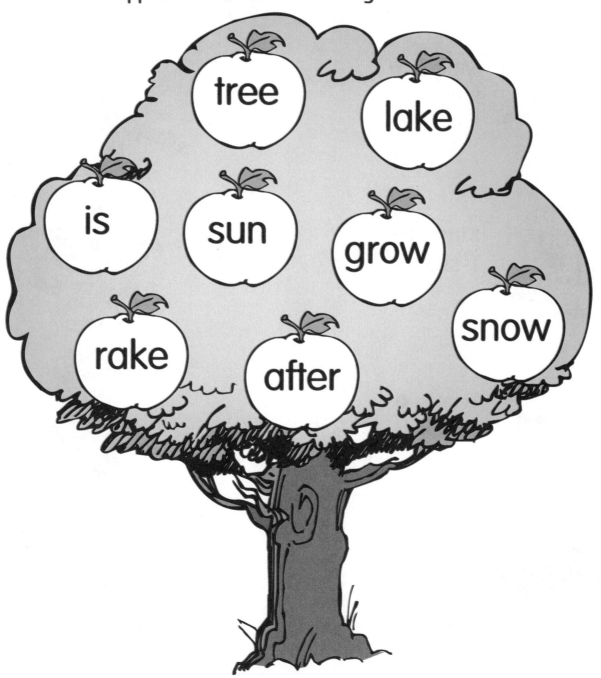

Skills:

Using **'s**
to Show
Possession

Summer Fun

When something belongs to one person,
add **'s** to the name of the person.

We swim in Amy's pool.

Draw a line to show to whom each thing belongs.

Meg's ●
kite

Tom

Kim's ●
T-shirt

Kim

Tom's ●
ball

Ben

Ben's ●
boat

Meg

Winter Fun

Write the name to show who owns each thing. Use 's.

1. Matt has skates.

_____ skates

2. Jan has boots.

_____ boots

3. Dan has a hat.

_____ hat

4. Maria has mittens.

_____ mittens

5. Ana has a sled.

_____ sled

6. Marco has a scarf.

_____ scarf

Skills:

Writing
Creative
Sentences

Identifying
Nouns

Around the Year

Finish each sentence to tell about the season. Circle the nouns in your sentences.

Winter

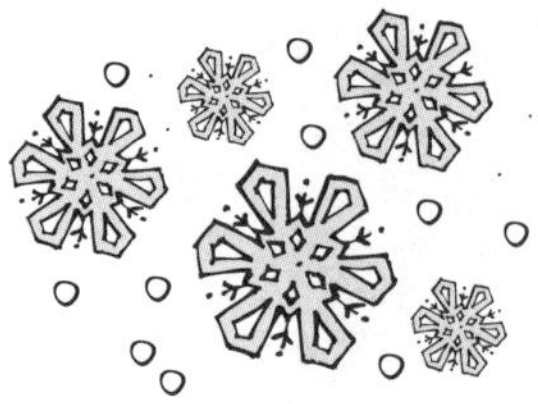

In the winter, I

_____

_____ .

Spring

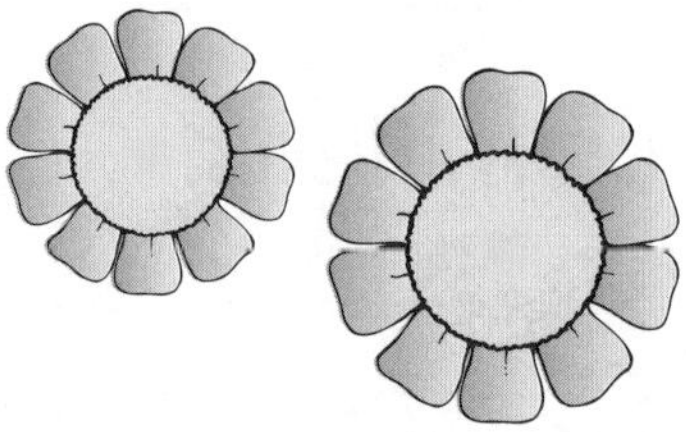

In the spring, I

_____

_____ .

Summer

In the summer, I

_____

_____ .

Fall

In the fall, I

_____

_____ .

Time of Year

Skills:

Writing a
Poem

Using **'s**
to Show
Possession

Finish the poem. Fill in the name of the season.

winter   spring   fall   summer

I like spring.

I like _____'s rain.

I like _____'s soft, quiet rain.

I like summer.

I like _____'s sun.

I like _____'s hot, hot sun.

I like fall.

I like _____'s colors.

I like _____'s red and yellow leaves.

I like winter.

I like _____'s snow.

I like _____'s white, white snow.

Story of the Year

My Spelling Test

Find the correct answer. Fill in the circle.

1. Which one is a naming word? (noun)
   - ○ swim
   - ○ lake

2. Which sentence shows that Ana owns something?
   - ○ These are Anas mittens.
   - ○ These are Ana's boots.

3. Which one tells to whom something belongs?
   - ○ Lee's bike
   - ○ red bike

Ask someone to test you on the spelling words.

1. _____

2. _____

3. _____

4. _____

5. _____

6. _____

7. _____

8. _____

4. Write the sentence correctly.

   the sum will mak Dans tree gro

   _____

   _____

Good Morning!

Wake up! It's morning. What do you **see**?
> The sun in the sky
> And birds in a tree.

Wake up! It's morning. What do you **hear**?
> Someone is singing
> A song soft and clear.

Wake up! It's morning. What do you **hold**?
> The covers around me
> To keep out the cold.

Wake up! It's morning. What do you smell?
> Someone is frying
> An egg, I can tell.

Wake up! It's morning. What do you eat?
> Warm oats and cold milk,
> And berries so sweet.

Find It!

Read the spelling words.
Check off the words you can find in the story.

✓ we	✓ me	✓ tree	✓ see
✓ hear	✓ hold	✓ smell	✓ eat

How many spelling words did you find? _____

Skills:

Spelling Words with Long **e**

Spelling Theme Vocabulary

Visual Memory

Spelling Practice

Read and Spell	Copy and Spell	Spell It Again!
1. we		
2. me		
3. tree		
4. see		
5. hear		
6. hold		
7. smell		
8. eat		

See and Write

Practice your spelling words. Write the missing letters.

we	me	tree
__ e	__ e	__ __ ee
w __	m __	tr __ __
__ __	__ __	__ __ __ __

see		eat
__ ee		__ __ t
s __ __		ea __
__ __ __		__ __ __

hear	hold	smell
__ ear	__ old	__ __ ell
h __ __ __	h __ __ __	sm __ __ __
__ __ __ __	__ __ __ __	__ __ __ __ __

Note: Read the directions to your child.

Can You See It?

Skills:

Spelling Words with Long **e**

Spelling Theme Vocabulary

Spelling Words in Context

Visual Discrimination

Choose the correct spelling. Write it on the line.

1. My new glasses help me/mi read. _____

2. Can you sey/see the pictures? _____

3. I will hould/hold the book for you. _____

4. Now wee/we can read together. _____

we	me	tree	see
hear	hold	smell	eat

Circle the spelling word in each bigger word.

meet   treetop   behold   seeds

hearing   smelly   beater   sweet

286   UNIT 5

Find the Verbs

Some words tell what is happening. These words are called verbs.

We smell the popcorn.
(What is happening)

Color the verbs.

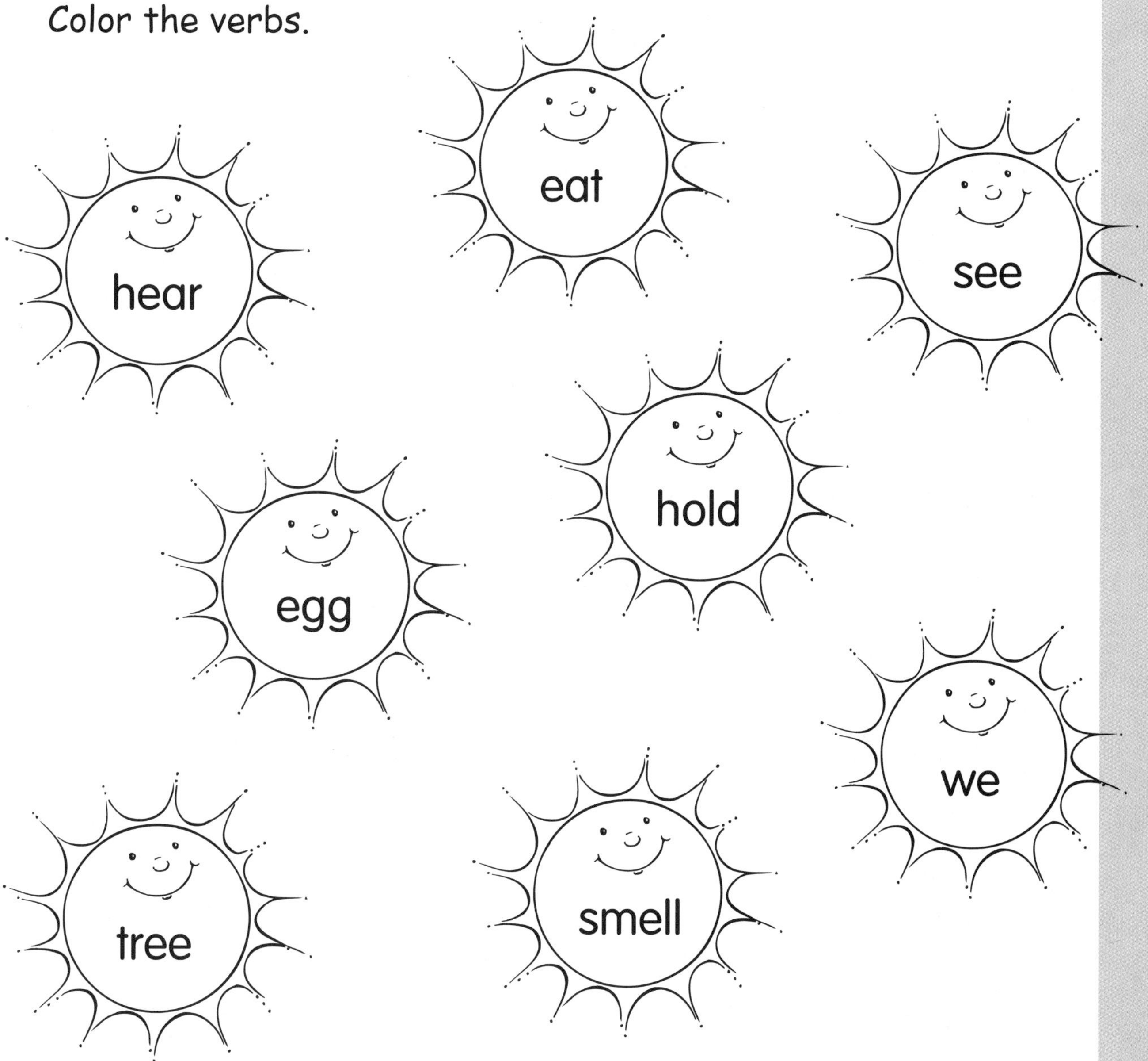

hear

eat

see

egg

hold

tree

smell

we

Using Pronouns

Some words take the place of names. These words
are called pronouns.

Rose likes ice cream.
She could eat it every day.

Dan and I like to dance.
We hear the music.

Use a word from the box to complete each sentence.

he	she	we	me

1. _____ are glad the sun is shining.

2. The birds seem to sing to _____.

3. My teddy bear looks like _____ is
   happy, too.

4. I can hear Dad. _____ is calling to
   _____.

5. What will _____ eat for breakfast?

6. Mom is cooking. _____ is making eggs.

I or Me?

▶ Use **I** when you are the person doing something.

I bake cookies with Mother.

Use **me** when something happens to you.

Mother gave me a cookie.

Fill in the blanks with **I** or **me**.

1. _____ have fun cooking.

2. Father and _____ make cookies.

3. He lets _____ help.

4. _____ put in flour and sugar.

5. Father helps _____ mix the batter.

6. _____ put the cookies on a plate.

7. Father gives _____ a taste.

8. _____ think they are good.

Skills:

Writing
Complete
Sentences

Using the
Pronoun I

Using My Senses

Write a sentence about **something you like to see, hear, touch, smell, and taste. Use I** in your sentences.

see

_____

_____

hear

_____

_____

touch

_____

_____

smell

_____

_____

taste

_____

_____

A Funny Noise

Skills:

Writing a
Creative Story

Using Spelling
Words in a
Composition

Finish the story. Use as many spelling words as you can.

we	me	tree	see
hear	hold	smell	eat

One day, I heard a funny noise. It was outside.

I went to look. I saw _____

_____

_____

_____

_____

_____

_____

✔ **Check Your Story**

◯ I used complete sentences.

◯ I used the words **I** and **me** correctly.

Good Morning! | My Spelling Test

Find the correct answer. Fill in the circle.

1. Which word tells what is happening?
   - ○ eat
   - ○ tree

2. Which pronoun goes in the blank?

   Sam gave _____ his book.
   - ○ I
   - ○ me

3. Which pronoun goes in the blank?

   Jenny can smell the flower.

   _____ likes flowers.
   - ○ We
   - ○ She

Ask someone to test you on the spelling words.

1. _____

2. _____

3. _____

4. _____

5. _____

6. _____

7. _____

8. _____

4. Write the sentence correctly.

   wee sea an apple on the tre

   _____

   _____

Sing a Song

A song needs notes. Hum a song you know. Can you hear the notes go up and down?

A song needs a beat. You can clap the beat of a song. Clap one–two–three–four!

Some songs have words. The words may be **happy**, **silly**, **sad**, or **nice**. Words help you feel the song.

So sing your song the way you feel it!

Find It! Read the spelling words.
Check off the words you can find in the story.

✓ so	✓ no	✓ note	✓ home
✓ do	✓ you	✓ nice	✓ sing

How many spelling words did you find? _____

Spelling Practice

Read and Spell	Copy and Spell	Spell It Again!
1. so	_____	_____
2. no	_____	_____
3. note	_____	_____
4. home	_____	_____
5. do	_____	_____
6. you	_____	_____
7. nice	_____	_____
8. sing	_____	_____

Can You Spell It?

Skills:

Spelling Words with Long **o**

Spelling Theme Vocabulary

Visual Discrimination

Writing Spelling Words

Mark an **X** on the misspelled words. Spell them correctly on the lines.

1. How doo we sound? _____

2. Will Troy singe with us? _____

3. He has a nise voice. _____

4. Play this not. _____

5. Can yu play a tune? _____

Fill in the boxes with the spelling words.

| home | nice | sing | you |

1.

3.

2.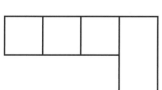

4.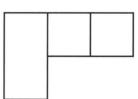

Rhyme Time

Skills:

Identifying
Rhyming
Words

Auditory
Discrimination

Circle two words in each row that rhyme with the first word.

1.	**sing**	bring	song	ring
2.	**note**	not	vote	boat
3.	**nice**	mice	twice	size
4.	**so**	no	to	go
5.	**you**	do	blue	snow
6.	**no**	too	show	so
7.	**home**	foam	Rome	come
8.	**do**	moo	no	you

Write a spelling word to finish each rhyme.

Does the king

Like to _____?

He sang it twice,

It was _____.

Is It a Sentence?

A sentence has a whole thought.

Sentence: **It is fun to play music.**

Not a sentence: **To play music**

If the words make a sentence, color the happy face.
If the words do <u>not</u> make a sentence, color the sad face.

1. The band

2. We play in a band

3. We keep the beat

4. With two sticks

5. I tap with the sticks

6. So no so no so

7. Ring the bell

8. Tap the triangle

Skills:

Using
Capital I

Looking for I

Circle the sentences that have a capital **I**.
Fix the sentences that do <u>not</u> have a capital **I**.

1. Rita and I have fun.

2. i turn on the radio.

3. I like to sing and dance.

4. When the music plays, i listen.

5. I show Rita the steps.

6. She and i practice at home.

7. i can snap my fingers.

8. Rita and I can teach you, too.

Sharpen Your Skills—Spell & Write • EMC 9719 • © Evan-Moor Corp.

We or Us?

Use **we** when you and other people do something.

> **We** learn the tune.

Use **us** when something happens to you and other people.

> Mr. Bell will teach **us** a song.

Fill in the each blank with **we** or **us**.

1. _____ go to music class.

2. _____ learn about notes.

3. Some of _____ sing high notes.

4. Two of _____ play the bells.

5. _____ learn to sing together.

6. Next week, _____ are in a show.

7. In the show _____ will sing and dance.

8. Will you sing with _____?

My Music

Do you play or sing music? What would you like to play? What would you like to sing? Write about it. Use some of your spelling words.

_____

_____

_____

_____

_____

Draw a picture of yourself making music.

✓ **Check Your Story**

○ I used complete sentences.

○ I used capital **I** correctly.

My Top Ten

Skills:

Writing a List

Make a list of songs you know. Draw a star by the song you like best.

1. _____

2. _____

3. _____

4. _____

5. _____

6. _____

7. _____

8. _____

9. _____

10. _____

Sing your song for someone.

Sing a Song

My Spelling Test

Find the correct answer. Fill in the circle.

Ask someone to test you on the spelling words.

1. Which one is a sentence?
   - ○ He plays a nice tune
   - ○ A note

2. Which word goes in the blank?

   _____ shake the bells.
   - ○ Us
   - ○ We

3. Which sentence has the correct capital letter?
   - ○ Travis and i like to sing.
   - ○ You and I like to dance.

1. _____

2. _____

3. _____

4. _____

5. _____

6. _____

7. _____

8. _____

4. Write the sentence correctly.

   doo us hum or sinng the nots

   _____

   _____

Be Safe

At school, Min and Adam learned how to be safe. A firefighter came to visit. He showed the children his gear and his truck. He told them how to stay safe. He gave them a list. It has a good rule to remember. If you see a fire, dial 9-1-1. Min and Adam like to play with toy fire trucks. They may want to fight fires one day.

Find It!

Read the spelling words.
Check off the words you can find in the story.

✓ day	✓ may	✓ stay	✓ play
✓ stop	✓ look	✓ rule	✓ safe

How many spelling words did you find? _____

Skills:

Spelling Words with **ay**

Spelling Theme Vocabulary

Visual Memory

Spelling Practice

Read and Spell	Copy and Spell	Spell It Again!
1. day	________	________
2. may	________	________
3. stay	________	________
4. play	________	________
5. stop	________	________
6. look	________	________
7. rule	________	________
8. safe	________	________

Write Your Words

Skills:

Spelling Words with **ay**

Writing Spelling Words

Visual Memory and Discrimination

Fill in the boxes with the spelling words.

day   may   stay   play

1.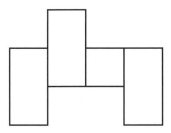

3.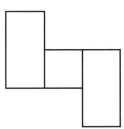

2.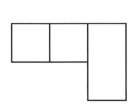

4.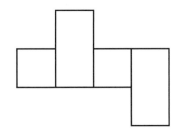

Finish the missing spelling words.

1. St_____ before you cross the street.

2. Be sure to l_____ both ways.

3. That is a good r_____ to follow.

4. It's up to you to be sa_____.

Skills:

Using
Sentence
Context
to Identify
Missing Words

Writing
Spelling Words

Using Vowel
Sounds

Play It Safe

Fill in the missing words.

may	stay	day	play

1. Will you _____ and play?

2. Do not _____ in the street.

3. You _____ get hurt.

4. Have a safe _____.

Write letters in the blanks to make spelling words.

oo	u	o	ay	a

d_____	m_____
st____p	r____le
s____fe	st_____
l___k	pl_____

Sharpen Your Skills—Spell & Write • EMC 9719 • © Evan-Moor Corp.

What Happened?

Skills:

Identifying and Writing Verbs

Using Sentence Context to Identify Missing Words

▶ Some words tell what is happening or what already happened. These words are called verbs.

> We **see** the red light.
> (What is happening)
>
> We **waited** to cross the street.
> (What already happened)

Fill in the blanks with words from the box. Circle the words that tell what happened.

do	stay	look	stop
play	fell	called	came

1. We try to _____ safe.

2. We know what to _____.

3. We do not _____ in the street.

4. We _____ at every corner.

5. We always _____ both ways.

6. One time, I _____ down in the street.

7. I _____ to my friend for help.

8. She _____ right away.

Skills:

Using Verbs **is** and **are**

Bike Safety

> Use **is** with one and **are** with more than one.
>
> That **is** a nice bike.
>
> Our bikes **are** the same color.

Fill in each blank with **is** or **are**.

1. Here _____ my new bike.

2. There _____ three bikes in our family.

3. What _____ the bike rule?

4. It _____ good to look for cars.

5. Two kids _____ at the stop sign.

6. This _____ a helmet.

7. It _____ safe to wear a helmet when you ride.

8. Our helmets _____ purple.

Important to Know

▶ Use **they** when several people do something.
Use **them** when something happens to several people.

> **They** got lost in the store.
>
> Mother couldn't find **them**.

Fill in each blank with **they** or **them**.

1. _____ asked the guard for help.

2. The guard helped _____.

3. What did _____ tell the guard?

4. _____ knew their mother's name.

5. Mother was so happy to see _____.

6. Do _____ know their phone number?

7. Tell _____ to learn their address.

Skills:

Writing
Complete
Sentences

Using
Picture Clues

Identifying
Verbs

Keep Safe

Tell how each child is being safe.

Circle a verb in each of the sentences you wrote.

School Rules

Skills:

Writing a
Creative Story

Using Spelling
Words in a
Composition

Read the safety rule. Write a story about a boy who didn't follow the rule. How many spelling words can you use in your story?

Rule: Walk, don't run in school.

day	stop	may	look
stay	rule	play	safe

_____

_____

_____

_____

_____

_____

_____

✔ **Check Your Story**

◯ I used complete sentences.

◯ I used capital letters correctly.

◯ I used punctuation marks.

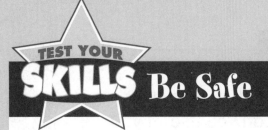

Be Safe

My Spelling Test

Find the correct answer. Fill in the circle.

Ask someone to test you on the spelling words.

1. Which word tells what is happening? (verb)
   - ○ look
   - ○ them

2. Which word goes in the blank?

   The fire _____ out.
   - ○ is
   - ○ are

3. Which word goes in the blank?

   Did _____ stop at the stop sign?
   - ○ them
   - ○ they

1. _____

2. _____

3. _____

4. _____

5. _____

6. _____

7. _____

8. _____

4. Write the sentence correctly.

   ### the rool says to stopp and looke

   _____

   _____

Note: Help your child read the story.

Away We Go!

How do you get from place to place?

Do you live in the city?
In the city, you might go by bus,
by train, or by car. You might
walk or ride a bike.

Do you live in the country?
In the country, you might
go by truck, by jeep, or
by tractor.

Do you want to go far, far away?
Do you want to float on the wind?
Take a hot-air balloon ride!

There are many ways to get from place to place.

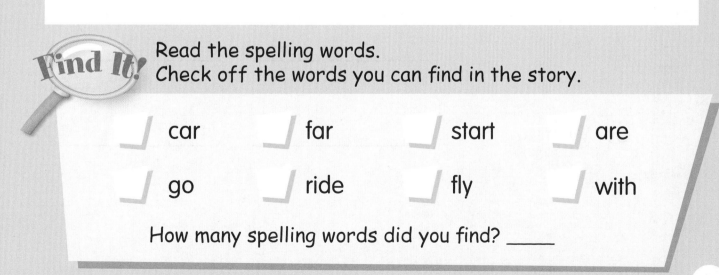

Find It! Read the spelling words.
Check off the words you can find in the story.

✓ car	✓ far	✓ start	✓ are
✓ go	✓ ride	✓ fly	✓ with

How many spelling words did you find? _____

Skills:

Spelling
Words with
R-Controlled
Vowel **ar**

Spelling
Theme
Vocabulary

Visual Memory

Spelling Practice

Read and Spell	Copy and Spell	Spell It Again!
1. car	_____	_____
2. far	_____	_____
3. start	_____	_____
4. are	_____	_____
5. go	_____	_____
6. ride	_____	_____
7. fly	_____	_____
8. with	_____	_____

Sharpen Your Skills—Spell & Write • EMC 9719 • © Evan-Moor Corp.

A Car Trip

Skills:

Using Sentence Context to Identify Missing Words

Writing Spelling Words

Visual Memory

Fill in the missing spelling words.

far	ride	go	start	are	car

1. We _____ going on a trip.

2. Dad will pack the_____.

3. We are ready to _____!

4. Carly and I can _____ in the back.

5. Mom will _____ the car.

6. How _____ is it to the ocean?

Circle the words that are spelled correctly.

1. with   witt

2. stort   start

3. fly   fliy

4. ryde   ride

Ride with Me

Skills:

Spelling Words with R-Controlled Vowel **ar**

Spelling Theme Vocabulary

Visual Memory

Practice your spelling words. Write the missing letters.

car	are	ride
___ ar	___ ___ e	___ ide
c ___ ___	ar ___	r ___ ___ e
___ ___ ___	___ ___ ___	___ ___ ___ ___

far		fly
___ ar		___ ___ y
f ___ ___		fl ___
___ ___ ___		___ ___ ___

start	go	with
___ ___ art	___ o	___ ith
st ___ ___ t	g ___	wi ___ ___
___ ___ ___ ___ ___	___ ___	___ ___ ___ ___

Sharpen Your Skills—Spell & Write • EMC 9719 • © Evan-Moor Corp.

Let's Lift Off!

Skills:

Identifying
and Writing
Verbs

▶ **Verbs** tell what is happening or what already happened.

> **We see the rocket.**
> **The rocket landed.**

Read each sentence. Write the word
that tells what is happening or what already happened. (verb)

1. We ride in a rocket. _____

2. See the rocket fly high. _____

3. It went to the moon. _____

4. Our rocket landed. _____

5. I walked on the moon. _____

6. Next, we go to Mars. _____

7. I start the rockets. _____

8. The ship goes home. _____

9. We see the Earth. _____

Skills:

Identifying
Contractions ·

Contraction Action

A contraction is a short way to write two words.

Do not go far.	It is a big ship.
Don't go far.	It's a big ship.

Draw a line to match each contraction with the two words
used to make it.

can't	they have
you'll	he is
they've	can not
she's	you will
he's	we are
I'm	let us
we're	I am
let's	she is

More Contractions

Skills:

Writing
Contractions
Using an
Apostrophe

The apostrophe takes the place of a letter or letters. A contraction uses an apostrophe. (')

does no̸t = doesn't

Rewrite each sentence using a contraction. Use an apostrophe.

We'll	Where's	it's	They're	don't

1. Where is that boat going?

   _____

2. I think it is a fishing boat.

   _____

3. We will sail this way.

   _____

4. I do not see land.

   _____

5. They are going fishing.

   _____

Skills:

Writing a
Creative Story

Up We Go!

Pretend you are taking a hot-air balloon ride. Look down. What do you see? Write about it. How many spelling words can you use?

car	far	start	are
go	ride	fly	with

✓ **Check Your Story**

◯ I used complete sentences.

◯ I checked my spelling words.

Train, Car, or Plane?

Think about a place you went. Answer the questions using complete sentences. Then draw a picture to show how you got there.

1. Where did you go?

_____

_____

2. Who went with you?

_____

_____

3. How did you get there?

_____

_____

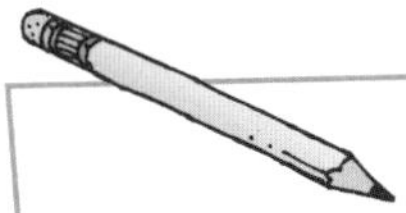

Draw a picture.

TEST YOUR SKILLS — Away We Go!

My Spelling Test

Find the correct answer. Fill in the circle.

1. Which word tells what is happening? (verb)
   - ○ ride
   - ○ car

2. Which word is the contraction for **have not**?
   - ○ have
   - ○ haven't

3. Which word is the contraction for **do not**?
   - ○ didn't
   - ○ don't

Ask someone to test you on the spelling words.

1. _____

2. _____

3. _____

4. _____

5. _____

6. _____

7. _____

8. _____

4. Write the sentence correctly.

   Lets goe for a rid in the care

_____

_____

On the Farm

The rooster crows, "Cock-a-doodle-do!" It's time for the farm animals to wake up. It's time for the farmer to wake up, too. The farmer eats fresh eggs for breakfast. Now it is time to walk down to the barn. Twinkle, the brown cow, waits for him. She knows it's milking time. The cats that live in the barn want to help. They want some of Twinkle's fresh milk, too!

Find It! Read the spelling words.
Check off the words you can find in the story.

| ☑ cow | ☑ now | ☑ down | ☑ town |
| ☑ brown | ☑ farm | ☑ barn | ☑ help |

How many spelling words did you find? _____

Spelling Practice

Read and Spell	Copy and Spell	Spell It Again!
1. cow	_____	_____
2. now	_____	_____
3. down	_____	_____
4. town	_____	_____
5. brown	_____	_____
6. farm	_____	_____
7. barn	_____	_____
8. help	_____	_____

See and Spell

Skills:

Spelling Words with **ow**

Spelling Theme Vocabulary

Visual Discrimination

Choose the correct spelling. Write it on the line.

1. Will you hepp/help us feed the chickens? _____

2. The feed is in the bern/barn. _____

3. Nowe/Now we get the eggs. _____

4. Then we can drive to town/tone. _____

Circle two words in each row that rhyme with the first word.

1. **down**	gown	town	done
2. **farm**	charm	ham	harm
3. **brown**	brow	clown	crown
4. **now**	low	cow	how

Skills:

Spelling Words with **ow**

Spelling Theme Vocabulary

Spelling Words in Context

Visual Discrimination

Our Farm

Mark an **X** on the misspelled words. Spell them correctly on the lines.

1. Sam lives on a fram. _____

2. Sam has a kow. _____

3. We will go done to see his cow. _____

4. She is broun with a white face. _____

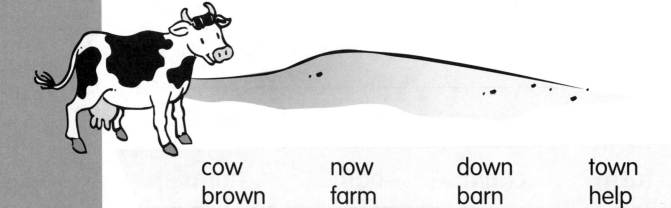

cow	now	down	town
brown	farm	barn	help

Circle the spelling word in each bigger word.

brownies   helper

farmhouse   barnyard

cowgirl   uptown

known   downstairs

Sharpen Your Skills—Spell & Write • EMC 9719 • © Evan-Moor Corp.

Finish the Sentences

Skills:

Using Sentence Context to Identify Missing Words

Using Ending Punctuation

A sentence that tells something ends with a period.(.)

We are going to the farm.

A sentence that asks something ends with a question mark. (?)

Would you like to visit a farm?

Fill in the blanks with words from the box below. End each sentence with a period or a question mark.

1. Our friends live on a _____

2. Have you ever been inside a red _____

3. They have horses, pigs, and a _____

4. Do you live on a farm or in _____

5. Is your horse black or _____

6. Let's go to town _____

| farm | now | barn | town | brown | cow |

Skills:

Writing
Contractions
Using an
Apostrophe

Contractions

A contraction is a short way to write two words.
A contraction uses an apostrophe. (')

We will plant the beans.
We'll plant corn, too.

Write the contraction for each pair of words. Use an apostrophe.

1. you will   _____

2. I am   _____

3. here is   _____

4. you are   _____

5. is not   _____

6. we have   _____

7. what is   _____

8. did not   _____

Is and Are

▶ Use **is** with one and **are** with more than one.

> The pear **is** in the basket.
>
> The apples **are** in the box.

Fill in each blank with **is** or **are**.

1. Our farm _____ a fruit farm.

2. That tree _____ a pear tree.

3. The pears _____ ready to pick.

4. There _____ boxes for the pears.

5. Here _____ the pear truck.

6. The apple trees _____ over there.

7. This _____ a sweet apple.

8. The apples _____ in a basket.

Skills:

Writing Asking
Sentences

Using
Question
Marks

Farm Questions

Think of three facts you know about farms. Write each fact as a question. End each question with a question mark.

1. _____

_____

2. _____

_____

3. _____

_____

Draw a picture of a farm.

On the Farm

Skills:

Writing a
Creative Story

Write a story about a class trip to a farm. Tell what the
children saw. Use as many spelling words as you can.

cow	now	down	town
brown	farm	barn	help

_____

_____

_____

_____

_____

_____

_____

_____

✔ Check Your Story

○ I used complete sentences.

○ I used a period or question mark at the end
of each sentence.

TEST YOUR SKILLS On the Farm

My Spelling Test

Find the correct answer. Fill in the circle.

Ask someone to test you on the spelling words.

1. Which punctuation mark goes at the end of the sentence?

   Do you live on a farm____

   ○ period (.)
   ○ question mark (?)

2. Which word is the contraction for **did not**?

   ○ don't
   ○ didn't

3. Which word goes in the sentence?

   These _____ the pears we picked.

   ○ is
   ○ are

1. _____

2. _____

3. _____

4. _____

5. _____

6. _____

7. _____

8. _____

4. Write the sentence correctly.

   does the brawn kow stay in the bran

   _____

   _____

Note: Help your child read the story.

Pet Show

We are having a pet show today.
Nick will bring a little bunny.
It is black and white.

Sierra will bring her kitten.
The kitten has a bell that
always tells where she is.

I will bring my funny puppy
to the pet show. His name
is Tucker. I am teaching
Tucker to sit. He is happy
when he gets a treat. He
wags his tail and licks
my face.

Can you come to our pet show?

Find It! Read the spelling words.
Check off the words you can find in the story.

☐ funny ☐ bunny ☐ puppy ☐ happy

☐ little ☐ kitten ☐ pet ☐ my

How many spelling words did you find? _____

Skills:

Spelling Theme Vocabulary

Visual Memory

Spelling Words with Double Consonants

Spelling Words That End with **y**

Read and Spell	Copy and Spell	Spell It Again!
1. funny	_____	_____
2. bunny	_____	_____
3. puppy	_____	_____
4. happy	_____	_____
5. little	_____	_____
6. kitten	_____	_____
7. pet	_____	_____
8. my	_____	_____

Pet Puzzles

Fill in the boxes with the spelling words.

funny	bunny	puppy	happy
little	kitten	pet	my

Skills:

Spelling Words with Double Consonants

Spelling Words That End with **y**

Visual Memory and Discrimination

1.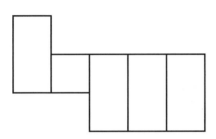

2.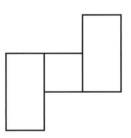

3.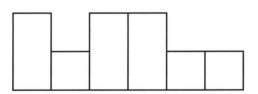

4.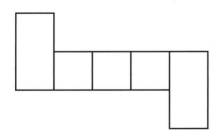

5.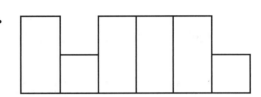

6.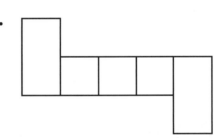

7.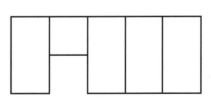

8.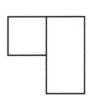

Skills:

Spelling Words
with Double
Consonants

Spelling Words
That End
with **y**

Spelling
Theme
Vocabulary

Visual Memory

Spelling Words
in Context

Choose a Word

Choose the correct spelling. Write it on the line.

1. My kittn/kitten likes to play. _____

2. It is a happy/happey cat. _____

3. Does your bunne/bunny eat carrots? _____

4. What kind of pat/pet would you like? _____

5. This is my/mi frog. _____

6. Your puppy/pupy is smart. _____

7. I have five litel/little fish. _____

8. A dog with a hat is funny/funey. _____

Fill in the missing letters to make spelling words.

n	p	t

ha __ __ y	li __ __ le	pu __ __ y
fu __ __ y	ki __ __ en	bu __ __ y

Correct Capitals

▶ **A sentence begins with a capital letter.**

My dog takes me for a walk.

Circle the sentences that begin with a capital letter.
Fix the letters that should be capitals.

1. My kitten is a good pet.

2. it likes to play with a ball of string.

3. the funny kitten got twisted up.

4. I had to help it.

5. now my kitten is happy.

6. what does your puppy play with?

7. Does the bunny like to play?

8. Every pet needs love.

Skills:

Capitalizing Names of People, Pets, and Specific Places and Things

Capitals for Names

The names of people, pets, and specific places and things begin with a capital letter.

April has two horses named Hanna and Harry.

She rides at Oak Tree Ranch.

Use red to circle the names of people and pets. Use blue to circle the names of special places and things.

1. Today the Texas State Fair begins.

2. April will take her horse.

3. She will brush Hanna's coat.

4. Carlos comes from Red River Ranch.

5. Carlos will ride in the ring.

6. He will ride a horse named Rex.

7. April and Carlos want a blue ribbon.

8. The blue ribbon says "First Place."

Pick Your Pronoun

▶ **Some words take the place of names. These words are called** pronouns.

Bunny Boo likes to hop around the yard.

She hops in the grass.

Fill in the blanks with words from the box below. Replace the underlined words.

1. My <u>dog</u> Trotter is a fast runner.

   _____ likes to play chase.

2. My <u>kittens</u> are Pepper and Spice.

   _____ look alike.

3. <u>Tina and I</u> have pet birds.

   The birds sing to _____.

4. <u>Mom and I</u> want a puppy.

   _____ want a little one.

we	he	us	they

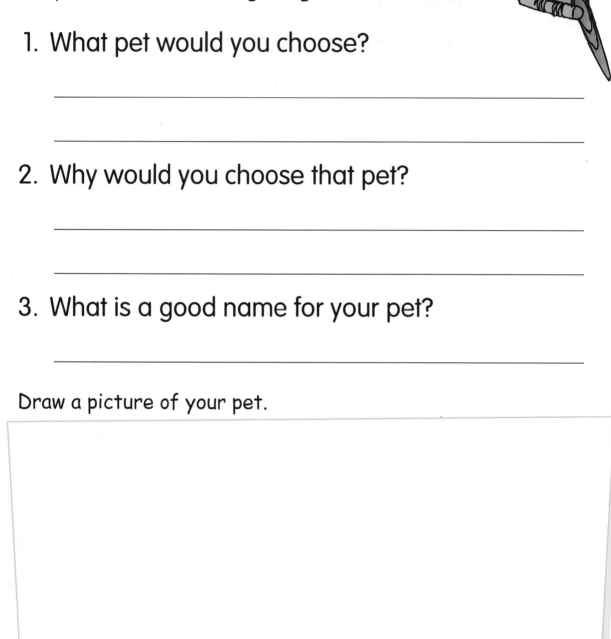

Skills:

Writing
Complete
Sentences

Capitalizing
the First Word
in a Sentence

Pet Report

Answer the questions using complete sentences. Use a capital letter at the beginning of each sentence.

1. What pet would you choose?

_____

_____

2. Why would you choose that pet?

_____

_____

3. What is a good name for your pet?

_____

Draw a picture of your pet.

Note: Read the directions to your child.

Make a Poster

The children are having a pet show. Make a sign for the show. Decorate your sign. How many spelling words can you use?

funny	bunny	puppy	happy
little	kitten	pet	my

Skills:

Creative Writing

Writing Information

Making a Poster

Pet Show

My Spelling Test

Find the correct answer. Fill in the circle.

1. Which sentence has the correct capital letter?
   - ○ the pet show is today.
   - ○ I like the kittens.

2. Which sentence has the correct capital letters?
   - ○ My dog went to Red's Puppy School.
   - ○ now clifford knows how to sit.

3. Which pronoun goes in the blank?

   Luke has a new kitten.
   _____ calls it Penny.
   - ○ He
   - ○ They

Ask someone to test you on the spelling words.

1. _____

2. _____

3. _____

4. _____

5. _____

6. _____

7. _____

8. _____

4. Write the sentence correctly.

   mi littel bunney is named sunny

   _____

   _____

Note: Help your child read the story.

Family Night

I love family night at my house. It is the same every week. We all help with dinner. Our dog Sam knows something is up. After dinner, we all wash the dishes. Then we choose a board game. My brother and I choose a game. We have fun playing games together. My mother and father play, too. We all have fun on family night.

Find It! Read the spelling words.
Check off the words you can find in the story.

| ☑ game | ☑ name | ☑ bake | ☑ family |
| ☑ mother | ☑ father | ☑ brother | ☑ sister |

How many spelling words did you find? _____

Skills:

Spelling Words with Long **a**

Spelling Theme Vocabulary

Visual Memory

Spelling Practice

Read and Spell	Copy and Spell	Spell It Again!
1. game	_____	_____
2. name	_____	_____
3. bake	_____	_____
4. family	_____	_____
5. mother	_____	_____
6. father	_____	_____
7. sister	_____	_____
8. brother	_____	_____

Word Search

Circle each spelling word.

game	name	bake	family
mother	father	sister	brother

sisternamebrothergamemotherfamilybakefather

gamenamemotherfatherbrotherfamilysisterbake

bakenamebrothergamefathersisterfamilymother

Circle the words that are spelled correctly.

1. muther   mother

2. name   nume

3. father   fathr

4. sistre   sister

5. gamm   game

6. family   famile

7. brother   bruther

8. backe   bake

Word Study

Fill in the spelling word for each sentence.

game   bake   mother   brother

1. Jim is my little _____.

2. My _____ asked me to watch him.

3. Let's play a _____.

4. Mother will _____ us some cookies.

Add the missing letters to make spelling words.

me   er   ke   ly

1. fath_____   5. moth_____

2. sist_____   6. broth_____

3. fami_____   7. ga_____

4. na_____   8. ba_____

Note: Read the directions to your child.

Names Have Capitals

Capitalizing Names of People, Pets, and Specific Places and Things

▶ **The names of people, pets, and specific places and things begin with a capital letter.**

> Emily is going to New York.
>
> She will take her dog Red.
>
> Her dad will drive the Ford truck.

Use red to circle the names of people and pets. Use blue to circle the names of special places and things.

1. Mike and Tony are brothers.

2. They live in Ohio.

3. Mike goes to Red Hill School.

4. Nemo is the name of Tony's fish.

5. He got the fish at Dave's Dive.

6. Their family is going to Mexico.

7. I will feed Nemo.

8. He likes Fine Fish Flakes.

Write the Nouns

Some words name things. These words are called nouns.

Harry read a story about a family.

Choose the noun. Write it in the sentence.

1. This is a good _____ to read.   **book**
                                              sing

2. My father reads it to us in _____.   **sleep**
                                              bed

3. I like the magic _____.   **look**
                                        skunk

4. The skunk's _____ is Miss Sweet.   **name**
                                             hear

5. The skunk takes a _____.   **hide**
                                         bath

6. That is a funny _____.   **story**
                                       think

Family Names

► **When something belongs to one person, add 's to the name of the person.**

Have you seen Uncle Ted's hat?

Who owns what? Write the name you choose in each blank. Use 's.

Aunt Beth	Mother	Grandpa	Ben	Leo
Mrs. Smart	Anna	Uncle Jay	Roy	

1. We are going to _____ farm.

2. I will ride _____ horse.

3. My brother can feed _____ goats.

4. We will eat _____ cake.

5. We can help pick _____ beans.

6. We will smell _____ flowers.

7. My sister can see _____ new kittens.

8. We can ride in _____ truck.

Skills:

Capitalizing the Names of People and Pets

Interviewing

Writing Complete Sentences

Pets Are Family, Too!

Ask two people to tell you the names of their pets. Draw a picture and write a sentence about each person and his or her pet. Use a capital letter to begin the names of people and pets.

Marta has a cat named Cookie.

All in the Family

Skills:

Writing a
Creative Story

Capitalizing
Names

What does your family like to do together? Write a story about something your family did. Use as many spelling words as you can.

game	name	bake	family
mother	father	brother	sister

_____

_____

_____

_____

_____

_____

_____

✔ Check Your Story

○ I used capital letters for names of people and pets.

○ I used capital letters for names of specific
places and things.

Family Night

My Spelling Test

Find the correct answer. Fill in the circle.

1. Which sentence has the correct capital letters?
   - ○ My sister and I go to Gus White School.
   - ○ My Brother's cat is named boots.

2. Which sentence uses **'s** correctly?
   - ○ I helped my brother find his books'.
   - ○ Where are Tim's books?

3. Which word is a noun?
   - ○ game
   - ○ funny

Ask someone to test you on the spelling words.

1. _____

2. _____

3. _____

4. _____

5. _____

6. _____

7. _____

8. _____

4. Write the sentence correctly.

   megs brothr and my sisster will play a gam

   _____

   _____

Note: Help your child read the story.

First-Grade Fun

First grade is lots of work! Mrs. Bell is a good teacher. She helps us learn to read, write, and spell. Now I can read a whole book on my own. I can read it to the class. I try to do my best in school. It's fun to spell and write. Mrs. Bell took a look at my work. Then she gave me a sticker. The sticker has a happy face. We work a lot in first grade. But I think first grade is fun!

Find It!

Read the spelling words.
Check off the words you can find in the story.

| ✓ book | ✓ good | ✓ look | ✓ took |
| ✓ take | ✓ read | ✓ think | ✓ work |

How many spelling words did you find? _____

Spelling Practice

Read and Spell	Copy and Spell	Spell It Again!
1. book	_____	_____
2. good	_____	_____
3. look	_____	_____
4. took	_____	_____
5. take	_____	_____
6. read	_____	_____
7. think	_____	_____
8. work	_____	_____

Spelling Time

Skills:

Spelling Words with **oo**

Spelling Theme Vocabulary

Auditory Discrimination

Fill in all the missing letters to make spelling words.

g __ __ d   b __ __ k

r __ __ d   l __ __ k

t __ k __   th __ nk

w __ __ k   t __ __ k

Circle two words in each row that rhyme with the first word.

1.	**book**	hook	lock	cook
2.	**take**	tock	rake	fake
3.	**work**	worm	jerk	perk
4.	**look**	lake	took	crook
5.	**read**	bead	seed	made
6.	**took**	look	make	book
7.	**good**	hood	stood	goat
8.	**think**	sing	sink	blink

Skills:

Spelling Words with **oo**

Spelling Theme Vocabulary

Visual Memory

Using Sentence Context to Identify Missing Words

Read and Spell

Choose the best word to finish each sentence. Write it on the line.

1. Will you _____ this to school?

    take   **think**   **took**

2. It was a _____ book.

    look   **book**   **good**

3. I think you can _____ well.

    read   **good**   **book**

4. _____ for another book to read.

    Took   **Look**   **Book**

5. Do you _____ there is a shark book?

    good   **work**   **think**

6. Find another good _____ to read.

    look   **took**   **book**

Circle the words that are spelled correctly.

1. wurk   work

2. tak   take

3. read   rede

4. theenk   think

A Whole Thought

▶ **A sentence has a whole thought.**

Sentence: **Math is what I like best.**

Not a sentence: **A math game**

If the words make a sentence, color the **YES** star. If the words do <u>not</u> make a sentence, color the **NO** star.

1. A math book

2. Here is my math book

3. I think math is fun

4. In a number

5. Six added to

6. You added three and three

7. Write the number

8. Your math work

Make It a Capital

The names of people, pets, and specific places and things begin with a capital letter.

We go to Big Creek School.

Mr. King is the music teacher.

We sing "America the Beautiful."

Cross out the words that do __not__ need a capital letter.

Teacher	Miss Pool	First Street School
School	Boston	City
Book	Iowa	State
Song	Helper	Mrs. Pine
Mr. Sims	Bus Driver	Curious George

Contractions

> A contraction is a short way to write two words.
> A contraction uses an apostrophe. (')
>
> you will = you'll

Rewrite each sentence using a contraction.
Use an apostrophe.

1. **Where is** the class?

   _____

2. **We are** at the computers.

   _____

3. **I will** play a word game.

   _____

4. Jessica said **she would** play.

   _____

5. She **did not** win the game.

   _____

   didn't   We're   I'll   Where's   she'd

Skills:

Writing
Complete
Sentences

Capitalizing
Names of
Specific Places

My School

Tell about your school. Answer each question with a complete sentence. Use capitals for names of specific places.

1. What is the name of your school?

_____

_____

2. On what street is your school?

_____

_____

3. In what city or town is your school?

_____

_____

4. In what state is your school?

_____

_____

5. In what country is your school?

_____

_____

Sharpen Your Skills—Spell & Write • EMC 9719 • © Evan-Moor Corp.

Book Magic

Skills:

Writing a
Creative Story

Using Spelling
Words in a
Composition

One day, the teacher opened a book to read to her class. Magic spilled out! The children found themselves in a faraway place. Where did they go? What did they see? How did they get back to school? Write a story. Use your spelling words.

book	good	took	look
take	read	think	work

_____

_____

_____

_____

_____

_____

✔ **Check Your Story**

○ I used complete sentences.

○ I checked my spelling words.

○ I used capitals for specific names and places.

First-Grade Fun

My Spelling Test

Find the correct answer. Fill in the circle.

Ask someone to test you on the spelling words.

1. Which one is a sentence?
   - ○ Your book
   - ○ I like your book

2. Which sentence has the correct capital letters?
   - ○ Our School is in california.
   - ○ Their school is in Texas.

3. Which word is the contraction for **you are**?
   - ○ you'll
   - ○ you're

1. _____

2. _____

3. _____

4. _____

5. _____

6. _____

7. _____

8. _____

SCHOOL XING

4. Write the sentence correctly.

she didnt werk at lincoln school

_____

_____

Test Your Skills-Record Form

Unit	Test Page	Topic	Test Your Skills Score (5 possible)	Spelling Test Score (10 possible)
1	252	At the Circus		
2	262	The Playground		
3	272	Fourth of July		
4	282	Story of the Year		
5	292	Good Morning!		
6	302	Sing a Song		
7	312	Be Safe		
8	322	Away We Go!		
9	332	On the Farm		
10	342	Pet Show		
11	352	Family Night		
12	362	First-Grade Fun		

© Evan-Moor Corp. • EMC 9719 • *Sharpen Your Skills—Spell & Write*

363

Pull-out Spelling Lists

Use these lists to give spelling tests, post on the refrigerator, and for extra practice.

Unit 1 At the Circus	Unit 2 The Playground	Unit 3 Fourth of July
1. can	1. up	1. hat
2. pan	2. us	2. hot
3. man	3. run	3. hand
4. cat	4. fun	4. sand
5. sat	5. jump	5. red
6. wish	6. to	6. blue
7. like	7. ship	7. white
8. lady	8. game	8. flag

Pull-out Spelling Lists

Use these lists to give spelling tests, post on the refrigerator, and for extra practice.

Unit 4 Story of the Year	Unit 5 Good Morning!	Unit 6 Sing a Song
1. make	1. we	1. so
2. shake	2. me	2. no
3. lake	3. tree	3. note
4. rake	4. see	4. home
5. sun	5. hear	5. do
6. snow	6. hold	6. you
7. grow	7. smell	7. nice
8. after	8. eat	8. sing

Pull-out Spelling Lists

Use these lists to give spelling tests, post on the refrigerator, and for extra practice.

Unit 7 Be Safe	Unit 8 Away We Go!	Unit 9 On the Farm
1. day	1. car	1. cow
2. may	2. far	2. now
3. stay	3. start	3. down
4. play	4. are	4. town
5. stop	5. go	5. brown
6. look	6. ride	6. farm
7. rule	7. fly	7. barn
8. safe	8. with	8. help

Pull-out Spelling Lists

Use these lists to give spelling tests, post on the refrigerator, and for extra practice.

Unit 10 Pet Show	Unit 11 Family Night	Unit 12 First-Grade Fun
1. funny	1. game	1. book
2. bunny	2. name	2. good
3. puppy	3. bake	3. look
4. happy	4. family	4. took
5. little	5. mother	5. take
6. kitten	6. father	6. read
7. pet	7. sister	7. think
8. my	8. brother	8. work

Answer Key

Page 243

At the Circus

May 31, 2005

Dear Grandpa,

Thank you for taking me to the circus. It was fun. I liked when the man and the big cat sat on a chair. I wish I could ride a horse like the lady in pink. I would stand up and ride.

I like the circus.
Let's go again!

Love,
Madison

Find It! Read the spelling words. Check off the words you can find in the story.

☐ can	☐ pan
✓ man	✓ cat
✓ sat	✓ wish
✓ like	✓ lady

How many spelling words did you find? __6__

Page 245

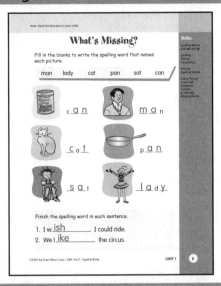

What's Missing?

Fill in the blanks to write the spelling word that names each picture.

man   lady   cat   pan   sat   can

c a n
m a n
c a t
p a n
s a t
l a d y

Finish the spelling word in each sentence.

1. I w __ish__ I could ride.
2. We l __ike__ the circus.

Page 246

Circus Rhymes

Draw a line to match the words that rhyme.

man — dish
cat — ran
wish — hat
like — bike

Write a spelling word to finish each rhyme.

Mrs. Brady is a __lady__

We had Dan open the __can__

What does Ann fry in the __pan__ ?

That clown __sat__ on his hat.

can   lady   sat   pan

Page 247

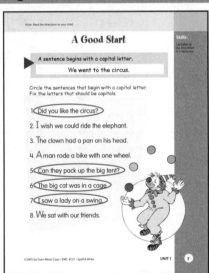

A Good Start

A sentence begins with a capital letter.

We went to the circus.

Circle the sentences that begin with a capital letter. Fix the letters that should be capitals.

1. (Did you like the circus?)
2. I wish we could ride the elephant.
3. The clown had a pan on his head.
4. A man rode a bike with one wheel.
5. (Can they pack up the big tent?)
6. (The big cat was in a cage)
7. (I saw a lady on a swing)
8. We sat with our friends.

Page 248

Tell Me Something

A sentence needs ending punctuation.
A sentence that tells something ends with a period. (.)

We see the circus tent.

Unscramble the words to make a sentence. End each sentence with a period.

1. We circus like the
   We like the circus.
2. The clown funny is
   The clown is funny.
3. flower He has a
   He has a flower.
4. It water sprays
   It sprays water.
5. wet We get
   We get wet.

Page 249

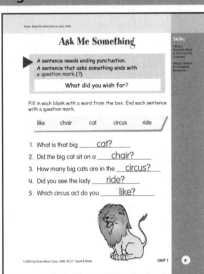

Ask Me Something

A sentence needs ending punctuation.
A sentence that asks something ends with a question mark. (?)

What did you wish for?

Fill in each blank with a word from the box. End each sentence with a question mark.

like   chair   cat   circus   ride

1. What is that big __cat?__
2. Did the big cat sit on a __chair?__
3. How many big cats are in the __circus?__
4. Did you see the lady __ride?__
5. Which circus act do you __like?__

Page 250

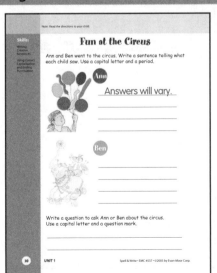

Fun at the Circus

Ann and Ben went to the circus. Write a sentence telling what each child saw. Use a capital letter and a period.

Ann
Answers will vary.

Ben

Write a question to ask Ann or Ben about the circus. Use a capital letter and a question mark.

Page 251

The Big Show

Finish the story. Use as many spelling words as you can.

can   pan   man   cat
sat   wish   like   lady

Ann and Ben played circus. They made a tent in the yard. Answers will vary.

✓ **Check Your Story**

○ I used a capital letter to begin each sentence.

○ I used a period or question mark at the end of each sentence.

Page 252

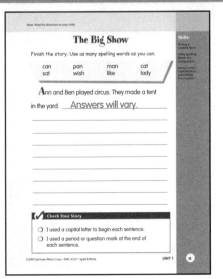

SKILLS At the Circus   **My Spelling Test**

Find the correct answer. Fill in the circle.

Ask someone to test you on the spelling words.

1. Which punctuation mark goes at the end of the sentence?
   We like the circus___
   ● period (.)
   ○ question mark (?)

2. Which punctuation mark goes at the end of the sentence?
   Did you see the big cat___
   ○ period (.)
   ● question mark (?)

3. Which sentence has the correct capital letter?
   ○ here is the circus Tent.
   ● Where is your ticket?

1. _____
2. _____
3. _____
4. _____
5. _____
6. _____
7. _____
8. _____

4. Write the sentence correctly.
   did you wich for a kat
   Did you wish for a cat?

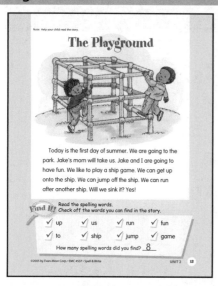

The Playground

Today is the first day of summer. We are going to the park. Jake's mom will take us. Jake and I are going to have fun. We like to play a ship game. We can get up onto the ship. We can jump off the ship. We can run after another ship. Will we sink it? Yes!

Find It! Read the spelling words.
Check off the words you can find in the story.

| ✓ up | ✓ us | ✓ run | ✓ fun |
| ✓ to | ✓ ship | ✓ jump | ✓ game |

How many spelling words did you find? __8__

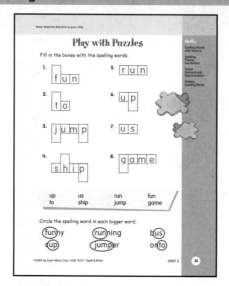

Play with Puzzles

Fill in the boxes with the spelling words.

1. f u n
2. t o
3. j u m p
4. s h i p
5. r u n
6. u p
7. u s
8. g a m e

up   us   run   fun
to   ship   jump   game

Circle the spelling word in each bigger word.

(fun)ny   (run)ning   (bus)
(cup)   (jump)er   on(to)

Can You Choose?

Choose the correct spelling. Write it on the line.

1. I like to gump/jump. ___jump___
2. How fast can you run/rum? ___run___
3. We play a ship/shep game. ___ship___
4. We had fen/fun. ___fun___
5. Will you play with uss/us? ___us___
6. I want to/toe swing. ___to___
7. Will he play a gam/game? ___game___
8. She may climb up/op. ___up___

Make word families. Write the words below in the correct box.

sun	bump	pup
bun	jump	cup
run	lump	up

cup
bun
jump
up
run
lump

Find the Sentence

A sentence has a whole thought.

Sentence: The three girls jump rope.
Not a sentence: The three girls

Read the two groups of words.
Write the group of words that makes a sentence.

1. Play ball with me / The ball
   ___Play ball with me.___

2. Kim and I / Kim runs to the park
   ___Kim runs to the park.___

3. Jump rope with us / With me
   ___Jump rope with us.___

4. Run fun sun / It is fun to run
   ___It is fun to run.___

Use a Capital

A sentence begins with a capital letter.

Dogs play in the park.

Does the sentence begin with a capital letter? Circle yes or no.

1. We run in the park.   (yes) no
2. go up the slide.   yes (no)
3. we have fun in the jump house.   yes (no)
4. Let's play a game.   (yes) no
5. I have a ball.   (yes) no

Write a sentence that goes with each picture. Use a capital letter to begin each sentence.

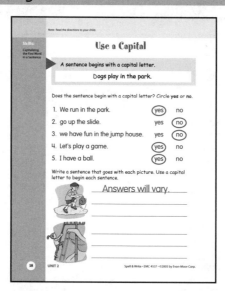

___Answers will vary.___

Capital I

The word I is always a capital letter.

You and I can play a game.

Color the ☺ if the sentence is correct. Fix the sentences that are not correct.

1. I like the park.   ☺
2. Ann and I can swing.   ☺
3. I like to go up.   ●
4. Max and I ride bikes.   ●
5. I have a blue bike.   ☺
6. May I ride your bike?   ☺
7. I can go fast.   ●
8. You and I can race.   ●

What Do You Do?

Write a sentence that begins with capital I.

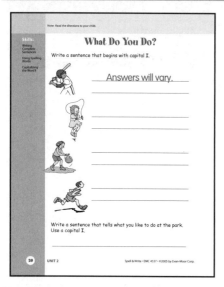

___Answers will vary.___

Write a sentence that tells what you like to do at the park. Use a capital I.

Friends Have Fun

Finish the story.

My friend's name is ___Answers will vary.___

We like to play _____

We also like to _____

My friend and _____ have fun.

Draw a picture of yourself and your friend playing. Write a sentence that tells about your picture.

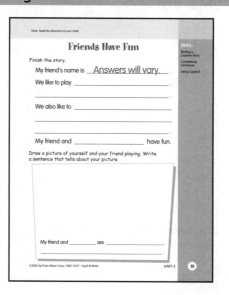

My friend and _____ are

TEST YOUR SKILLS — **The Playground**

Find the correct answer. Fill in the circle.

1. Which one is a sentence?
   ○ A slide
   ● A slide is fun

2. Which sentence has the correct capital letter?
   ○ my bike Is red.
   ● Your bike is blue.

3. Which sentence has the correct capital letter?
   ● Dad and I like to ride.
   ○ Dad and i have fun.

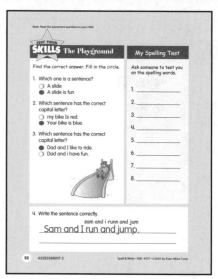

4. Write the sentence correctly.
   sam and i runn and jum
   ___Sam and I run and jump.___

My Spelling Test

Ask someone to test you on the spelling words.

1. _____
2. _____
3. _____
4. _____
5. _____
6. _____
7. _____
8. _____

Page 263

Fourth of July

Note: Help your child read the story.

Zack and Mia found a note on the door. They read the note. Then they asked Mom for paper. Zack made a red and white hat. Mia made red and blue flowers for her bike. Can you guess why?

Here is what the note said:

> Calling All Kids!
> Come to Our March!
> It's in the Park.
> Bring your Bike.
> Be there at Noon.
> You will get a flag!
> You will get drinks
> and snacks!

Find It! Read the spelling words. Check off the words you can find in the story and note.

✓ hat ✓ hot ✓ sand ✓ hand
✓ red ✓ white ✓ blue ✓ flag

How many spelling words did you find? __5__

©2005 by Evan-Moor Corp. • EMC 4537 • Spell & Write   UNIT 3   23

Page 265

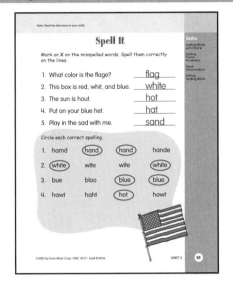

Spell It

Note: Read the directions to your child.

Mark an X on the misspelled words. Spell them correctly on the lines.

1. What color is the flage? ___flag___
2. This box is red, whit, and blue. ___white___
3. The sun is hout. ___hot___
4. Put on your blue het. ___hat___
5. Play in the sad with me. ___sand___

Circle each correct spelling.

1. hamd **hand** hand hande
2. **white** wite wite **white**
3. bue bloo **blue** **blue**
4. hawt haht **hot** howt

Skills:
Spelling Words with Short a
Spelling Theme Vocabulary
Visual Discrimination
Writing Spelling Words

©2005 by Evan-Moor Corp. • EMC 4537 • Spell & Write   UNIT 3   25

Page 266

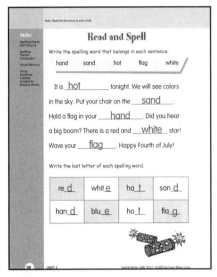

Skills:
Spelling Words with Short a
Spelling Theme Vocabulary
Visual Memory
Using Sentence Context to Identify Missing Words

Read and Spell

Note: Read the directions to your child.

Write the spelling word that belongs in each sentence.

hand   sand   hot   flag   white

It is __hot__ tonight. We will see colors in the sky. Put your chair on the __sand__. Hold a flag in your __hand__. Did you hear a big boom? There is a red and __white__ star! Wave your __flag__. Happy Fourth of July!

Write the last letter of each spelling word.

| re_d_ | whit_e_ | ha_t_ | san_d_ |
| han_d_ | blu_e_ | ho_t_ | fla_g_ |

26   UNIT 3   Spell & Write • EMC 4537 • ©2005 by Evan-Moor Corp.

Page 267

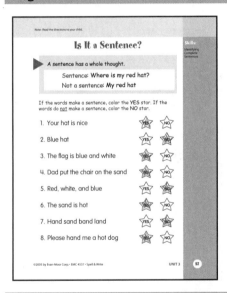

Skills:
Identifying Complete Sentences

Is It a Sentence?

Note: Read the directions to your child.

A sentence has a whole thought.

Sentence: Where is my red hat?
Not a sentence: My red hat

If the words make a sentence, color the YES star. If the words do **not** make a sentence, color the NO star.

1. Your hat is nice   YES **NO**
2. Blue hat   YES **NO**
3. The flag is blue and white   **YES** NO
4. Dad put the chair on the sand   **YES** NO
5. Red, white, and blue   YES **NO**
6. The sand is hot   **YES** NO
7. Hand sand band land   YES **NO**
8. Please hand me a hot dog   **YES** NO

©2005 by Evan-Moor Corp. • EMC 4537 • Spell & Write   UNIT 3   27

Page 268

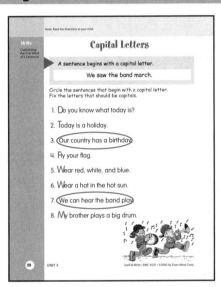

Skills:
Capitalizing the First Word of a Sentence

Capital Letters

Note: Read the directions to your child.

A sentence begins with a capital letter.

We saw the band march.

Circle the sentences that begin with a capital letter. Fix the letters that should be capitals.

1. Do you know what today is?
2. Today is a holiday.
3. (Our country has a birthday)
4. Fly your flag.
5. Wear red, white, and blue.
6. Wear a hat in the hot sun.
7. (We can hear the band play)
8. My brother plays a big drum.

28   UNIT 3   Spell & Write • EMC 4537 • ©2005 by Evan-Moor Corp.

Page 269

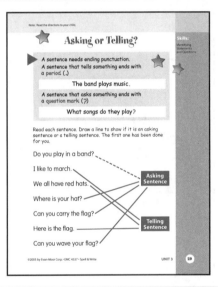

★ **Asking or Telling?**

Note: Read the directions to your child.

Skills:
Identifying Statements and Questions

A sentence needs ending punctuation. A sentence that tells something ends with a period. (.)

The band plays music.

A sentence that asks something ends with a question mark (?)

What songs do they play?

Read each sentence. Draw a line to show if it is an asking sentence or a telling sentence. The first one has been done for you.

Do you play in a band?
I like to march.
We all have red hats.
Where is your hat?
Can you carry the flag?
Here is the flag.
Can you wave your flag?

Asking Sentence
Telling Sentence

©2005 by Evan-Moor Corp. • EMC 4537 • Spell & Write   UNIT 3   29

Page 270

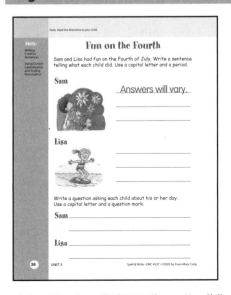

Skills:
Writing Creative Sentences
Using Correct Capitalization and Ending Punctuation

Fun on the Fourth

Note: Read the directions to your child.

Sam and Lisa had fun on the Fourth of July. Write a sentence telling what each child did. Use a capital letter and a period.

Sam   _Answers will vary._

Lisa

Write a question asking each child about his or her day. Use a capital letter and a question mark.

Sam _____

Lisa _____

30   UNIT 3   Spell & Write • EMC 4537 • ©2005 by Evan-Moor Corp.

Page 271

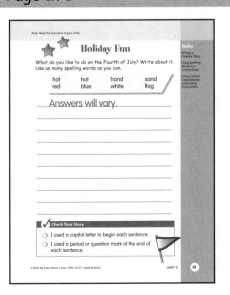

★ ★ **Holiday Fun**

Note: Read the directions to your child.

What do you like to do on the Fourth of July? Write about it. Use as many spelling words as you can.

hat   hot   hand   sand
red   blue   white   flag

Answers will vary.

Skills:
Writing a Creative Story
Using Spelling Words in a Composition
Using Correct Capitalization and Ending Punctuation

✓ **Check Your Story**
○ I used a capital letter to begin each sentence.
○ I used a period or question mark at the end of each sentence.

©2005 by Evan-Moor Corp. • EMC 4537 • Spell & Write   UNIT 3   31

Page 272

Note: Read the assessment questions to your child.

TEST YOUR SKILLS Fourth of July

Find the correct answer. Fill in the circle.

1. Which punctuation mark goes at the end of the sentence?
Did you march with the band___
○ period (.)
● question mark (?)

2. Which one is a sentence?
○ The white sand
● The sand is hot

3. Which sentence has the correct capital letter?
● This hat is too big for me.
○ my Red hat is just right.

4. Write the sentence correctly.
my flag is rad, white, and blu
My flag is red, white, and blue.

My Spelling Test

Ask someone to test you on the spelling words.

1. _____
2. _____
3. _____
4. _____
5. _____
6. _____
7. _____
8. _____

32   ASSESSMENT 3   Spell & Write • EMC 4537 • ©2005 by Evan-Moor Corp.

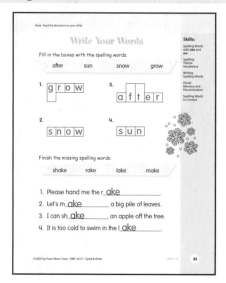

Page 273

Story of the Year

The story of the year goes like this:

In the **spring**, baby birds and lambs are born. The days get warmer. Little plants begin to grow.

Summer brings long days of hot sun. The garden is full of flowers and bees. We go to the beach.

In the **fall**, leaves turn yellow, red, and brown. They fall from the trees. We rake them up.

Winter comes and brings the cold. A bear sleeps. The lake has a cover of ice. We have fun in the snow. We make tracks.

Year after year, the story goes on. First spring comes, then summer, fall, and winter.

Find It! Read the spelling words. Check off the words you can find in the story.

✓ make ☐ shake ✓ lake ✓ rake
✓ sun ✓ snow ✓ grow ✓ after

How many spelling words did you find? 7

Page 275

Write Your Words

Fill in the boxes with the spelling words.

after   sun   snow   grow

1. g r o w
2. s n o w
3. a f t e r
4. s u n

Finish the missing spelling words.

shake   rake   lake   make

1. Please hand me the r**ake**
2. Let's m**ake** a big pile of leaves.
3. I can sh**ake** an apple off the tree.
4. It is too cold to swim in the l**ake**

Page 276

Choose One

Choose the correct spelling. Write it on the line.

1. The sum/sun is hot. — **sun**
2. Dad will take us to the lake/lak. — **lake**
3. We can mack/make a sand pile. — **make**
4. See it groo/grow. — **grow**
5. I will sake/shake off the sand. — **shake**
6. Alan has a pail and a rake/roke. — **rake**
7. The sand is as white as snow/snoe. — **snow**
8. Let's play aftr/after we swim. — **after**

Make word families. Write the words below in the correct box.

sun   grow   shake   snow   lake   run

low	fun	make
grow	sun	shake
snow	run	lake

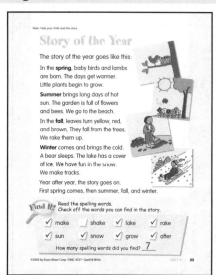

Page 277

Nouns Name Things

Some words name things. These words are called nouns.

The lady has a blue hat.

Color each apple that names something.

(apples: tree, lake, is, sun, grow, rake, after, snow)

Page 278

Summer Fun

When something belongs to one person, add 's to the name of the person.

We swim in Amy's pool.

Draw a line to show to whom each thing belongs.

Meg's kite — Tom
Kim's T-shirt — Kim
Tom's ball — Ben
Ben's boat

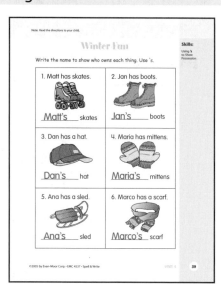

Page 279

Winter Fun

Write the name to show who owns each thing. Use 's.

1. Matt has skates. — **Matt's** skates
2. Jan has boots. — **Jan's** boots
3. Dan has a hat. — **Dan's** hat
4. Maria has mittens. — **Maria's** mittens
5. Ana has a sled. — **Ana's** sled
6. Marco has a scarf. — **Marco's** scarf

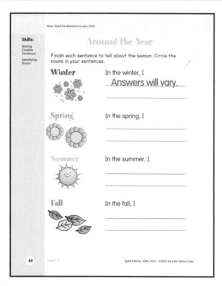

Page 280

Around the Year

Finish each sentence to tell about the season. Circle the nouns in your sentences.

Winter — In the winter, I
Answers will vary.

Spring — In the spring, I

Summer — In the summer, I

Fall — In the fall, I

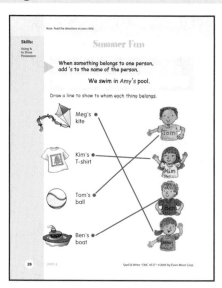

Page 281

Time of Year

Finish the poem. Fill in the name of the season.

winter   spring   fall   summer

I like spring.
I like **spring** 's rain.
I like **spring** 's soft, quiet rain.

I like summer.
I like **summer** 's sun.
I like **summer** 's hot, hot sun.

I like fall.
I like **fall** 's colors.
I like **fall** 's red and yellow leaves.

I like winter.
I like **winter** 's snow.
I like **winter** 's white, white snow.

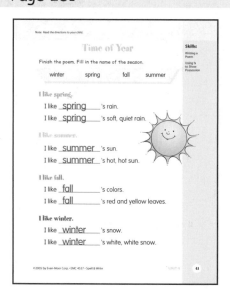

Page 282

TEST YOUR SKILLS — Story of the Year   **My Spelling Test**

Find the correct answer. Fill in the circle.

Ask someone to test you on the spelling words.

1. Which one is a naming word? (noun)
   ○ swim
   ● lake

2. Which sentence shows that Ana owns something?
   ○ These are Anas mittens.
   ● These are Ana's boots.

3. Which one tells to whom something belongs?
   ● Lee's bike
   ○ red bike

1. _____
2. _____
3. _____
4. _____
5. _____
6. _____
7. _____
8. _____

4. Write the sentence correctly.
   the sum will mak Dans tree gro
   The sun will make Dan's tree grow.

Good Morning!

Wake up! It's morning. What do you **see**?
The sun in the sky
And birds in a tree.

Wake up! It's morning. What do you **hear**?
Someone is singing
A song soft and clear.

Wake up! It's morning. What do you **hold**?
The covers around me
To keep out the cold.

Wake up! It's morning. What do you smell?
Someone is frying
An egg, I can tell.

Wake up! It's morning. What do you eat?
Warm oats and cold milk,
And berries so sweet.

Find It! Read the spelling words.
Check off the words you can find in the story.

✓ we   ✓ me   ✓ tree   ✓ see
✓ hear   ✓ hold   ✓ smell   ✓ eat

How many spelling words did you find? 7

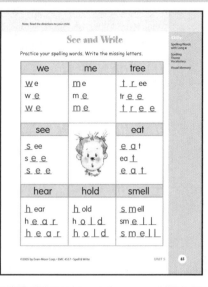

See and Write

Practice your spelling words. Write the missing letters.

we	me	tree
w e	m e	t r ee
w e	m e	tr ee
w e	m e	t r ee

see		eat
s ee		e at
s ee		ea t
s ee		e at

hear	hold	smell
h ear	h old	s m ell
h ear	h old	sm ell
h ear	h old	smell

Can You See It?

Choose the correct spelling. Write it on the line.

1. My new glasses help me/mi read.   me
2. Can you sey/see the pictures?   see
3. I will hould/hold the book for you.   hold
4. Now wee/we can read together.   we

we	me	tree	see
hear	hold	smell	eat

Circle the spelling word in each bigger word.

meet   treetop   behold   seeds
hearing   smelly   beater   sweet

Find the Verbs

Some words tell what is happening. These words are called verbs.

We smell the popcorn.
(What is happening)

Color the verbs.

egg   we   tree

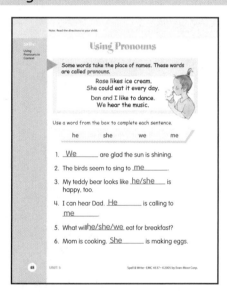

Using Pronouns

Some words take the place of names. These words are called pronouns.

Rose likes ice cream.
She could eat it every day.
Dan and I like to dance.
We hear the music.

Use a word from the box to complete each sentence.

he   she   we   me

1. We are glad the sun is shining.
2. The birds seem to sing to me.
3. My teddy bear looks like he/she is happy, too.
4. I can hear Dad. He is calling to me.
5. What will he/she/we eat for breakfast?
6. Mom is cooking. She is making eggs.

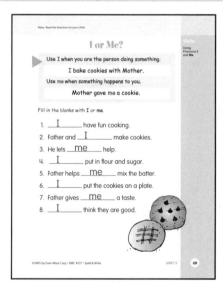

I or Me?

Use I when you are the person doing something.

I bake cookies with Mother.

Use me when something happens to you.

Mother gave me a cookie.

Fill in the blanks with I or me.

1. I have fun cooking.
2. Father and I make cookies.
3. He lets me help.
4. I put in flour and sugar.
5. Father helps me mix the batter.
6. I put the cookies on a plate.
7. Father gives me a taste.
8. I think they are good.

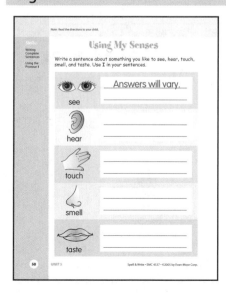

Using My Senses

Write a sentence about something you like to see, hear, touch, smell, and taste. Use I in your sentences.

see   Answers will vary.

hear

touch

smell

taste

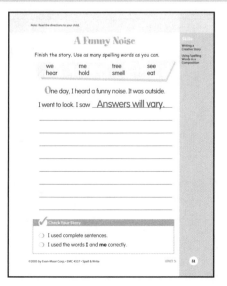

A Funny Noise

Finish the story. Use as many spelling words as you can.

we	me	tree	see
hear	hold	smell	eat

One day, I heard a funny noise. It was outside.
I went to look. I saw Answers will vary.

Check Your Story
○ I used complete sentences.
○ I used the words I and me correctly.

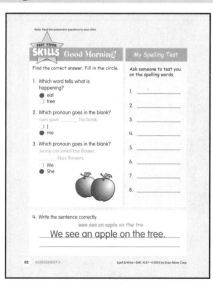

TEST YOUR SKILLS Good Morning!   My Spelling Test

Find the correct answer. Fill in the circle.

Ask someone to test you on the spelling words.

1. Which word tells what is happening?
● eat
○ tree

2. Which pronoun goes in the blank?
Sam gave _____ his book.
○ I
● me

3. Which pronoun goes in the blank?
Jenny can smell the flower.
_____ likes flowers.
○ We
● She

4. Write the sentence correctly.
wee sea an apple on the tre
We see an apple on the tree.

1. _____
2. _____
3. _____
4. _____
5. _____
6. _____
7. _____
8. _____

Page 293

Sing a Song

A song needs notes. Hum a song you know. Can you hear the notes go up and down?

A song needs a beat. You can clap the beat of a song. Clap one—two—three—four!

Some songs have words. The words may be **happy, silly, sad,** or **nice.** Words help you feel the song.

So sing your song the way you feel it!

Find It! Read the spelling words. Check off the words you can find in the story.

| ✓ | so | ☐ | note | ✓ | home |
| ☐ | do | ✓ | you | ✓ | nice | ✓ | sing |

How many spelling words did you find? __5__

Page 295

Can You Spell It?

Mark an X on the misspelled words. Spell them correctly on the lines.

1. How doo we sound? _____ do
2. Will Troy singe with us? _____ sing
3. He has a nise voice. _____ nice
4. Play this not. _____ note
5. Can yu play a tune? _____ you

Fill in the boxes with the spelling words.

home   nice   sing   you

1. h o m e
2. s i n g
3. n i c e
4. y o u

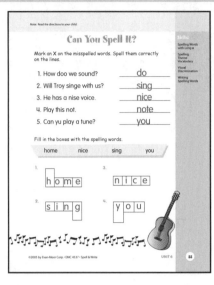

Page 296

Rhyme Time

Circle two words in each row that rhyme with the first word.

1.	**sing**	(bring)	song	(ring)
2.	**note**	not	(vote)	(boat)
3.	**nice**	(mice)	(twice)	size
4.	**so**	(no)	to	(go)
5.	**you**	(do)	(blue)	snow
6.	**no**	too	(show)	(so)
7.	**home**	(foam)	(Rome)	come
8.	**do**	(moo)	no	(you)

Write a spelling word to finish each rhyme.

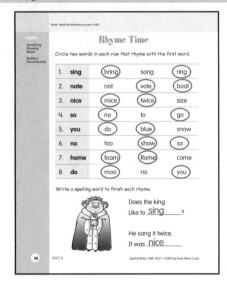

Does the king Like to **sing** ?

He sang it twice, It was **nice** .

Page 297

Is It a Sentence?

▶ A sentence has a whole thought.

Sentence: **It is fun to play music.**

Not a sentence: **To play music**

If the words make a sentence, color the happy face. If the words do **not** make a sentence, color the sad face.

1. The band	☺	☹
2. We play in a band	☺	☹
3. We keep the beat	☺	☹
4. With two sticks	☺	☹
5. I tap with the sticks	☺	☹
6. So no so no so	☺	☹
7. Ring the bell	☺	☹
8. Tap the triangle	☺	☹

Page 298

Looking for I

Circle the sentences that have a capital I. Fix the sentences that do **not** have a capital I.

1. (Rita and I have fun)
2. I turn on the radio.
3. (I like to sing and dance)
4. When the music plays, I listen.
5. (I show Rita the steps)
6. She and I practice at home.
7. I can snap my fingers.
8. (Rita and I can teach you, too)

Page 299

We or Us?

▶ Use **we** when you and other people do something.

We learn the tune.

Use **us** when something happens to you and other people.

Mr. Bell will teach us a song.

Fill in the each blank with **we** or **us.**

1. __We__ go to music class.
2. __We__ learn about notes.
3. Some of __us__ sing high notes.
4. Two of __us__ play the bells.
5. __We__ learn to sing together.
6. Next week, __we__ are in a show.
7. In the show __we__ will sing and dance.
8. Will you sing with __us__ ?

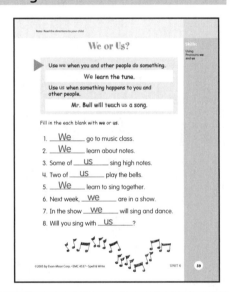

Page 300

My Music

Do you play or sing music? What would you like to play? What would you like to sing? Write about it. Use some of your spelling words.

___Answers will vary.___

Draw a picture of yourself making music.

Check Your Story
- ☐ I used complete sentences.
- ☐ I used capital I correctly.

Page 301

My Top Ten

Make a list of songs you know. Draw a star by the song you like best.

1. ___Answers will vary.___
2. _____
3. _____
4. _____
5. _____
6. _____
7. _____
8. _____
9. _____
10. _____

Sing your song for someone.

Page 302

TEST YOUR SKILLS Sing a Song | My Spelling Test |

Find the correct answer. Fill in the circle.

1. Which one is a sentence?
   - ● He plays a nice tune
   - ○ A note

2. Which word goes in the blank?
   _____ shake the bells.
   - ○ Us
   - ● We

3. Which sentence has the correct capital letter?
   - ○ Travis and i like to sing.
   - ● You and I like to dance.

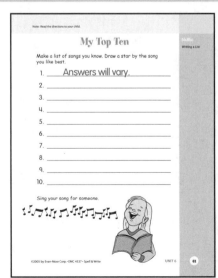

My Spelling Test

Ask someone to test you on the spelling words.

1. _____
2. _____
3. _____
4. _____
5. _____
6. _____
7. _____
8. _____

4. Write the sentence correctly.
doo us hum or sing the nots
___Do we hum or sing the notes?___

Page 303

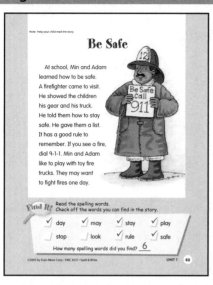

Be Safe

At school, Min and Adam learned how to be safe. A firefighter came to visit. He showed the children his gear and his truck. He told them how to stay safe. He gave them a list. It has a good rule to remember. If you see a fire, dial 9-1-1. Min and Adam like to play with toy fire trucks. They may want to fight fires one day.

 Read the spelling words. Check off the words you can find in the story.

✓ day	✓ may	✓ stay	✓ play
stop	look	✓ rule	✓ safe

How many spelling words did you find? 6

Page 305

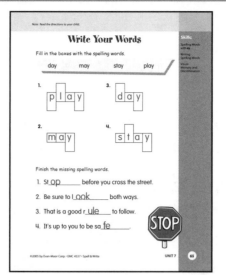

Write Your Words

Fill in the boxes with the spelling words.

day   may   stay   play

1. `p l a y`
3. `d a y`
2. `m a y`
4. `s t a y`

Finish the missing spelling words.

1. St op before you cross the street.
2. Be sure to l ook both ways.
3. That is a good r ule to follow.
4. It's up to you to be sa fe.

Page 306

Play It Safe

Fill in the missing words.

may   stay   day   play

1. Will you stay and play?
2. Do not play in the street.
3. You may get hurt.
4. Have a safe day.

Write letters in the blanks to make spelling words.

oo   u   o   ay   a

d ay	m ay
st o p	r u le
s a fe	st ay
l oo k	pl ay

Page 307

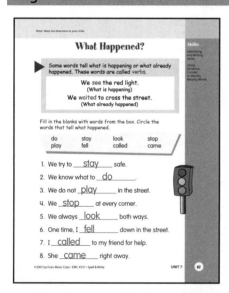

What Happened?

Some words tell what is happening or what already happened. These words are called verbs.

We see the red light.
(What is happening)
We waited to cross the street.
(What already happened)

Fill in the blanks with words from the box. Circle the words that tell what happened.

| do | stay | look | stop |
| play | fell | called | came |

1. We try to stay safe.
2. We know what to do.
3. We do not play in the street.
4. We stop at every corner.
5. We always look both ways.
6. One time, I fell down in the street.
7. I called to my friend for help.
8. She came right away.

Page 308

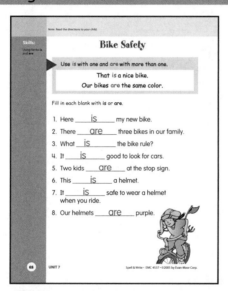

Bike Safety

Use is with one and are with more than one.

That is a nice bike.
Our bikes are the same color.

Fill in each blank with is or are.

1. Here is my new bike.
2. There are three bikes in our family.
3. What is the bike rule?
4. It is good to look for cars.
5. Two kids are at the stop sign.
6. This is a helmet.
7. It is safe to wear a helmet when you ride.
8. Our helmets are purple.

Page 309

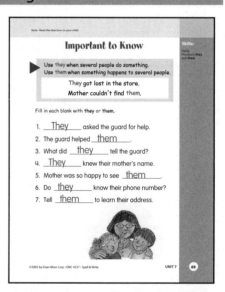

Important to Know

Use they when several people do something. Use them when something happens to several people.

They got lost in the store.
Mother couldn't find them.

Fill in each blank with they or them.

1. They asked the guard for help.
2. The guard helped them.
3. What did they tell the guard?
4. They knew their mother's name.
5. Mother was so happy to see them.
6. Do they know their phone number?
7. Tell them to learn their address.

Page 310

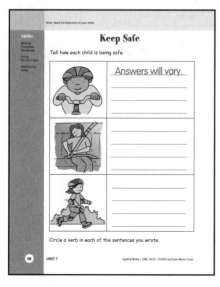

Keep Safe

Tell how each child is being safe.

Answers will vary.

Circle a verb in each of the sentences you wrote.

Page 311

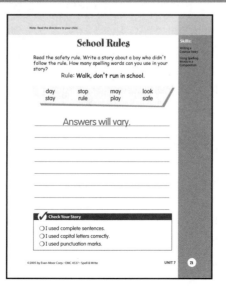

School Rules

Read the safety rule. Write a story about a boy who didn't follow the rule. How many spelling words can you use in your story?

Rule: Walk, don't run in school.

day   stop   may   look
stay   rule   play   safe

Answers will vary.

Check Your Story
- ○ I used complete sentences.
- ○ I used capital letters correctly.
- ○ I used punctuation marks.

Page 312

TEST YOUR SKILLS Be Safe

Find the correct answer. Fill in the circle.

1. Which word tells what is happening? (verb)
   - ● look
   - ○ them

2. Which word goes in the blank?
   The fire _____ out.
   - ● is
   - ○ are

3. Which word goes in the blank?
   Did _____ stop at the stop sign?
   - ○ them
   - ○ they

4. Write the sentence correctly.
   the rool says to stopp and looke
   The rule says to stop and look.

My Spelling Test

Ask someone to test you on the spelling words.

1. _____
2. _____
3. _____
4. _____
5. _____
6. _____
7. _____
8. _____

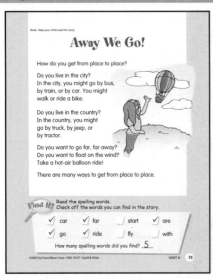

Away We Go!

Note: Help your child read the story.

How do you get from place to place?

Do you live in the city?
In the city, you might go by bus,
by train, or by car. You might
walk or ride a bike.

Do you live in the country?
In the country, you might
go by truck, by jeep, or
by tractor.

Do you want to go far, far away?
Do you want to float on the wind?
Take a hot-air balloon ride!

There are many ways to get from place to place.

Find It! Read the spelling words.
Check off the words you can find in the story.

✓ car　✓ far　　start　✓ are
✓ go　✓ ride　　fly　　with

How many spelling words did you find? __5__

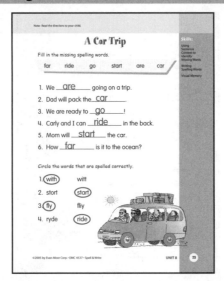

A Car Trip

Note: Read the directions to your child.

Fill in the missing spelling words.

far　ride　go　start　are　car

1. We __are__ going on a trip.
2. Dad will pack the __car__.
3. We are ready to __go__!
4. Carly and I can __ride__ in the back.
5. Mom will __start__ the car.
6. How __far__ is it to the ocean?

Circle the words that are spelled correctly.

1. (with)　witt
2. stort　(start)
3. (fly)　fliy
4. ryde　(ride)

Skills:
Using Sentence Context to Identify Missing Words
Spelling Spelling Words
Writing Theme Vocabulary
Visual Memory

Ride with Me

Note: Read the directions to your child.

Practice your spelling words. Write the missing letters.

car	are	ride
_c_ ar	_a_ r e	_r_ ide
c a r	ar _e_	r ide
c a r	a r e	r i d e
far		**fly**
_f_ ar		_f_ l y
f a r		fl _y_
f a r		_f_ _l_ _y_
start	**go**	**with**
s t _art_	_g_ o	_w_ ith
s t _a_ rt	g o	wi _th_
s t a r t	_g_ _o_	_w_ _i_ _t_ _h_

Skills:
Spelling Words with R-Controlled Vowel ar

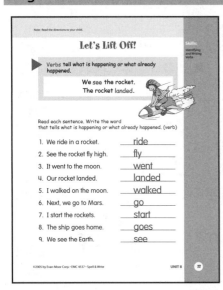

Let's Lift Off!

Note: Read the directions to your child.

Verbs tell what is happening or what already happened.

We see the rocket.
The rocket landed.

Read each sentence. Write the word
that tells what is happening or what already happened. (verb)

1. We ride in a rocket. __ride__
2. See the rocket fly high. __fly__
3. It went to the moon. __went__
4. Our rocket landed. __landed__
5. I walked on the moon. __walked__
6. Next, we go to Mars. __go__
7. I start the rockets. __start__
8. The ship goes home. __goes__
9. We see the Earth. __see__

Skills:
Identifying and Writing Verbs

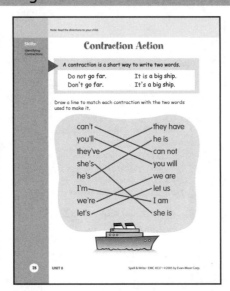

Contraction Action

Note: Read the directions to your child.

A contraction is a short way to write two words.

Do not go far.　　It is a big ship.
Don't go far.　　It's a big ship.

Draw a line to match each contraction with the two words used to make it.

can't　　　they have
you'll　　　he is
they've　　can not
she's　　　you will
he's　　　we are
I'm　　　let us
we're　　　I am
let's　　　she is

Skills:
Identifying Contractions

More Contractions

Note: Read the directions to your child.

The apostrophe takes the place of a letter or letters. A contraction uses an apostrophe. (')

does not = doesn't

Rewrite each sentence using a contraction. Use an apostrophe.

We'll　Where's　it's　They're　don't

1. Where is that boat going?
   __Where's__
2. I think it is a fishing boat.
   __it's__
3. We will sail this way.
   __We'll__
4. I do not see land.
   __don't__
5. They are going fishing.
   __They're__

Skills:
Writing Contractions Using an Apostrophe

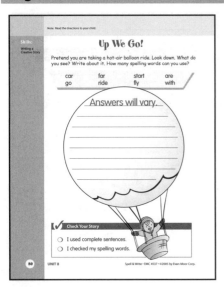

Up We Go!

Note: Read the directions to your child.

Pretend you are taking a hot-air balloon ride. Look down. What do you see? Write about it. How many spelling words can you use?

car　far　start　are
go　ride　fly　with

Answers will vary.

Check Your Story
○ I used complete sentences.
○ I checked my spelling words.

Skills:
Writing a Creative Story

Train, Car, or Plane?

Note: Read the directions to your child.

Think about a place you went. Answer the questions using complete sentences. Then draw a picture to show how you got there.

1. Where did you go?
   Answers will vary.

2. Who went with you?

3. How did you get there?

Draw a picture.

Skills:
Writing Complete Sentences

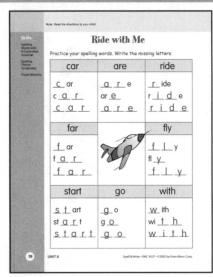

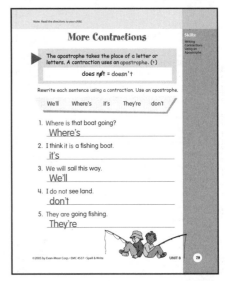

TEST YOUR SKILLS　Away We Go!　　My Spelling Test

Note: Read the assessment questions to your child.

Find the correct answer. Fill in the circle.

1. Which word tells what is happening? (verb)
   ● ride
   ○ car

2. Which word is the contraction for **have not**?
   ○ have
   ● haven't

3. Which word is the contraction for **do not**?
   ○ didn't
   ● don't

4. Write the sentence correctly.
   Lets goe for a rid in the care.
   __Let's go for a ride in the car.__

Ask someone to test you on the spelling words.

1. _____
2. _____
3. _____
4. _____
5. _____
6. _____
7. _____
8. _____

ASSESSMENT 8

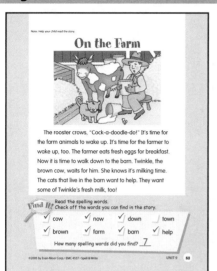

Page 323 — On the Farm

Note: Help your child read the story.

On the Farm

The rooster crows, "Cock-a-doodle-do!" It's time for the farm animals to wake up. It's time for the farmer to wake up, too. The farmer eats fresh eggs for breakfast. Now it is time to walk down to the barn. Twinkle, the brown cow, waits for him. She knows it's milking time. The cats that live in the barn want to help. They want some of Twinkle's fresh milk, too!

Find It! Read the spelling words. Check off the words you can find in the story.

✓ cow ✓ now ✓ down ☐ town
✓ brown ✓ farm ✓ barn ☐ help

How many spelling words did you find? 7

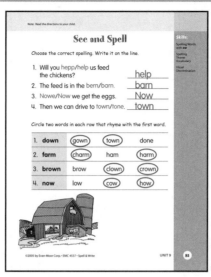

Page 325 — See and Spell

Note: Read the directions to your child.

See and Spell

Choose the correct spelling. Write it on the line.

1. Will you hepp/help us feed the chickens? — help
2. The feed is in the bern/barn. — barn
3. Nowe/Now we get the eggs. — Now
4. Then we can drive to town/tone. — town

Circle two words in each row that rhyme with the first word.

1. down — (gown) (town) done
2. farm — (charm) ham (harm)
3. brown — brow (clown) (crown)
4. now — low (cow) (how)

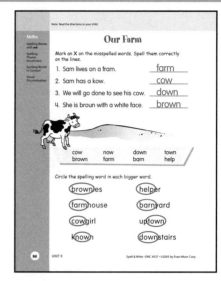

Page 326 — Our Farm

Note: Read the directions to your child.

Our Farm

Mark an X on the misspelled words. Spell them correctly on the lines.

1. Sam lives on a fram. — farm
2. Sam has a kow. — cow
3. We will go done to see his cow. — down
4. She is broun with a white face. — brown

| cow | now | down | town |
| brown | farm | barn | help |

Circle the spelling word in each bigger word.

(brown)ies   (helper)
(farm)house   (barn)yard
(cow)girl   up(town)
(known)   (down)stairs

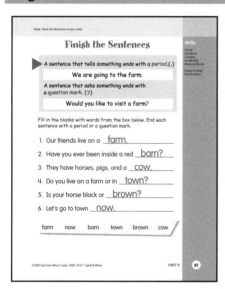

Page 327 — Finish the Sentences

Note: Read the directions to your child.

Finish the Sentences

A sentence that tells something ends with a period. (.)
> We are going to the farm.

A sentence that asks something ends with a question mark. (?)
> Would you like to visit a farm?

Fill in the blanks with words from the box below. End each sentence with a period or a question mark.

1. Our friends live on a farm.
2. Have you ever been inside a red barn?
3. They have horses, pigs, and a cow.
4. Do you live on a farm or in town?
5. Is your horse black or brown?
6. Let's go to town now.

| farm | now | barn | town | brown | cow |

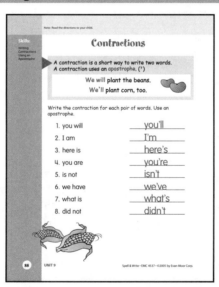

Page 328 — Contractions

Note: Read the directions to your child.

Contractions

A contraction is a short way to write two words. A contraction uses an apostrophe. (')
> We will plant the beans.
> We'll plant corn, too.

Write the contraction for each pair of words. Use an apostrophe.

1. you will — you'll
2. I am — I'm
3. here is — here's
4. you are — you're
5. is not — isn't
6. we have — we've
7. what is — what's
8. did not — didn't

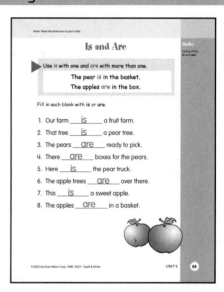

Page 329 — Is and Are

Note: Read the directions to your child.

Is and Are

Use is with one and are with more than one.
> The pear is in the basket.
> The apples are in the box.

Fill in each blank with is or are.

1. Our farm is a fruit farm.
2. That tree is a pear tree.
3. The pears are ready to pick.
4. There are boxes for the pears.
5. Here is the pear truck.
6. The apple trees are over there.
7. This is a sweet apple.
8. The apples are in a basket.

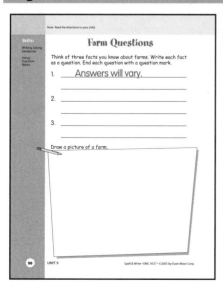

Page 330 — Farm Questions

Note: Read the directions to your child.

Farm Questions

Think of three facts you know about farms. Write each fact as a question. End each question with a question mark.

1. Answers will vary.
2.
3.

Draw a picture of a farm.

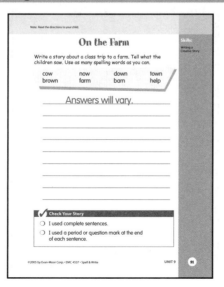

Page 331 — On the Farm

Note: Read the directions to your child.

On the Farm

Write a story about a class trip to a farm. Tell what the children saw. Use as many spelling words as you can.

| cow | now | down | town |
| brown | farm | barn | help |

Answers will vary.

✓ Check Your Story
○ I used complete sentences.
○ I used a period or question mark at the end of each sentence.

Page 332 — On the Farm

Note: Read the assessment questions to your child.

TEST YOUR SKILLS — On the Farm   My Spelling Test

Find the correct answer. Fill in the circle.

1. Which punctuation mark goes at the end of the sentence?
Do you live on a farm___
○ period (.)
● question mark (?)

2. Which word is the contraction for **did not**?
○ don't
● didn't

3. Which word goes in the sentence?
These _____ the pears we picked.
○ is
● are

4. Write the sentence correctly.
does the brawn kow stay in the bran
Does the brown cow stay in the barn?

Ask someone to test you on the spelling words.

1.
2.
3.
4.
5.
6.
7.
8.

Page 333

Pet Show

We are having a pet show today.
Nick will bring a little bunny.
It is black and white.

Sierra will bring her kitten.
The kitten has a bell that
always tells where she is.

I will bring my funny puppy
to the pet show. His name
is Tucker. I am teaching
Tucker to sit. He is happy
when he gets a treat. He
wags his tail and licks
my face.

Can you come to our pet show?

Find It! Read the spelling words.
Check off the words you can find in the story.

- ✓ funny ✓ bunny ✓ puppy ✓ happy
- ✓ little ✓ kitten ✓ pet ✓ my

How many spelling words did you find? __8__

Page 335

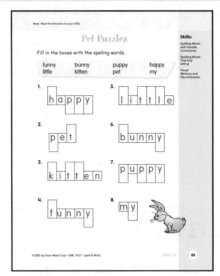

Pet Puzzles

Fill in the boxes with the spelling words.

funny bunny puppy happy
little kitten pet my

1. h a p p y
2. p e t
3. k i t t e n
4. f u n n y
5. l i t t l e
6. b u n n y
7. p u p p y
8. m y

Skills:
Spelling Words with Double Consonants
Spelling Words That End with y
Visual Memory and Discrimination

Page 336

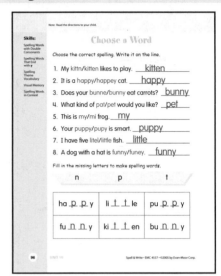

Skills:
Spelling Words with Double Consonants
Spelling Words That End with y
Spelling Theme Vocabulary
Visual Memory
Spelling Words in Context

Choose a Word

Choose the correct spelling. Write it on the line.

1. My kittn/kitten likes to play. __kitten__
2. It is a happy/happey cat. __happy__
3. Does your bunne/bunny eat carrots? __bunny__
4. What kind of pat/pet would you like? __pet__
5. This is my/mi frog. __my__
6. Your puppy/pupy is smart. __puppy__
7. I have five litel/little fish. __little__
8. A dog with a hat is funny/funey. __funny__

Fill in the missing letters to make spelling words.

n p t

| ha p p y | li t t le | pu p p y |
| fu n n y | ki t t en | bu n n y |

Page 337

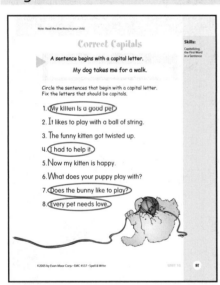

Correct Capitals

A sentence begins with a capital letter.

My dog takes me for a walk.

Circle the sentences that begin with a capital letter.
Fix the letters that should be capitals.

1. (My kitten Is a good pet)
2. It likes to play with a ball of string.
3. The funny kitten got twisted up.
4. (I had to help it)
5. Now my kitten is happy.
6. What does your puppy play with?
7. (Does the bunny like to play?)
8. (Every pet needs love)

Skills:
Capitalizing the First Word in a Sentence

Page 338

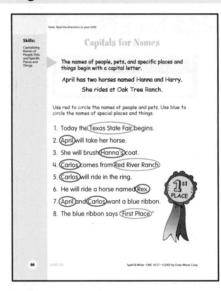

Skills:
Capitalizing Names of People, Pets, and Specific Places and Things

Capitals for Names

The names of people, pets, and specific places and things begin with a capital letter.

April has two horses named Hanna and Harry.
She rides at Oak Tree Ranch.

Use red to circle the names of people and pets. Use blue to circle the names of special places and things.

1. Today the (Texas State Fair) begins.
2. (April) will take her horse.
3. She will brush (Hanna's) coat.
4. (Carlos) comes from (Red River Ranch).
5. (Carlos) will ride in the ring.
6. He will ride a horse named (Rex).
7. (April) and (Carlos) want a blue ribbon.
8. The blue ribbon says (First Place)."

1ST PLACE

Page 339

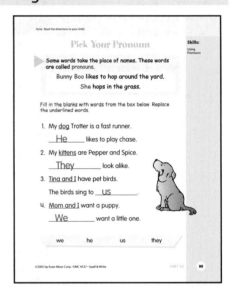

Skills:
Using Pronouns

Pick Your Pronoun

Some words take the place of names. These words are called pronouns.

Bunny Boo likes to hop around the yard.
She hops in the grass.

Fill in the blanks with words from the box below. Replace the underlined words.

1. My dog Trotter is a fast runner.
   __He__ likes to play chase.
2. My kittens are Pepper and Spice.
   __They__ look alike.
3. Tina and I have pet birds.
   The birds sing to __us__.
4. Mom and I want a puppy.
   __We__ want a little one.

we he us they

Page 340

Skills:
Writing Complete Sentences
Capitalizing the First Word in a Sentence

Pet Report

Answer the questions using complete sentences. Use a capital letter at the beginning of each sentence.

1. What pet would you choose?
   __Answers will vary.__

2. Why would you choose that pet?

3. What is a good name for your pet?

Draw a picture of your pet.

Page 341

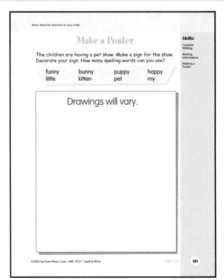

Make a Poster

The children are having a pet show. Make a sign for the show. Decorate your sign. How many spelling words can you use?

funny bunny puppy happy
little kitten pet my

Drawings will vary.

Skills:
Creative Writing
Writing Information
Making a Poster

Page 342

TEST YOUR SKILLS **Pet Show**

Find the correct answer. Fill in the circle.

1. Which sentence has the correct capital letter?
   ○ the pet show is today.
   ● I like the kittens.

2. Which sentence has the correct capital letters?
   ● My dog went to Red's Puppy School.
   ○ now clifford knows how to sit.

3. Which pronoun goes in the blank?
   Luke has a new kitten.
   _____ calls it Penny.
   ● He
   ○ They

4. Write the sentence correctly.
   mi littal bunny is named sunny
   __My little bunny is named Sunny.__

My Spelling Test

Ask someone to test you on the spelling words.

1. _____
2. _____
3. _____
4. _____
5. _____
6. _____
7. _____
8. _____

Page 343

Family Night

I love family night at my house. It is the same every week. We all help with dinner. Our dog Sam knows something is up. After dinner, we all wash the dishes. Then we choose a board game. My brother and I choose a game. We have fun playing games together. My mother and father play, too. We all have fun on family night.

Find It! Read the spelling words. Check off the words you can find in the story.

✓ game · name · bake · ✓ family
✓ mother · ✓ father · ✓ brother · sister

How many spelling words did you find? __5__

Page 345

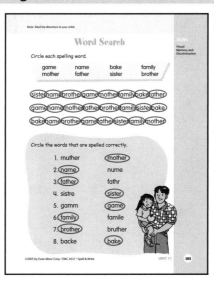

Word Search

Circle each spelling word.

game · name · bake · family
mother · father · sister · brother

sister name brother game mother family bake father
game name mother father brother family sister bake
bake name brother game father sister family mother

Circle the words that are spelled correctly.

1. muther — **mother**
2. **name** — nume
3. **father** — fathr
4. sistre — **sister**
5. gamm — **game**
6. **family** — famile
7. **brother** — bruther
8. backe — **bake**

Page 346

Word Study

Fill in the spelling word for each sentence.

game · bake · mother · brother

1. Jim is my little __brother__.
2. My __mother__ asked me to watch him.
3. Let's play a __game__.
4. Mother will __bake__ us some cookies.

Add the missing letters to make spelling words.

me · er · ke · ly

1. fath__er__
2. sist__er__
3. fami__ly__
4. na__me__
5. moth__er__
6. broth__er__
7. ga__me__
8. ba__ke__

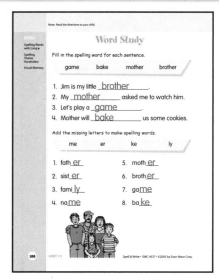

Page 347

Names Have Capitals

The names of people, pets, and specific places and things begin with a capital letter.

Emily is going to New York.
She will take her dog Red.
Her dad will drive the Ford truck.

Use red to circle the names of people and pets. Use blue to circle the names of special places and things.

1. (Mike) and (Tony) are brothers.
2. They live in (Ohio).
3. (Mike) goes to (Red Hill School).
4. (Nemo) is the name of (Tony's) fish.
5. He got the fish at (Dave's Dive).
6. Their family is going to (Mexico).
7. I will feed (Nemo).
8. He likes (Fine Fish Flakes).

Page 348

Write the Nouns

Some words name things. These words are called nouns.

Harry read a story about a family.

Choose the noun. Write it in the sentence.

1. This is a good __book__ to read. — book / sing
2. My father reads it to us in __bed__ — sleep / bed
3. I like the magic __skunk__. — look / skunk
4. The skunk's __name__ is Miss Sweet. — name / hear
5. The skunk takes a __bath__. — hide / bath
6. That is a funny __story__. — story / think

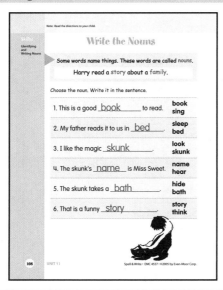

Page 349

Family Names

When something belongs to one person, add 's to the name of the person.

Have you seen Uncle Ted's hat?

Who owns what? Write the name you choose in each blank. Use 's.

Aunt Beth · Mother · Grandpa · Ben · Leo
Mrs. Smart · Anna · Uncle Jay · Roy

1. We are going to __Answers will vary.__ farm.
2. I will ride _____ horse.
3. My brother can feed _____ goats.
4. We will eat _____ cake.
5. We can help pick _____ beans.
6. We will smell _____ flowers.
7. My sister can see _____ new kittens.
8. We can ride in _____ truck.

Page 350

Pets Are Family, Too!

Ask two people to tell you the names of their pets. Draw a picture and write a sentence about each person and his or her pet. Use a capital letter to begin the names of people and pets.

Marta has a cat named Cookie.

Answers will vary.

Page 351

All in the Family

What does your family like to do together? Write a story about something your family did. Use as many spelling words as you can.

game · name · bake · family
mother · father · brother · sister

Answers will vary.

✓ **Check Your Story**
○ I used capital letters for names of people and pets.
○ I used capital letters for names of specific places and things.

Page 352

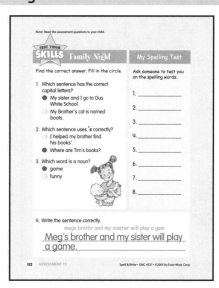

TEST YOUR SKILLS — **Family Night** | **My Spelling Test**

Find the correct answer. Fill in the circle.

Ask someone to test you on the spelling words.

1. Which sentence has the correct capital letters?
 ● My sister and I go to Gus White School.
 ○ My Brother's cat is named boots.

2. Which sentence uses 's correctly?
 ○ I helped my brother find his books'.
 ● Where are Tim's books?

3. Which word is a noun?
 ● game
 ○ funny

1. _____
2. _____
3. _____
4. _____
5. _____
6. _____
7. _____
8. _____

4. Write the sentence correctly.
megs brother and my sisster will play a gam

__Meg's brother and my sister will play a game.__

Page 353

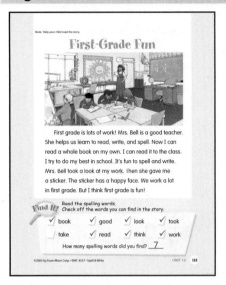

First-Grade Fun

First grade is lots of work! Mrs. Bell is a good teacher. She helps us learn to read, write, and spell. Now I can read a whole book on my own. I can read it to the class. I try to do my best in school. It's fun to spell and write. Mrs. Bell took a look at my work. Then she gave me a sticker. The sticker has a happy face. We work a lot in first grade. But I think first grade is fun!

Find it! Read the spelling words. Check off the words you can find in the story.

✓ book ✓ good ✓ look ✓ took
  take ✓ read ✓ think ✓ work

How many spelling words did you find? **7**

Page 355

Spelling Time

Fill in all the missing letters to make spelling words.

g o o d   b o o k
r e a d   l o o k
t a k e   th i nk
w o r k   t o o k

Circle two words in each row that rhyme with the first word.

1.	**book**	(hook)	lock	(cook)
2.	**take**	tock	(rake)	(fake)
3.	**work**	worm	(jerk)	(perk)
4.	**look**	lake	(took)	(crook)
5.	**read**	(bead)	(seed)	made
6.	**took**	(look)	make	(book)
7.	**good**	(hood)	(stood)	goat
8.	**think**	sing	(sink)	(blink)

Page 356

Read and Spell

Choose the best word to finish each sentence. Write it on the line.

1. Will you ___take___ this to school?
   take think took

2. It was a ___good___ book.
   look book good

3. I think you can ___read___ well.
   read good book

4. ___Look___ for another book to read.
   Took Look Book

5. Do you ___think___ there is a shark book?
   good work think

6. Find another good ___book___ to read.
   look took book

Circle the words that are spelled correctly.

1. wurk (work)
2. tak (take)
3. (read) rede
4. theenk (think)

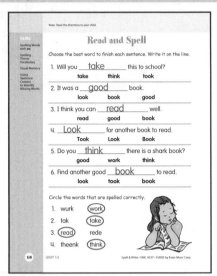

Page 357

A Whole Thought

A sentence has a whole thought.

Sentence: Math is what I like best.
Not a sentence: A math game

If the words make a sentence, color the YES star. If the words do not make a sentence, color the NO star.

1. A math book — YES / **NO**
2. Here is my math book — **YES** / NO
3. I think math is fun — **YES** / NO
4. In a number — YES / **NO**
5. Six added to — YES / **NO**
6. You added three and three — **YES** / NO
7. Write the number — **YES** / NO
8. Your math work — YES / **NO**

Page 358

Make It a Capital

The names of people, pets, and specific places and things begin with a capital letter.

We go to Big Creek School.
Mr. King is the music teacher.
We sing "America the Beautiful."

Cross out the words that do not need a capital letter.

Teacher	Miss Pool	First Street School
~~School~~	Boston	~~City~~
~~Book~~	Iowa	~~State~~
~~Song~~	Helper	Mrs. Pine
Mr. Sims	~~Bus Driver~~	Curious George

Page 359

Contractions

A contraction is a short way to write two words. A contraction uses an apostrophe. (')

you will = you'll

Rewrite each sentence using a contraction. Use an apostrophe.

1. **Where is** the class?
   Where's the class?

2. **We are** at the computers.
   We're at the computers.

3. **I will** play a word game.
   I'll play a word game.

4. Jessica said **she would** play.
   Jessica said she'd play.

5. She **did not** win the game.
   She didn't win the game.

didn't We're I'll Where's she'd

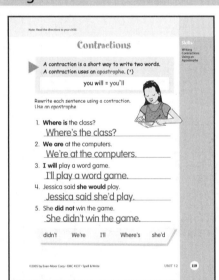

Page 360

My School

Tell about your school. Answer each question with a complete sentence. Use capitals for names of specific places.

1. What is the name of your school?
   Answers will vary.

2. On what street is your school?

3. In what city or town is your school?

4. In what state is your school?

5. In what country is your school?

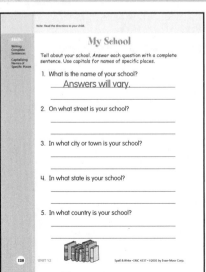

Page 361

Book Magic

One day, the teacher opened a book to read to her class. Magic spilled out! The children found themselves in a faraway place. Where did they go? What did they see? How did they get back to school? Write a story. Use your spelling words.

book good took look
take read think work

Answers will vary.

✓ **Check Your Story**
○ I used complete sentences.
○ I checked my spelling words.
○ I used capitals for specific names and places.

Page 362

TEST YOUR SKILLS First-Grade Fun

Find the correct answer. Fill in the circle.

1. Which one is a sentence?
   ○ Your book
   ● I like your book

2. Which sentence has the correct capital letters?
   ○ Our School is in california.
   ● Their school is in Texas.

3. Which word is the contraction for **you are**?
   ○ you'll
   ● you're

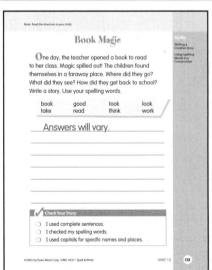

4. Write the sentence correctly.
   she didnt werk at lincoln school
   She didn't work at Lincoln School.

My Spelling Test

Ask someone to test you on the spelling words.

1. _____
2. _____
3. _____
4. _____
5. _____
6. _____
7. _____
8. _____